NO
NAY
NEVER
NO MORE

NOEL HEAVEY

Mushroom King Publishing

First published in Ireland 2014
by
Mushroom King Publishing

ISBN 978-0-9930074-0-8

Typeset in Avenir and Trajan
Printed and bound by Nicholson & Bass
Design and layout: Paula Nolan

Dedicated to the memories of my cousin
Anne Canning of Portstewart and
late of Quigley's Point, Donegal who came
to my aid when I needed it and later inspired
me with her courage.

Also dedicated to the memory of
Dougie Braiden of Kildare, a good writer
who loved to write and have a laugh.

And my other cousin, Frank Morrissey
of Essex, a very witty man.

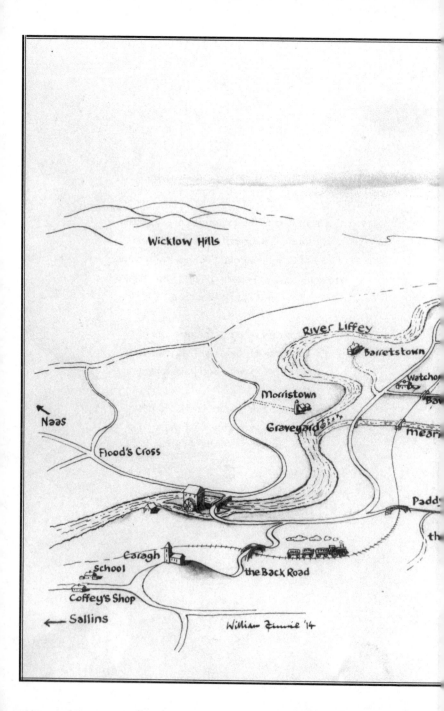

Wicklow Hills

River Liffey

Barretstown

Watcho

Morristown

Bov

Naas

Graveyard

mear

Flood's Cross

Padd

the

Caragh

School

the Back Road

Coffey's Shop

← Sallins

William Zinnie '14

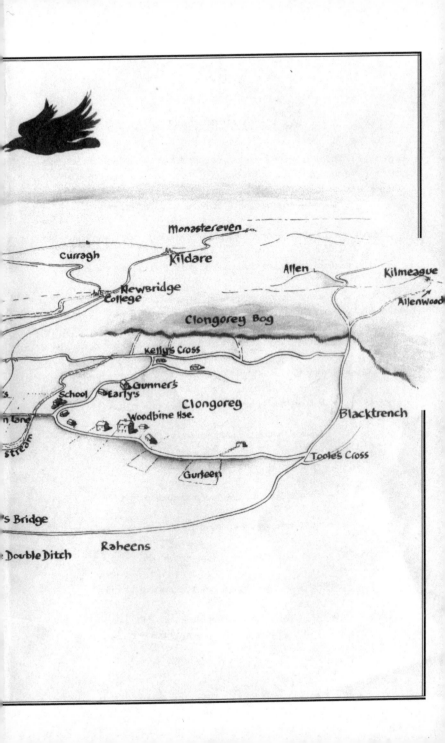

Acknowledgments

Rosemary Kearney, Aileen Saunders, Sandra Behan, Jim O'Riordan, Stephen Harding, Kevin Maher, Dougie Braiden (RIP), Paraig Walshe, Ruth Pertwick Ryan, Judy Fusco Linnane, Audrey Harwood and Martin O Ceardubhain who all wrote, listened, and shared their opinions in NUIM Maynooth.

John McKenna, Patrick Semple, Orla Murphy who imparted wisdom in NUIM.

Hilary Semple who generously read and proofed in the early stages.

Mary Linehan, Martina McCormack, Michael Doyle, Pauline Clooney, Rob Wolfe, Orla McAlinden, Carmel Walshe, Marian Henry, Brendan Bartley, Eileen Keane, Terry Moore, Mary Cosgrove who listened and shared and gave their opinions at various times in the Liffey Writers Circle at KYT in Newbridge.

Maria Murphy and Anne Marie Dillon for reading the sensitive stuff.

Willie Finnie for his wonderful map of Clongorey.

The Nationalist for the match report on page 259

Suzanne Power my editor.

Paula Nolan my designer and guiding light.

Aileen Heavey for finding the photographs.

Bernadette for putting up with me.

All the people mentioned in the course of the stories.

Richard Meehan and Evanne Black and all the people who will help me shift copies of this book.

Contents

INTRODUCTION 9
MOOREFIELD 11
EARLY SCHOOLDAYS 17
CHANGING TIMES 23
A LETTER TO CAP 30
SAVING HAY 37
SAVING TURF 40
PIGS 46
TALES OF MY MOTHER 54
HIS AND HERS 61
DOMINUS, DOMINE, DOMINUM 68
A TRIP TO SALLINS 75
THE FACTS OF LIFE 83
ALF TUPPER'S PROTÉGÉ 87
MY FIRST HOP 91
ANGST 94
BALL GAMES 102
BELFIELD 109
NEW YORK: 1. FINDING MY FEET 115
NEW YORK: 2. STAR GAZING 124
LOST LOVE IN TIMES OF FLATLAND 130
OFFALY 135
WARRENSTOWN 139
SEVENTIES LONDON 150

AFTER EIGHT YEARS DANCING...................................161

A STRANGE NIGHT ON THE TOWN 166

A CHANCE ENCOUNTER....................................170

THE AGS AND THE MIAMI.................................172

GARDENS OF IRELAND......................................178

CORFU 181

EUREKA...186

PROSPEROUS: 1. A STUDENT RECOLLECTION 192

PROSPEROUS: 2. MY FIRST YEAR AS A TEACHER...196

CELERY...200

THE CEARD TEASTAS...205

THE BIG QUESTION..208

FROM A JACK TO A KING 213

BACK TO BELFIELD...220

SCOTLAND THE BRAVE.....................................224

ACROSS THE THRESHOLD 229

CLONGOREY..233

STRAWBERRIES AND BERLIN 239

1978: 1. LIFE..248

1978: 2. FOOTBALL...252

1978: 3. THE JACK HIGGINS 259

1978: 4. ANOTHER LIFE 260

KEEP HER GOING SONNY 263

JAY..269

THE MAN WITH THE HORRIBLE FACE 277

THE APOGEE..280

A SATURDAY EVENING IN AUGUST..................283

INTRODUCTION

A few years ago, I wrote down a rough version of how I came to win two cups at a sporting event in Sallins a long time ago. I thought I'd forgotten all about this but writing seemed to turn on the tap. Memories and words spluttered at first but after a while they began to flow.

Around the same time Marty Taaffe told my wife, Bernadette, of an earlier event, when he'd accompanied me on trip to Sallins meat factory with a sick cow. This, too, I'd forgotten but after a few hours at the keyboard, I was back on the road again, feeling all the excitement and emotion that I'd felt that day a very long time ago.

Memories, ideas and possibilities now began to flood into my brain, but I wasn't at all confident that I could write a story well enough that anyone would be bothered to read it. I rang John McKenna, whom I love listening to on the radio programme *Sunday Miscellany*, to ask for help. He told me of the creative writing course he was involved with at National University of Ireland, Maynooth (NUIM).

Here I met a dozen kindred spirits. We wrote, we listened, we laughed and we cried and when it was all over we knew we could write at a standard that people might read and enjoy. But the dilemma was: to write about what?

I was born in 1950, which means I'm old enough to remember the ways of fifties Ireland. All this was blown away with the coming of Gay Byrne and his *Late Late Show* on television; The Beatles, The Rolling Stones, The Kinks and Manfred Mann on Radio Luxembourg, and then there was our version of Rock and Roll – the Showbands. I loved them all and the wonderful excitement they brought into my life. I wrote and I wrote and I wrote.

The events and people described in the following pages are as I remember them. Many years have passed. Others may well recall things differently, but I have described people and happenings as I saw them. I sincerely hope this does not cause offence, disappointment or hurt to anyone. The primary purpose of my writing these stories is that extra ordinary people and happenings be not forgotten.

Each of the fifty stories in this volume stand alone, with a beginning, middle and end. They are roughly in chronological order, but can be read in any order.

Somewhere along the way it occurred to me that many of the things and people I was writing about were no more. This put me in mind of a song I've been singing since forever, a half line of which I've used as the e title for my little book of stories of the way things were.

> I've been a wild rover for many's the year
> And I spent all my money on whiskey and beer,
> And now I'm returning with gold in great store,
> I never will play the wild rover no more.
>
> And it's no nay never, no nay never no more;
> Will I play the wild rover, no nay never, no more.

Noel Heavey
Clongorey.
July 9th, 2014.

MOOREFIELD

Me, my father in his painting overalls and Marie c1953 The Sheds in the background housed turf, a cow, two pigs and our toilet

Ours was a small tin-roofed home just beyond Artillery Place, Moorefield, on the Curragh side of Newbridge. Five happy souls lived in this little house, comprised of just a kitchen and a bedroom. In my memory the outside door is open and the sweet scent of wallflowers tumbles into the kitchen. The mustardy coloured dresser is the dominant piece of furniture. The lino around it is worn thin. Everything we need seems to be in, on or hung from the dresser. Outside there is a shed which houses two pigs, a few hens and a black cow and also our dry toilet, which has a separate little door.

My mother's time here was probably the happiest of her life. Born and reared in Lislary on the Atlantic shore of North Sligo, she left school at thirteen years of age to work in the laundry of the nearby Lissadell House. Before long she moved north to Derry where she lived with her aunt Bella, and eventually secured a job with The Red Cross, before she emigrated to

London during the war. I think this may have had something to do with an American soldier. She rarely spoke of this part of her life except for her oft-expressed admiration for the sharp wit and spirit of the Cockneys she knew in dangerous times.

She never spoke of the American, but I overheard my father shouting about him once when they were having a fierce row. Mother's sister, my aunt Sally told me one time that she later became engaged to a 'really nice fellow' called Tom who was a professional boxer from Mayo. 'She just never met him again' after she was swept off her feet by 'the Kildare man.' Sally didn't seem too keen on my father. He had caused quite a furore by defecting from the Kildare football team when it went on tour to London in 1947. He was still 'thick' after being dropped for the previous summer's Leinster final against Laois, following a malicious report that he had been seen coming from a soccer game in Naas 'with his football boots on the carrier of his bicycle.'

They married and lived in London for a while before they moved back to have their first-born in Kildare. Mother's face would brighten up anytime she spoke wistfully of the excitement, glamour and wonderful friends she left behind her in London, where she had worked as a waitress. Those first couple of years when they moved from a rented flat to a shared house in Clongorey, from there moving into a lonely house at the end of a long narrow cul-de-sac, were hard for my mother. 'I often didn't speak to a single soul from morning 'til night.' She would say of her time there. Things changed when they bought the little cottage on three quarters of an acre in Moorefield. Over the years, I often heard them relate how they cycled the eight or so miles from Gingerstown, on the Naas side of Caragh, to Moorefield, pulling a pram between them that contained baby me and all their worldly possessions.

When I think of the time of my life when we lived in

Moorefield, a jumble of wonderful images flash before me. My mother is always smiling. She has jet-black hair and a 'cow's lick' of it falls down over her eyes. She flicks it back with a toss of her head and says something funny as she puts a clip in it. The other adults smile and laugh as they look at her because mother is a beautiful looking lady with a warm personality and a devil-may-care attitude. People love being close to her.

Mother holding Marie, Sheila McGovern holding a dog,
me and a friend holding baby Veronica c 1954

A couple of her friends share the blanket spread out on the ground. We are having a picnic under a radiant sun shining in a clear blue sky. Veronica is the baby, not yet six months and is held by Sheila McGovern's friend, whose name I never knew. My other sister Marie and I are playing with the adults. When the baby cries one of us gives her a soother and rocks her 'til she falls asleep. Red and orange nasturtium flowers with their peculiar scent, ramble along the pathway running down to the gate. My father flits in and out of the picture. He too is always smiling and well-groomed with a straight parting on one side and always the whiff of Brylcreem.

Even when we lived in Moorefield there was always a strong connection to Clongorey, a country place about four miles north-east of Newbridge, just off the back road to Naas. Father was born, bred and reared in Clongorey. He must have cut and saved turf there when I was about five, because he hired a youth from up the road to bring it home and I was his helper. He, being the driver of the black pony, sat on the front of the load while I sat at the back. When we came to Kelly's Cross on the bog road in the heart of Clongorey, I recognised where we were and jumped from the load of turf without saying a word to him. I ran all the way down to my granny's, who at this stage lived in Ivy House about half a mile down the Clongorey road. She started to quiz me about where I'd come from. I couldn't explain myself properly, and I started to cry. Shortly before this, the same long-legged youth gave me the loan of a silver dog chain in return for letting him put his hand down the front of my trousers. He fiddled around with me for a few minutes before he finished, then he took back the chain and warned me not to tell anyone. My granny must have suspected something was amiss and spoke to my father, in order for him to take some sort of appropriate action, because the long legged youth never bothered me again.

The first thing I ever loved was a little red bike my father bought for me that summer. It was very small, the smallest bike I'd ever seen, but it took me a long time and many falls before I learned how to ride it. At the time I had a sort of guardian angel by the name of Marie McGovern, who although only eight or nine years older than me, was my second mother. It was Marie who held the little bike and ran alongside me as I strove to complete my first major challenge in life. There were falls, grazed knees and tears. Marie felt my pain and kept me in plasters until I mastered it and could even ride under the crossbar. Up to this point I probably struggled to hold my own

14

with Sean Bradley and Padge Kehoe in the little gang we had, but the bike changed things. It wasn't that I became 'top dog' or anything but the others now had to be nice to me if they were to have any chance of having 'a go on the bike.'

Sean, who lived in Number 3 Artillery Place, was the one who usually came up with ideas that sometimes landed us in trouble. Padge lived in Number 10 and was the one who had to give assent before we'd try out these ideas. Sean's father always had a great smile for me, anytime he saw me. He used to call me over with a wag of his finger for me to sing him a song that I'd made up called 'The Bloody Oul Cow.' This was inspired by our black cow that had a proclivity for kicking the bucket into which she was milked, usually by Mother. Sometimes there would be an audience of children at milking time particularly when the milker was my father. He would encourage us to hold our mouths open into which he would then squirt strigs of warm milk. He was a good shot but still missed more often than not and some mothers didn't like the smell of spilt milk reeking from their children and their clothes. The children weren't bothered by this and found ways to circumvent their mothers' strictures.

Marion Jackson and Anne Coyle also lived in Artillery Place and were around the same age as us. They were inclined to be a bit bossy but this didn't stop us from playing together. An upside down barrow became an imaginary truck. It was a squeeze for everyone to fit on board but we managed. When it was right way up and there was an adult or teenager to push it, it became the real deal. Once, after a day's summer rain, it became a paddling pool but it turned over and everyone was thoroughly soaked. The same mothers who complained about the smell of stale milk really had it in for my father now. They must have got to him because the barrow was locked in the shed and that was that.

Sean Bradley had two older brothers, Con and Larry, who each year organised a chase game called 'The Phantom.' Older children of Artillery Place would dress up, wear scary masks then chase the younger ones. Having given us a good lead, they would hunt us down one by one until we were all captured and brought back to the den, in reality a ramshackle tent at the back of the big sheds. Here we would be shouted at loudly until we cried. It was a harmless enough game, but because of the hype leading up to it we were in terror before it even happened. I cannot recall ever being more scared than when The Phantom was close at hand and about to pounce.

Just as scary but in a very different way was a game invented by the girls called 'Doctors and Nurses'. This involved being examined by nurses who, as it turned out, weren't all that keen on being examined by the doctors. They would give us a few quick peeks but it was unsatisfactory compared to what we'd let them do to us. A few days later they came up with a variation on the theme. We had to kneel down, close our eyes and keep them closed until a frock was draped over our head whereupon we were allowed a split-second to see their knickers. Then we had to close our eyes tightly again. The object of the exercise was to identify which of the angels sitting before us was the owner of the different coloured underwear. It's over half a century now since we played this little game but I can still recall with absolute clarity the frilly white knickers of the girl who came up with the idea in the first place. Something stirred inside me which I didn't understand except I recall that it was a much nicer feeling than being caught by the phantom or having to take the loan of a silver dog chain.

EARLY SCHOOLDAYS

One day my mother bought me a schoolbag and a pencil case. The next thing I remember was her leading me by the hand, into the school opposite the parish church, at the other end of Newbridge, and handing me over to a nun called Sister Philomena, who stood behind a huge desk in a large bright classroom. This was my first time ever to see a nun. She wore a black veil on her head down to the middle of her back and a black habit covered the rest of her from the neck down to the ground. I couldn't even see her feet as she floated around the classroom. A set of large black rosary beads hung from her waist. The colour black was set off with a startling white breastplate that to me looked like a gigantic dribbler. All this made a singular impression on me that has stood the test of time.

The first thing that caught my eye in the classroom was a rocking-horse in the corner. It was some time before I discovered that this was for pupils who did something to especially please Sister Philomena. I cannot remember anyone ever getting onto that rocking-horse. What I do remember is a boy with black hair who everyday spent hours and hours trying to unravel a loose ball of yellow strings which were all knotted up. I heard someone say he was given this task because he was slow witted but this made no more sense to me then than it does now.

There were about thirty pupils in my class and while I can recall many of the boys, to this day I cannot remember any girls being in the same room, even though I am assured they were there; nor can I remember anything we ever learned. Padge Kehoe, Sean Bradley and I stuck together that first year and well into the second. But by the time we were in first class we had been subsumed into a gang of which Tommy McCormack was the leader. Our main activity was collecting boxes after school. Our walk home was along the entire length of the main street with shops, shops and more shops all on the one side.

'Boxes? Boxes? Any empty boxes?' We'd call out as we went from shop to shop. Eddie O'Connors Newsagent, Dolans Toy Shop and Keegan's Hardware were the best ones for keeping them aside for us. Some of the very large cardboard boxes we had acquired in Keegan's needed two or more to carry them up the street. These were great for making carriages to pull or push along shiny linoleum floors.

'Parcels' was a completely different game. This involved parcelling a box with brown paper and twine like the way they did in drapery stores. We'd then tie a length of fish line to this and leave it on the middle of the road while we hid. When someone pulled up in a car or dismounted from a bicycle to investigate, we'd make it disappear by pulling it into our hiding place behind the hedge.

Having observed my mother gutting herrings one particular Friday, we thought we'd bring this trick to a new level. We retrieved the guts of several fish, which had a truly vile smell, and placed them into a shoe box. Then we parcelled the box as neatly as we could with brown paper and string. We left it on the middle of the road outside our gate and hid in our usual spot. A big green car duly came along. There was a man and a woman in it.

I recognised the driver as Mr Roche, the boss of the Rope Factory, impeccably dressed in a dark coloured suit, white shirt and a tie. We giggled with excitement when he stooped to pick up the parcel. He opened it after he got back into his car.

We didn't giggle however when he then got back out of the car and marched up the path to our house, with the box in his hands. He knocked on the kitchen door and spoke to my mother as he handed her the opened box. Mother was very angry. She ordered Padge and Sean home. I went to go with them. We ran when she called me back, but she ran after us and caught me before I reached the end of the garden. She then reddened my bum for me in front of the others, pulled me back to the house as I roared crying, gave me another few whacks and put me up to bed. That was the end of the fish-gut parcels.

One day towards the end of the school year there was a big outdoor party organised for the whole school. This was held in the playground. Everyone had been instructed to bring in a drink and something nice to eat. The message must've gotten a little mixed up by the time it reached my mother because she had packed me off with thick cheese sandwiches. To add to my sense of mortification, instead of a bottle of orange, I was given cow's milk in a brown Guinness bottle, with a cork made of tightly rolled up newspaper.

A frolicsome atmosphere pervaded the playground that day. But this wasn't picked up on by the little boy who hadn't any biscuits or orange and who wouldn't take either the brown stout bottle with the newspaper cork, or the thick cheese sandwiches, out of his school-bag. I must have been a picture of misery because one of the older girls came over with a concerned look on her face. She had straight short hair and smiled warmly as she spoke to me. After she looked into my school-bag, she went back to look into her own, then came back over to me again. This time she handed me a small bottle of orange and some of her Mikado biscuits, which were nice and soft and very tasty. I recognised her as one of the older girls from the Cash family that lived next door to my aunt Rose in Roseberry, on the Clongorey side of the town.

Many, many years later I introduced myself to a middle aged woman as we shopped for breakfast cereals in Dunnes Stores, Newbridge. I had recognised her as the Cash girl who had been so kind to me. She smiled the same smile as she did that day but became slightly embarrassed when I very belatedly thanked her for the kindness she had shown a miserable little boy in that playground so long before. I'm not sure if she even remembered the incident but we both enjoyed our reminisces of times long passed. She then turned the tables on me when she introduced me to her son, who had come up behind us. Now it was my turn to blush as I recognised Glen Ryan, my latter-day football hero who was shortly to captain Kildare in the All Ireland final against Galway in Croke Park.

One day as I walked home from school I saw a great commotion at the Moorefield end of the town, where the shops on one side of the street ended and the houses began. Next, I saw smoke belching through a hole in the roof of the Irish Ropes Factory on the opposite side of the street. That evening after my father came home from work on The Curragh, he was still dressed in his painter overalls. He wasn't his usual self at all. He sat down with his elbows on the table and his head in his hands. Mother came over and put her arms around him.

He was sniffling and when I looked into his face I saw that he was crying. I then started to cry as well thinking we were both crying about the fire in the Ropes factory. But no, my father was crying because he had just heard of the death of his friend Andy Moore, a prominent and much loved man in the town. His death was a terrible tragedy. He had gone into the local Jockey hospital, to have an ingrown toenail removed, but died during the operation.

Mother and Father both went to a thing called 'the funeral' leaving us in the care of Padge Kehoe's mother, a kind-hearted, bespectacled lady. She donned her black overcoat and brought us down to the Protestant church at the end of Artillery Place, where a small crowd of women and children had gathered to watch the cars crawl past on their way down to the Parish church. I was struck by the sadness and the silence.

'The hearse is down at the Parish,' someone muttered after what seemed a long time.

'That's a full mile down the town,' said Mrs Kehoe as she blessed herself.

I looked back up towards Scanlon's shop. The cars were still coming.

One day shortly after this, I came into the kitchen to see, this time, my mother sitting down by the table with my father's arms around her.

'What are we to do now? She sighed as she looked up at him.

'I don't know.' He said. He called me over and lifted me up into his arms. Mother stood up then and hugged the two of us. I tasted salt on her cheeks; this puzzled me but I was happy to receive hugs and kisses from the two people I loved most. Father had just been laid off from his job as a painter with the Board of Works and apparently this was very worrying. There was much talk but no work. All that winter there wasn't much laughter in our little house but at a certain point the atmosphere changed. Father had gone to see an elderly gentleman called Larry Fulham who owned a small farm in Clongorey. It was for sale by public auction but Larry Fulham let it be known that he was anxious that my father should have 'the place.' When my mother produced her Post office savings book, Father took it and went to see Mr Fulham again.

Shortly after this I remember climbing a stairs for the first time in my life, to stand in a large room with a rich creamy coloured paint on the walls. We were in a large old house in the middle of the country, with a strange acrid smell of smoke and dampness. Mother became agitated when she discovered a bees nest in the corner of the room. Father was excited and looked over at me.

'Well son, what do you think?' he asked.

'I want to go home,' I replied. A strange look passed between Father and Mother. Then she came over and held me close.

'He'll get used to it,' said my father as he shrugged his shoulders and turned away.

They bought the house before the auction and shortly after this our lovely little home in Moorefield was sold. A black car came for Mother, Marie and Veronica. Father and I travelled in the cab of the lorry that took away all our furniture along with my little red bike. I was excited at the prospect of what lay in front of me. I just couldn't process that this was the end of my days as a townie, the end of nuns, gangs, boxes and all that would have happened if our father and mother hadn't bought Woodbine House in Clongorey.

CHANGING TIMES

My First Holy Communion. This was taken outside the
Parish church in Newbridge in Spring 1957

'Be back in time for your dinner.' Always my mother's parting instruction when she'd see me jump on the little red bike to pedal out of the haggart. Father's finishing time after he regained his job as a painter with the Board of Works on The Curragh was half past five. His cousin *Sticks* Murphy used to give him a lift to the bottom of The Baune Lane from where he cycled up home to be at the dinner table for five minutes to six. Woe betide any family member who wasn't sitting down on time.

Looking back, it seems incongruous, but the abiding memory I have of my little red bike towards the latter end of 1957 – my first year living in Clongorey as a six-year-old recently moved from Moorefield – is cycling to wakes. It had been ages since anyone local had died, but in the space of a few months Mick Tidd, Bridgie O'Rourke, Charlie O'Rourke, Minnie Kelly and Mrs Conlon all passed away and I was at all their wakes. I picked up news of their deaths from other pupils who also planned on going to the wake as soon as school was over for the day. I didn't know any of the people concerned, but I wasn't going to miss out on anything as exciting as cycling up to a dead person's house and sprinkling holy water on a white worn out face held in place with a black tie or headscarf.

I was nearly seven years old and I felt myself to be very important, saying prayers and looking every bit as serious as the adults sitting around drinking tea, eating sandwiches and smoking free cigarettes. The only thing was I couldn't understand how white sheets covering the mirrors in the room sped a soul on the way to heaven, nor could anyone explain it to me.

An even earlier memory was the ride with my father and about twenty other cyclists from Clongorey to Clogherinkoe for a football game. This time I was on the crossbar of my father's bicycle perched on the special little seat with my feet resting on the small steps attached to the frame. There were seven Kellys on that Clongorey team, two Taaffes, Snowball Conlon, my father Paddy, but called Sappy by everyone who knew him, and his cousins Buddy, Andy and Seamus.

There were a couple of cars but the majority of the team and supporters cycled all those miles to the Meath border on that sunny Sunday. That day seems so long ago now but I am still fascinated with the exotic sound of Clogherinkoe and emotional at the memory of being so close to my dad. I hear the steady whirr of rubber on road, as each man takes it in turn to lead out 'the posse.'

He told me things that day that have never left me. How the local school teacher called Mrs Fulham used to own Woodbine House before the time of the Clongorey evictions. She was part of the Plan of Campaign and when the bailiffs knocked on her door to evict her, she opened the upper sash of what was now our bedroom window and 'destroyed them with the contents of the chamber pot.' A few of the others overheard him telling the story and there was much laughter and guff about the antics.

'They evicted her; but because it was the only local house made of bricks, they retained it as a barracks for the "emergency men" whose job was to preserve the landlord's version of law and order.' He said this to me that day. He also told me of how owning Woodbine House and the land was a dream come true for him and my mother.

For the three young children though, the move from the town to the country was quite a shock. Candles and an oil lamp with a double wick were the means by which we lit up that cold dark house, with its two rooms downstairs and two bedrooms upstairs. One for the girls, the other I shared with my parents. The first sight that greeted me on waking each winter's morning was thick Jack Frost patterns on the back window.

I well remember a particular scene, viewed through that bedroom window during our first winter, when my mother and I cried from the bottom of our hearts. Our cow had died in the cow-byre after trying all night to give birth to her calf. Her flank was cut open and the body of the calf was slung across her gaping wound. Snow covered the yard and continued to fall as the bodies were winched up into the knacker's truck.

Michael Rowe, the vet from Naas, had spent the whole night with my father and flashlights and the oil lamp trying to save the situation. I came down that morning to the three adults crying in our kitchen over the tragedy of it all. That evening my uncle Martin, or Gunner as he was called, hunted a red shorthorn cow into our yard. He told me her name was Katie. She was his gift to us to replace our loss. We never looked back.

From the same upstairs window the previous autumn, we had gazed in wonder at a golden ball making its way across the dawn sky above Byrne's hedge. It was the Russian Sputnik with a dog on board. I wondered at the time how can a dog drive a sputnik? I have often wondered since if there wasn't more than a grain of truth in words I overheard from Johnny Dempsey, when discussing the matter one evening with my father:

'There'll never again be a proper summer after that fuckin sputnik was put up there.' Johnny was an elderly gentleman from Dereens, who worked alongside my father for the Board of Works and normally never used bad language.

The following summer was the wettest on record. Bertie Watchorn's combine harvester sank in the Gurteen field and had to be abandoned until the following spring.

A tilly lamp was the first sign of progress, it gave off a hissing sound and it took a while to give off its full glow. The paraffin oil had to be primed by a rapid pumping action and lighting a scissors-like apparatus, soaked in methylated spirits, was necessary to get it going, but its light was brighter than a dozen or more candles. Our electric radio, which we'd brought from Newbridge, was now useless but my mother bought a second hand PYE radio at an auction in Brophy's Showrooms behind the Palace cinema in Newbridge. This was powered by two transparent wet cell batteries which had to be charged up in McLoughlin's shop on the main street in Newbridge every so often. I remember a commotion when the living room curtains were destroyed by brushing against one of the batteries on the window sill. Apparently the top of one of the batteries had come loose during my mother's cycle up the Baune Lane, on her way home and the acid which had spilled down the side of the battery burnt the curtains.

My father was a friend and active supporter of Billy Norton, a Labour Party minister in the Coalition Government. Mr Norton, who had big jowly cheeks, used his political influence to bring The Rural Electrification Scheme to Clongorey in 1959. Most people signed up, but some were reluctant because they didn't want any truck with the Labour Party. In the end everyone signed up except for three households, who just didn't want it. Jimmy Kelly the electrician and his apprentice wired the houses. Each room had a brown round light switch and one or two plug sockets. There was tremendous excitement when the electricity was switched on. The first appliance in our house was a washing machine with a hand wringer. The washboard and galvanised bath were now redundant and there was no more hand wringing for my mother. Nevertheless the utensils were retained for years, just in case.

One evening during that second summer, a car with a bicycle in the boot drove into our front yard. It was a dark green Hillman ZW 99, driven by our father. Suddenly his life and ours were changed forever. Going for a pint or ten to Allen, Caragh, Newbridge or Naas became easy. After this my mother would often rise from her bed late at night, let down the front window to listen for the sound of the Hillman. There would be no sleep until it rolled into the yard. This was a hard time, but the abiding memory I have of our first car is of

Sunday evenings when father and I would drive the ten miles or so to Allenwood, to visit my Aunt Kitty who owned the shop at the Crossroads. The road as far as Kilmeague was long and lonely, but the stepped design of the village houses going up the hill always fascinated me. A few miles on there was the first of four canal bridges; he would rev up the engine to take the hills at speed, in order to produce an exquisite tingle in our bellies. I cannot recall him ever discussing this with me, but I know he enjoyed it every bit as much as I did.

Aunt Kitty was a very kind lady who plied us with thickly buttered Ryvita, tea and cake. She had a television with a great picture because of the high aerial. Telefis Eireann had begun broadcasting on New Years eve 1961. Sunday night programmes were brilliant. The Flintstones were on at seven o'clock. My favourite bit each week was at the start of the programme, when Fred would push a bird's long thin beak down to play a rock-disc on his stone age record player. After a while I became more sophisticated and preferred Richard Boone in 'Have Gun, Will Travel.' He had a lightning fast draw. I tried to emulate him by practicing initially with a bit of a stick from my pocket. When Santa brought me a gun and holster set I very quickly became the fastest draw in Clongorey.

Around this time my mother and I were alone in the back kitchen one sunny afternoon when Father Bennett, our parish priest, walked in through the open door without knocking.

He wore a soutane which was buttoned down the front from his neck to his ankles. The previous Sunday he had read out 'the station offerings' from the altar. He had started with the local big farmers and the shopkeeper who had contributed five pounds each and continued his way down the list, calling out the names and their contributions, until he came down to the people who had only contributed half a crown. These would be called out in a very desultory tone indeed. That Sunday as he worked his way through the list, a child had started to cry. Mother and I happened to be sitting beside my Aunt Josie whose baby quickly became the centre of attention.

'Will the mother of that child please control it, or go down to the room at the back of the church?' An almighty tension developed as the priest and the whole congregation waited for my Auntie to walk. She blushed and hushed her child but never budged. Mother was livid with the attitude of the priest, who was highly regarded in Caragh for organising fund raising events to build a new church, There was talk now of him starting a collection to build a new school there as well.

Now standing on the floor of our back kitchen, Fr Bennett who had a rather brusque manner came straight to the point.

'I'm very disappointed with the half crown ye found fit to contribute to the stations,' he said to my mother as she stood there staring back at him.

'It was all we could afford and you were lucky to get it.' She never flinched as she looked him in the eye. I was sitting on the green flour box beside the range and was totally transfixed by this exchange between the red faced priest and my mother, growing paler by the minute.

'You seem to be doing very well here, ten shillings is the least ye should be able to contribute.'

When he said this, my mother looked at him for some fairly long seconds before quietly moving to the tea chest at the far side of the range. She picked up the poker, raised it above her head and said quietly but very firmly.

'You are nothing only a bully, now get out of this house and don't come back.'

Father Bennett was speechless, after a few seconds he turned on his heel and walked out the door with the soutane billowing in his wake. He never came back.

A LETTER TO CAP

Even after all these years I find it difficult when I recall the way you left us. Stiff as a poker, with your neck extended backwards, your three and a half legs stretched out rigid like iron rods. You took your last agonised breath in front of me on the floor of the shed that Sunday morning in early spring. Normally you'd be wagging the tail ready and able to fall in beside me for the day.

So well do I remember now the time in my life I shared with you and how you came to be with us. You were part of a deal. My father had placed a small ad in the Leinster Leader:

'For Letting. Twenty acres of grassland. Apply Box no 207.'

He had just been given the deeds for the twenty acre field in Barrettstown by the Land Commission. At that point we had no stock for the land, hence the small ad. The only response it elicited was from an elderly Wicklow man, who needed good land to fatten sheep. Both parties wanted it to work but there was reluctance from my father who had no experience of sheep farming whatsoever.

'I'll never be able to mind them and I'm afraid they'll break out all over the place,' he said.

'You needn't worry, we'll leave you a collie dog. He's only young but he's good and you can hold on to him, even after we take back the sheep.' He opened the back of the Morris Minor van and there you were with your wiry black and white coat.

Forlorn, you stood there with a long snout and brown roundy eyes looking at the four human beings looking at you. You didn't wag the tail, but you didn't growl or pull back either when I rushed up and threw my arms around you. Father spat on his hand and whacked the offered hand of the Wicklow man. His son told me your name was Cap.

I loved you from the beginning but you broke my heart that first week. The Wicklow men had said to keep you in for a few days until you got used to the place. You were locked up in the shed and I spent as much time with you as I could. On the fourth morning I rushed to let you out but you weren't there. We looked everywhere. You were gone. I was inconsolable.

The following Sunday the Wicklow men drove into the yard with you in the back of the van. It had taken you three days and three nights to make your way back to Lacken, on the far side of Blessington, a distance of well over twenty miles from Clongorey. My heart jumped in my chest when I saw you. A little wag of the tail was all you gave, but you came to me all the same. Somehow or other we both knew then there would be no more rambling. After this we grew very close, playing and just being together. I was eight years old and you became the brother I didn't have. My father at this stage had to cycle to and from work each mday and most of the herding work fell to my mother and I. We would check the sheep at least once a day. Sometimes they were off up at the far side of the field. A sign and a shout from me was all it would take for you to set off on a loop to bring them around for me to count them.

The following summer my mother procured a setting of turkey eggs which hatched out to become a flock of turkey poults. These were reared in the haggart. They would scratch around the place all day but would show little inclination to come in at night. Each evening you found and gently nuzzled those poults out from under nettles and briars. We never lost a turkey poult, but there was the terrible death that befell the most prominent of them.

All that summer we minded those turkeys. By September they had grown enormously. One of them was significantly bigger and had developed an attitude that made both of us wary of him. He would stick out his neck, fluff out his feathers and charge at anything or anyone that came near the others. He was their king and protector.

When December came around, a small ad was placed in the Leader: 'Turkeys for Sale'. One Saturday father and mother had to go to the town and I was left in charge. I was instructed by my father on the price he needed for the turkeys and to tie a piece of baler twine around the leg of whichever turkey anyone chose and that he'd kill and pluck it for them to collect that evening.

Two people called; a woman and her husband. I was so proud to conduct the sale and when they picked out The King. I spancelled him with the baler twine left out for the job. As always you were by my side, when, along with my father I opened that shed door to be confronted by a sickening spectacle that has left its mark on me. The remains of The King lay dead on the floor, his head and gullet were ravaged. An eye and his beak were separated out from the rest of the head and blood was splattered all over the shed and on every single one of the twenty or so turkeys. You instantly started barking and charged in to scatter those murderous bastards. Always after this I hated turkeys, even on my Christmas plate. That King turkey had spent most of his short life watching out for others, but when he was down and helpless they picked him to pieces.

As the years went by our cattle herd grew. Cows, calves, yearlings, stores, springers, we had them all. They grazed all together in the Gurteen field and Crofton's Bottoms. Each evening all I had to do was stand at the gate and shout 'Cows' and you'd head off down the field to return within minutes with all seven or eight cows for milking. Any of the others who tried to come, you rebuffed.

One winter day my mother sent me down to the Gurteen

to bring home the black cow that was up against calving. As always you trotted behind me, It lashed rain. The drains were full and the fields were flooded. We found her in the furthest corner of Crofton's Bottoms. We were too late. A big bull calf sat there in the rain shivering and too weak to stand. I picked him up and headed for the gate. Rushes and drains had to be traversed in the company of a delirious cow, She spent most of the time charging at you but nearly knocked me several times on our very difficult journey to the road.

We eventually arrived at the cattle ring, which I used to throw bales of hay into from the pony and cart parked on the road. There was a large area of muck around the cattle ring, and this I now had to traverse. The calf was heavy and slippery and my arms were very tired as the rain pelted down on us. I decided that the only thing to do was to bull through the muck and hope for the best. This I did, but in the process I walked out of my boots . Barefoot and shivering on the side of the road the twelve year old boy looked at his wellington boots stuck in the mire, then said to you:

'Fuck this for a game of cowboys, I'm going to have nothing to do with farming.' Your response was a slight wag of the tail.

One day down in Barrettstown we were trying to bring home a rogue heifer who was bulling. She wanted none of it and a battle of wills developed between us and her. Twice we had her on the Baune Lane heading for home, but each time she turned and bested us to return to the herd. Twice you brought her back onto the lane but then inexplicably you went to her head rather than her heels and caused her to burst back again. I was so frustrated and vexed that I kicked you on your flank as hard as I could and gave you the belt of a stick I wanted to give to that heifer. I left her where she was, but what bothered me more than you'd ever know was that I'd broken that trust

33

there was between us.

The guilt I felt for maltreating you has never left me. I was instantly remorseful as you yelped and howled, you poor thing. I knew I had hurt you considerably. Our relationship recovered to what it nearly was before, but harm was done that day and thereafter it was never quite the same between us.

One evening you were hit by a car, my father said the driver was drunk but the end result was your hind leg was broken. It healed, but it was now shortened and bent up and for all intents and purposes you became a three-legged dog. You never let it stop you from doing anything but you were well slowed down and weren't inclined to do too much for anyone except for me. By this time I was a pupil in Newbridge College and in truth the halcyon days of the boy and the dog were behind us.

One night a cousin of my father's from Monasterevin came to visit. Ber Smyth had heard of you and now that he'd started into sheep he wondered if my father would give him the loan of you for a couple of months. He said he was desperate. The two of them went up to Mulrennan's for a pint and to discuss the matter further. I went to bed.

'Where's Cap?' I asked my father, when I came down the following morning.

'I gave a loan of him to Ber, he's my cousin and he's badly stuck.'

'He's my dog ..... in Monasterevin, for fuck's sake, you shouldn't have done it.' I blurted straight out.

'Don't you dare use that language to me......Look it's only a loan he'll be back in a couple of months.' I had never spoken to Father like this before and I knew I was very close to getting a belt. I was incandescent but I could see from his demeanour that my father wasn't at all impressed with himself. I let it go but I really really missed the welcoming wag of the tail anytime I came into the yard.

Weeks slipped into months; there was no word of you being returned. One Saturday night I dreamt I saw you drag your withered leg through the bottom bar of our gate. I awoke and went to tell my mother of my dream but she was down in the kitchen rattling dishes getting ready for the breakfast. Suddenly she shouted out at the top of her voice:

'Noel, Noel , come down quick.'

I rushed out to the landing, but before I took the first step you were in the hallway at the bottom of the stairs. You twirled around and around and barked wildly when you saw me, then for the first and only time in your life, you clattered up that steep stairs, into my grateful and unbelieving grasp.

You'd undertaken another epic journey and had come home from Monasterevin.

Sometime after this there was that awful moment, when I caught you in O'Grady's field trying in vain to keep up with a pack of four or five other dogs who were worrying, more than worrying sheep. I never hit you again after that episode on the Baune Lane but I grabbed you and brought you home. This time it was your turn to be guilty, you wouldn't look me in the eye but skulked over to the hay shed, with your tail between your legs. My father decided that you were to be locked up every night in the empty pig shed that had been the scene of the turkey King's murder. I was so careful to ensure this was done each night.

That week Bertie Watchorn had three 'in lamb' ewes suffer an appalling death from marauding dogs. In a fit of apoplexy that Saturday evening, he went around Clongorey with a bagful of raw meat laced with strychnine and stopped at the houses he knew had dogs. Four dogs that I know of died as a result of this. Including you. Stiff as a poker, with your neck extended backwards, your three and a half legs stretched out rigid like iron rods, you took your last agonised breath in front of me on the floor of the shed that Sunday morning in early spring. All hell broke loose and Bertie came under ferocious pressure especially from my father. He had actually called into our home that night and had slipped you the poisoned meat as he came in the door, just before I locked you up. It was sort of understandable what he did, but it caused enormous bitterness.

Shortly after this, Bertie emigrated to Canada. Two Christmases later an envelope arrived with a Canadian stamp. There was a card inside with long note from Bertie. The only bit of it I remember was the heartfelt apology for what he'd done to you that night. My father wrote him back a letter saying 'what's in the past is in the past'. When he returned to resume farming where he'd left off, Bertie and my father became friends once more. However I kept my distance.

Years later when I was a student in UCD, I accidentally met Bertie one night at the greyhound track in Harold's Cross. He asked if I'd join him for a 'bit of grub?'I did so and I let myself enjoy listening to a man who'd been a huge part of my childhood. We chatted of this and that without ever once mentioning your name. We didn't have to. Your presence dominated the reconciliation which happened that night. When he reached across the table to shake my hand, I took it with a good heart.

I fancied I saw a tail swish as you waited for me to leave so that you could fall in and trot behind me one last time.

SAVING HAY

'Jesus, I hope it doesn't rain.' My mother said, more in the way of a prayer than a sigh.

Later on that same morning she cycled down The Baune Lane to look at the hayfield on her rickety old bicycle. As she passed me, I noticed her lips moving without her speaking, rosary beads in her left hand as it grasped the handlebars. Once she heard the rat-a-tat of the mower, the rosary beads were kept close at hand. Memories of trying to save hay in small fields right next to the Atlantic Ocean off Lislary in County Sligo would flood back to her. There would be thoughts and talk of little else until the hay was cocked.

'I can't help it,' she would say to my father's exasperated admonishments to:

'Stop driving me out of my mind.'

The men, including her brothers in law, were cocking hay in the middle of our field. Rain clouds were threatening to bring this work to a standstill by that afternoon. She handed me a basket of sandwiches and the kettle in a shopping bag with strict instructions:

'Run over and get them to drink the tea before it goes cold.'

She didn't want her *in laws* to see how tense she was, so she hopped up on her bicycle and was gone before they knew she was there. I'd been told by Father to remain on the headland with Cap where he could keep an eye on me. I was delighted now to have the excuse to run over to where the men were working to tell them about the tea and the sandwiches.

Father's stepfather, Jay, was atop the hay rake, driving his white mare, Molly, across the field. Every five or six swards he pulled the lever to leave the hay in big fluffed up rows. Uncle Jimmy drove his mare, Kitty, along these rows to gather it.

37

Seven or eight gathers was sufficient to make a large cock of hay. Jack Kelly, our neighbour and my Uncle Martin, known far and wide as The Gunner, shook huge forkfuls into the space which quickly took the shape of a haycock as they worked around it.

I ran out to the middle of the field to where the men were working. Cap came running after me. There was little talk and I could hear the distinct rattle off the hay, which along with the uniquely sweet smell was a sure sign that it was fit. The sun shone through breaks in the clouds as Father walked from the previous cock to the next, with a ball of twine in an old bucket, a wooden rake with a couple of teeth missing and a two grain fork.

It was his field and for this reason he was the one to finish each cock into the shape of a dome, with all the semidried stalks of grass or 'trawneens' as they were called, perfectly aligned to throw off the rain. Father loved sucking the juice from trawneens and always seemed to have one stuck in his mouth when he was working at hay.

It was a matter of considerable pride to the brothers for the cocks to be well made and in a straight row. This took concentration as well as a certain rhythm, and it was probably for this reason I wasn't surprised to be told:

'Go back and mind the tea and sandwiches for us, we'll be over in a few minutes.' Also I think father was half afraid that Jay might run me over. We were walking back when Cap saw a rabbit and took off after him along the headland.

Alone, back at the gate, the sharp smell from the sandwiches got the better of me. I contemplated my mother's basket and pulled back the greaseproof paper to get a proper look at them. I liked fresh sliced pan sandwiches, especially when dripping with mashed hard boiled eggs and chopped scallions mixed with dollops and dollops of salad cream. I absolutely loved salad cream.

Whether it was the smell, the hunger or a streak of devilment, the nine year old boy made a fair hole in that basket of sandwiches. I even gave one to Cap when he came back from his futile chase of the rabbit, but he didn't like the salad cream and left it out of his mouth. As the meithel walked purposefully towards their lunch it dawned on me, there weren't now enough sandwiches for the men and that I might be in trouble. I wasn't wrong. First there was disbelief that I could have eaten so much. This they knew from the crusts which I'd foolishly left in the basket. If looks and comments could kill, I'd have been killed that afternoon as the sun broke from between the cloud.

Birds sang lazy sweet notes in the hawthorn bushes behind us while I withered from the comments and disappointment in my father's eyes, when he realised all that was left for him to eat were a few crusts and the sandwich that the dog hadn't eaten.

Mother came down again for the basket and the cups but mostly to see to see how the work was progressing. The rain clouds were no more as the sun broke through. Mother's eyes radiated happiness as she contemplated the straight rows of haycocks.

'They'll be finished before seven' she said. She cycled back up The Baune Lane. Cap and I trotted up behind her. I said nothing about the sandwiches. She'd find out soon enough.

SAVING TURF

There was something almost sacred about how father regarded the bog. He had an innate understanding and appreciation of it, probably because much of his childhood from late Spring to early Summer was spent there. Money was scarce and the means of earning it even scarcer with no state support whatsoever for hard pressed families.

During The Emergency, as the years between 1939 and 1945 were called in Ireland, there was a huge demand for turf because of the scarcity of coal. Clongorey people with a turf bank on the bog suddenly had a significant source of income at their disposal, provided they were prepared to work hard and put in long hours, there being no bog mechanisation at the time. Each of the seven children, in my father's family participated in the effort. As a consequence they came to know all about the saving of turf and developed a real understanding and appreciation of its value.

After every Easter, Father and I would go into our *turf-bank*, which became my father's when he purchased the place from Larry Fullam. He brought me with him more for the company than anything else. I loved the strangeness of the still black water in the bog-holes next to the high banks of turf and the feeling of walking on a sponge when I walked into the askeen.* This became much more pronounced when I chanced to walk on the surface of the raised bog which Clongorey people called the fan*. He spent a couple of days clearing the drains and readying the turf bank for cutting later that summer. For drain clearing he used a long handled tool called a drag, which he'd borrowed from my Uncle Jimmy. I thought of this as a long handled four grain fork with bent tines. Father loved watching water flow and loved teaching his only son how water always found its own level.

After he was satisfied that water coming into the bog hole from the raised bog could flow out to the mearn drain unimpeded, he would climb up to The Fan to prepare the turf bank for cutting. Mother had him warned not to let me ramble on top of the raised bog for fear that I would disappear into one of the many fissures, or cracks as he called them, close to the face of the turf banks. Maybe it was something to do with knowing I was treading on forbidden ground but I loved being on The fan. I always managed to sneak up there, from where I could see the steeples of five churches.

In Clongorey bog a perch of turf was reckoned to be sufficient for to heat a family home for one year. To mark out a perch my father stepped out an area of high bog, so that the new section of turf to be cut would finish up seven yards long by five yards wide. To get to this he cut a series of huge chunks off the raised bog, and rolled them into the water of the bog hole, ten feet below. The hole was what was left, following a previous years extraction of turf. These cubes were called 'falls' with the area of each face being about three and a half feet. These made a huge splash when rolled off the top of the new turf bank, into the water far below. All year, I would look forward to the excitement of those splashes.

He then jumped down into the boghole to cut off the pieces jutting above surface of the water, until it was all levelled off and the water was pushed out of the bog hole, into the drain which he'd cleared the day before. The foundations having being set in place, he then overlaid this with bushes, which he'd breasted from the hawthorn hedge at the back of our house. Onto the bushes, we spread specially pulled heather from The fan and finally old mouldy hay from the bottom of the rick in the haggart.

He made a sort of ritual out of preparing tools and equipment

41

for that first morning as we loaded up the pony's cart, to drive into the bog to begin to cut. We were never all that early and after we reached Kelly's Cross on the Bog Road, the white shirts of others already at work stood out against the dark background. As we drew closer I could see that each man had made a covering for his head out of his handkerchief. Father was an expert for making these *bog-hats*. The technique was to tie a knot at each corner and pull it tight. It was perfect for protecting my head from the heat of the sun.

Sometimes, a gust of wind would send particles of dry turf mull swirling into the air. It was very distressing, and common enough when one of these tiny particles ended up in my eye. Father would then take off his *bog-hat*, loosen it, so it again became a handkerchief. The corner of this was then inserted into his mouth so that it was wetted and stiffened with spittle. He would then pull me close, tenderly open my eyelash so that he could spot the particle which he would then deftly remove with the stiffened corner of the handkerchief.

'There, the little fecker is gone.' He would say then give a little grin.

'Thanks Da.' I would blink a few times to assure myself it was gone. I'd then rub my eyes and enjoy the sublime moment of closeness and love, before we resumed our work. First he'd cut four or five floors of spongy white turf or sphagnum. This was soft and easily cut with a wing sleane, but would be very difficult to get dry enough to burn. It gave off little heat. Mother used to say it was fit only for lighting a fire. The next five or six floors of brown turf were permeated with whigs. Whigs were composed of fibrous material and were almost impossible to cut with the downward motion of a wing sleane, as they stuck on it's cutting edge. Instead they had to be 'mullocked' out with a spade or a breast sleane after it had been back cut with a hay knife.

'These fuckin whigs have my heart broke.' He would say at times like this.

'The feckers!' I'd reply.

Once, I chanced to use the word 'fuckers' instead. His head jerked up and he said:

'Don't use that word.'

I never consciously did say it to him again either, until much later in life. Whether it was Father or me in my late teens, cutting through whigs was a hungry business and after a few hours of it, our eyes would pleadingly skim the horizon for sight of my mother cycling in with her two shopping bags swinging from the handlebars. A small fire would have been lit first thing in the morning and the kettle of water boiled on this.

Mother's sandwiches never tasted so good as they did after a morning of 'mullocking whigs.' It usually took us three or four days of to cut down to the yellow turf. He showed me the traces of birch fossilised in this, of which there were three or four or five floors immediately above the water which came up from the bottom. Immediately below yellow was the black turf, which was the best because of the way it had been compressed by the weight of matter laid down on top of it over thousands and thousands of years. Black turf was highly regarded as fuel because of the heat it gave off. Father used to say that it was 'better than coal.'

Black turf lies in situ below the level of the permanent water table. That day it was literally underwater and it took great skill and determination on my father's part to harvest every sod. The technique to do this was to divide the bottom into two or three sections, beginning with the one next to the drain. Each section had to be bottomed out in a day. The management of water was of the utmost importance and was facilitated greatly by digging a *scub-hole* two sods deeper than the bench of black turf he was working on. This instantly drained all the water from the rest of the section but it had to be kept from overflowing, by emptying the hole every few minutes.

When the cart was full of slippery saturated sods, I led our white pony further out the askeen to tip up the cart so that the sods slipped out and scattered on the askeen. This was his opportunity to empty the scub-hole with a deep enamel basin attached to a long pole for ease of throwing the water up and over the *indam*. The *indam* was a twelve inch thick wall of black turf, next to the water in the drain which prevented the water from flowing back in on top of the cutter. It was a matter of huge pride to my father that he harvested every single sod of black turf. If I let a sod slip back down into the water he would order me down to recover it with a two grain fork. If the cutter didn't know what he was doing, incoming water would get the better of him and the bottom with the black turf still in situ would have to be abandoned. Father was a true bogman and had little enough respect for anyone who left black turf in a bottom. Me going out with the pony to scatter the turf was also his opportunity to attack the buttermilk. He would have brought several large lemonade bottles of buttermilk to the bog with him on the morning he was about to tackle the bottom. These he kept cool by immersion in the soft muck of the scub-hole.

'Bottoming' was a race against time and incoming water to extract 'the black gold.' The last floor consisted of a red sod which was useless for burning but was wing sleaned out in any case and left on the edge of the boghole with the underlying grey lac still attached as a badge of honour for all to see that every sod had been extracted.

When the cutting was over Father was inclined to leave the turning and footing of turf to his wife and children. I hated footing turf with a vengeance. It was back breaking work

44

usually done with clouds of midges hovering over me. They must have regarded me as some sort of delicacy because more often than not I would come home from footing turf with lumps all over me as big as carbuncles. My sister Marie didn't seem to mind footing turf, and was good at it too. I'm not sure about Veronica.

Black turf had to be watched very carefully. It took a certain amount of sunshine to dry it out and for this reason we scattered it on the askeen. Once it was dry however it had to be thrown into heaps because if it were left untended on the flat for as little as a couple of days it became extremely brittle and would disintegrate into almost nothing. As the turf dried we threw it into bigger and bigger heaps until it was fit enough to bring home.

I loved the job of bringing home turf whether by pony and cart with high creels or driving the tractor which became the way after Father purchased the blue Fordson Major. This had come with a trailer which was really the body of a lorry and was far too heavy for the bog. Father's Uncle Mike was a blacksmith and he converted a horse cart into a tractor trailer to bring home turf. I loved whizzing up and down the Clongorey road in the driving seat of the big blue tractor with the small trailer and the breeze blowing back my hair. I was all of twelve years old and king of the road.

*Askeen is the spreading ground usually located on the cutaway or low bog. It is usually adjacent to the turf being cut.
*Fan is the surface of the raised or high bog.

PIGS

I couldn't understand why the fuss over a little chip of white enamel missing from a basin, I may have said something to that effect but neither lady had the slightest interest in what an eleven year old boy had to say on the matter.

'Put it under the washing machine, it'll do for bringing out clothes,' Mrs Watchorn, the lady of the house was adamant.

'Missus If I can't use this as the second basin .... blood is going to go all over the yard and there won't be enough for the puddings.' Mrs Wallace, the silver haired house maid, was equally adamant.

'Oh alright so but make sure you strain it,' said the gentle lady of the house at the end of the Baune Lane. She also was silver haired but chair bound because of rheumatics or some such ailment.

Loud pig squeals in the front yard quickly ended any further discussion. I rushed out, Bertie, her son and my father's friend, had just hit the pig, a belt on the head with a mallet. As the stunned animal lay on the ground my father slipped a rope around its hind legs. Bertie's father, who wasn't called 'The Boss' for nothing, issued instructions left, right and centre as he stood leaning on the car between the half opened door and the driver's seat. He had a stick in his hand.

Three stout poles had been lashed together to form a tall tripod. My father had to climb a chair to thread the rope through the eye of the pulley suspended from the apex of the tripod. Then they hauled mightily on the rope until the pig's head was suspended a foot or so above the ground. They secured the rope to a stout hook on one of the poles.

'Come on with the basin', shouted Bertie. Mrs Wallace ran as quickly as she could and placed it under the head before retiring. When Bertie slit the pig's throat from ear to ear the blood gushed forth. A couple of minutes later Mrs Wallace handed Bertie the second basin, the one with the missing enamel chip, which he held between the pig's head and the other basin on the ground, this her ladyship deftly removed without spilling a single drop although it was full to the brim. I stood there, transfixed by the goings on. Then a barrow was brought out.

'Go on inside to the women,' my father ordered when Bertie laughed as he answered my question by telling me that the barrow was for 'the guts.' I decided I'd seen enough and hopped up on my little red bicycle and pedalled home to my mother to tell her all the news. This ritual had been practiced around Clongorey for aeons, and was second nature to the adults involved. I think it was on this day that 'The Boss' convinced my father that he 'should get into pigs.'

First stop was the Spring Show in Dublin. We spent a whole day traipsing around looking at pigs, more pigs and everything to do with pigs. Someone sold my father a thick book with a picture of pigs on the blue cover. This became his bible for the next three or four years.

That summer Dan Doherty from Caragh arrived to build the pig-sheds. I appointed myself as his helper. One of the tasks allocated to me was to slit the empty paper bags in which pig rations had come. These were then put on top of netting wire strung between the joists. Another job was to fill the barrow with dry 'turf mull' to go on top of the bags. This insulation idea was just one of many gleaned from the blue book.

Also my father set up a series of lectures by an agricultural instructor called PJ Keenan, in the school. I was allowed to attend; I was fascinated by the slides and a thing called an overhead projector. Around this time we dug a well and installed a pump and plumbed water to the pigs' sheds as well

Pigs in the yard of our pig shed that Dan Doherty built

as into the kitchen. Within jig-time we had developed one of the most modern pig farms in the whole parish.

Around the time I became a teenager, our first sow whom we called Missus Nutt, an imposing animal with a personality to match, took up residence. When she came in heat we hunted her down the Baune Lane to Watchorn's 'Department' Boar. This huge brute had an intriguing piece of equipment shaped like a corkscrew which he used for putting sows in pig.

I became fascinated by this but discussions on the topic were not encouraged by my father or mother. We duly counted down the three months, three weeks and three days to our first litter of piglets. Father stayed up all night and the following morning he came into us all excited to announce:

'She has seventeen banbhs but only sixteen teats.'

By the time we all rushed out to welcome our new additions this situation was resolved. Missus Nutt had inadvertently crushed two of her litter as she lay down to suckle.

My father was raging that one of these wasn't the little runt who was only half the size of the others. The banbhs spent most of the time sleeping under the infrared light suspended in the corner. Feeding time was when Missus Nutt grunted in a particular sequence. She was very careful about how she lay down, but after the first day or so the little ones were nimble enough to avoid her in any case.

In time we built up a herd of eight sows, and became entitled to a grant from the Department of Agriculture to buy our own boar. This was a considerable relief to me, for whatever about escorting an 'in heat' sow a mile or so down the Baune Lane, escorting her back was most challenging, except for Missus Nutt who didn't need anyone to escort her anywhere.

The sows slept together most of the time. They had the run of the Long Field which in short time was all but ruined because of their rooting. Father decided this had to be stopped. His solution was to ring their snouts. This entailed looping each sow's top jaw with a slender rope behind her tusks and tying the rope to a pole set in concrete, then inserting two rings into the soft tissue that separated the nostrils by squeezing them in with a pliers-like instrument. The squeals that day were the most piercing sounds I'd ever heard, but there was no more rooting, because nose-rings caused pain anytime they came in contact with the ground.

When a sow was about to farrow, she would be moved into her own house and yard.

'Can I stay up with Missus Nutt tonight on my own?' I asked my father. I'd stayed up with farrowing sows before but it was just to keep my father company. She was restless and we knew she would give birth that night.

'She's a huge belly on her; it'll be a big litter. I'm afraid you'd fall asleep and that you might let her lie on them,' said my father as he we both looked in over the timbered wall that separated the farrowing area from the rest of the shed. Missus Nutt grunted as she looked back up at us.

'Ah Da, you know that won't happen. Didn't you show me what to do?'

'Well OK, I'll set the clock for six, and come out to check how things are before I go to work'.

So I took on the responsibility of bringing a litter of piglets into the world while the rest of the family went to bed. I tuned the transistor radio to 208 Radio Luxembourg which I normally listened to under blankets. Around one o'clock the first little piglet arrived and immediately jumped up and spent several moments trying to re-enter the passage from which he had just emerged. I deftly picked him up and placed him under the infrared light in the corner. I turned off the radio and settled myself for a serious night of birthing. I waited and waited but no other piglet appeared. Several times I was about to go into the house to waken my father, but I was afraid they'd all come together if I left my vigil.

Father appeared, sometime before six. When he saw the single piglet he started to grill me intensively. I quickly realised he suspected I'd fallen asleep and that all piglets bar one were crushed and possibly buried by me. The more I implored him to believe me, the more suspicious he became. He thought this might have something to do with me listening to the transistor radio. It took years for him to stop mentioning it. I'm not sure if he ever came around to believing, I hadn't fallen asleep listening to 'that rotten pop music.'

Thankfully Missus Nutt went on to have many fine big litters. There was one particular occasion when she became extremely cross as she suckled her banhms. Father was at work, but this was urgent and couldn't wait 'til evening, so mother phoned Bertie who, as always, answered her plea for help. He sized up the situation immediately and asked my mother for a scissors. He had spotted that one of the piglets had a wayward tooth that had to be clipped. With difficulty we managed to remove the truculent Missus Nutt and bolted the gate that separated her from her litter. Mother and I watched proceedings from an internal window in the adjoining shed.

Bertie grabbed the piglet and clipped the tooth. It was hard to believe that a piglet so tiny could create such a racket. Within seconds we heard the gate being burst open and almost immediately Missus Nutt burst through the door as if it were made of matchwood.

She charged at the man holding her piglet, her jaws open for the chop. Bertie dropped the banbh and vaulted head first straight through the window. The bottom block of this window was exactly four foot nine inches above the ground. Bertie, with his 'bit of a belly' and in wellington boots was a most unlikely candidate to perform such an athletic feat, but he did.

'Do you know O'Sheas on the far side of the Hill Of Allen?' Father asked me as he drank the last dregs of tea before heading for work.

'Yeah, what about them'? I replied.

'They have a spare farrowing crate, will you collect it with the tractor?'

'OK.'

'Be careful,' he said, as he rushed out the door.

I was delighted to make my first major foray with the blue Fordson Major and the heavy back of a lorry with which I'd brought home the turf. There was however one problem, the brakes were in very poor condition and practically useless, but

I had learned to compensate for this by the judicious use of the throttle and changing down the gears. My mother shook holy water at the tractor as her thirteen year old son drove out the gate.

Everything went well until on the return journey, I decided to take a shortcut down the narrow Granghiggen road. I went to change down the gears but I was freewheeling down the steep hill and could not get them to engage. Within seconds I was doing maybe thirty miles an hour down that narrow road. My heart thumped nearly out of my chest. I stood up to jump off but 'funked it.' Eventually we came to a stop. I was shaking after the fright but I said a little prayer to Our Lady and silently thanked my mother for sprinkling the holy water.

Around the mid sixties, the bottom fell out of the pig trade for the small producer. By this time Father had made the acquaintance of Jimmy Barry, the manager of the GRA kennels in Naas. These were owned by an English company that was prepared to offer thirty shillings a week for each greyhound pup reared. The pigs were sold off, including Missus Nutt, and from then on I had to sweep dog shit rather than pig dung off the floor of the pig yard. It just didn't seem fair.

Many years later, I was having a drink one Sunday afternoon in Welds public house opposite the canal bridge in Robertstown. I reminisced about Missus Nutt to a gentleman by the name of Price. I told him that after one trip down the Baune Lane when she was in heat; she got to know the way herself and that each subsequent time she came 'round' she would rattle the gate with her nose until it opened. Then she'd walk the mile or so down the Baune Lane to Watchorn's boar, do her business and then walk home – all on her own. He agreed she was a remarkable animal indeed. Then he told me of a particular sow he knew himself.

'She was owned by the people across there.' He pointed to a house on the other side of the canal. 'Whenever she was in heat, she'd make her own way across the bridge, into the yard behind us and present herself to Charlie Weld's boar. One particular day the bridge was damaged and she couldn't come across, so she ambled back to that low spot on the bank.' He said pointing to the spot. 'She knew that she could swim but also knew her only stroke was the doggie paddle and that if she used this with her sharp trotters she would slit her throat.' He hesitated.

'So what did she do?' I enquired

'She took a deep breath, walked into the canal and across the bottom to come out the far side and then went on to visit the boar.' I looked him in the eye. He looked straight back at me.

'Then she went to the same spot on the bank, took a deep breath and walked back home across the bottom of the canal again.'

He finished his tale, I shook my head, finished my drink and thanked him for his company as we both shook hands. I drove home smiling all the way.

TALES OF MY MOTHER

Mother loved auctions. The first thing she checked for when the *Leinster Leader* came in the door each Thursday evening were the auctions on the back page. She especially loved ones with the addendum 'House Contents.' Mother didn't get to all the auctions she would have wanted, nor did she always buy at the ones she went to. She never let her bid price rise above what she considered to be a bargain. She loved bargains even more than auctions. There was many a row when my father, who with a puss on him would give out about:

'All the rubbish coming into the house.'

The truth of the matter was that nearly all the finer things in our home came from my mother going to auctions. I was with her the day she purchased the sideboard and the mahogany table with the Queen Anne legs in Brophy's showrooms, behind the Palace cinema in Newbridge. She paid something like fifteen shillings for a revolving bookcase and five boxes of books at the auction in Dr Roundtree's house, after he died. All our large mirrors came from the auction of fittings from Roycroft's drapery store after it closed. Father passed a caustic remark when he went to collect these that it was a wonder she didn't buy the pulley system with the brass cups. She held her tongue and didn't rise to the bait. I would have loved her to have bought that pulley system and I know she would too but ours was a small farm not a sprawling shop.

Mother worked so hard. At one stage there were five cows to be milked by hand, as well as calves and pigs to be fed each morning and night. She had purchased three huge crockery dishes at an auction in Rathangan and into one of these she strained the milk after each milking. The following morning the thick layer of cream would be skimmed off and poured into the churn. When this was just under half full she would insert the paddle and which ever of her children was nearest got the job of turning the handle of the paddle until butter appeared. Churning wasn't always straight forward, it seemed to me to be a very complex process altogether. Sometimes the butter was reluctant to form and on these occasions Mother could get very tense and rather cross. For this reason I tried to dodge churning as often as I could but this was easier said than done.

I was ten or eleven before I put myself in to learn how to milk. Young and all as I was, I suspected I was letting myself in for much hardship, but Father at the time had to cycle to work for to be in The Curragh for eight o'clock. Much of the hard physical work fell to Mother and I and my two sister's did things inside the house. In my memory, I see Mother in her light blue dress and wellington boots and I carrying two full buckets each of *Paul & Vincent* freshly mixed pig food across to the pig enclosures. We step up onto the railway sleepers that Father had carefully placed on concrete blocks along the outside of the wall to make it easier for us to lift the buckets over the top, invert them against the plastered wall and pour evenly along the trough to the delight of up to twelve squealing squabbling fatteners trying to get their snouts in first.

'They'll be ready in time for Christmas.' She remarks before adding 'make sure you comb that hair before you go into school.'

'Yes Ma.'

'Come on in, we'll have a cup of tea, before you go.'

I loved being close to her but there weren't too many mornings when I was early for school.

Chrissie was a young woman who came to work for my mother. She lived in our home for a time and Ma regarded her as one of the family. Chrissie was a free spirit and would say or do whatever came into her head. There was much laughter between the two and a mutual fondness as well. Another great friend was Mrs Curley who kept Mother abreast of all the news in the locality. Mrs Curley's husband had died before she moved into the 'schoolteachers residence', next door. They were the best of friends but for whatever reason they never used each other's first names. It was 'Mrs Curley this' and 'Mrs Heavey that' whenever one of them referred to the other.

The McStays were family friends from Dublin who often came to visit. Usually this was pre-arranged. On one particular day, mother and I were alone in the back kitchen when Mr McStay drove into the yard. We weren't expecting him and I instantly knew Mother was alarmed because there was little or no food in the house.

'Run out quick and get me a small bucket of black turf,' she ordered as she went to the press to get a new apron.

'Arra Mick, how wonderful to see you.' I heard her say as I ran to the turf shed. When I came in with the bucket of turf, he was sitting on the large green box beside the range.

'I've a new gundog in the boot that I want to try out.' He said as she stoked up the fire. She then found an old copy of the *Leinster Leader* and spread it out on the table.

'Sorry Mick, there's something I need in that box.' He stood up and she took out a couple handfuls of oats which she placed into to her apron, this she'd folded and held by the other hand. Both of us watched as she moved to the doorway, sprinkled the oats on the step and called out in the high falsetto voice, she reserved for calling hens.

'Chuck, chuck chuck chuck chuck. Chuck, chuck chuck chuck chuck.' Before she had uttered the final 'chuck' there were about a dozen hens on the step gobbling up oats.

Mother reached down calmly and took one the hens by

the neck. She grabbed its legs and stretched the neck until all flapping of the wings had stopped. The legs kicked back violently as she placed it on the old newspaper spread out on the table. She plucked the feathers onto this and when finished washed, dressed and trussed up the hen for the oven, which was now rising to the required temperature. All the time she talked about the weather and this and that. Mr McStay didn't say much. When she was finished, she opened the door of the range, wrapped up the mess of feathers, head and guts and threw the lot into the blazing fire.

'Mick, I'll have the dinner on the table at half five. That'll give you time to try out that dog.'

Mr McStay rose then. He asked if I could accompany him down to the Gurteen. The gun-dog could get no scent but we rambled through the rushes in the bottom of the Gurteen, chatting about this and that as was our way. At one point he looked at me:

'Noel, your mother is a remarkable woman.'

My uncle minded the animals on the few occasions we went on holidays. The only places I remember going to were Mother's sister's family in Portstewart and to their home place in Lislary, on the shores of Sligo Bay ten miles beyond the town. Mother left home when she was sixteen and hadn't been back too often since then. She loved it though and her heart would rise up as soon as she spotted Benbulben just before driving into Sligo town. She would lilt, sing and talk about the wonderful scenery until we drove into *Uncle Tom's* yard on the edge of the Atlantic ocean.

I barely remember my granny, who wore a long black skirt and whose grey hair was tied in a bun on the back of her head. Uncle Tom was great fun and I traipsed around after him everywhere he went. Everyone thought him to be a

Mugshot of 'My Brother' Tommy, taken in a kiosk

confirmed bachelor but he surprised them all by starting to court a woman called Margaret Conway from Ballyconnell soon after his mother died. Within a year they were married. Within another, their first baby, *Mary*, was born.

Around this time we'd had a telephone installed in the hall. It was the first and at the time, the only telephone in Clongorey or Blacktrench. Its installation had saved my teacher's life and rapidly became the means by which urgent news, both good and bad, came to the fifty or so families living in our area. I developed a sharp ear to discern the tone of my father or mother's voice coming through the hall door when they answered a call. They often had to go to someone else's home with bad news.

One particular night mother came from the hall, all smiles after speaking to her brother Tom on the telephone. He had

My Uncle Tom, coming out the door of his home in Lislary Co. Sligo, to jump on his bicycle

rung to tell her that Margaret had given birth to a son and that they were going to call him Tom. This news put her in great form. As the weeks went by there were more telephone calls, but increasingly there were no smiles when she'd leave down the phone. In late September there was a particular telephone call. Mother answered and when she came back into the living room she was crying. My uncle Tom's wife, Margaret had died. Two little babies were left without their mother.

It was a desperate time. Our aunt Josie minded us as Mother and Father drove off to attend the funeral in Sligo. Father came back after a few days but he was alone. A few days later Mam arrived back to us. She had with her a blue carry cot with a hood on it. When I looked in, all I could make out was a little head with black hair.

'His name is Tommy.' My mother said.

The arrival of the little baby changed things in our family. Veronica was no longer the youngest and now she had to fight for attention as the focus switched to the little mite in the cot. My sister Marie and I competed now to see which of us were allowed lift and feed him. For the most part I had to settle for sniffs of baby oil but I did get to hold him a few times. I even learned how to change his nappy. Uncle Tom came to stay with us a few times but his heart wasn't in it. He really resented the loss of the love of his life and became a rather sad man. There were a few visits to Sligo for young Tommy but while there was never a formal adoption or even a formal chat as far as I know; it quickly became obvious that I had a little brother at long last, and that he was a Clongorey lad through and through.

HIS AND HERS

On my first day in Clongorey school Mrs Partridge formed the opinion that I couldn't read, even though I'd completed first class in Newbridge and made my First Holy Communion the previous May. She moved me across the room and back into First Class alongside my cousin Vincent, PJ Earley, Robbie Curley and about seven others. I was delighted but my mother came down to remonstrate the following day. There was loud talk from both women but I was left where I'd been put.

I remember the second-hand reader book with its illustrations of Paul who had a car and Mary who had a chair. When I learned the trick of relating letters of the alphabet to sounds I sensed I'd made a breakthrough and thus it proved as I went on to read that little book from cover to cover within a few nights. Thereafter I was bored for the rest of the year while reading was beaten into some of the others with her thick brown stick.

Being slapped with a stick was part and parcel of going to school. I'd hold out the hand to await my punishment in nervous apprehension, complete with grimaces and blinking eyes, as she ranted on to herself about how she wasn't going to put up with sloppy work, wrong sums, misspelt words or whatever. Pulling back the hand before the blow was struck wasn't a good idea, as she would then grab the wrist and use extra force in the downward swing. One of the first things I learned the hard way was to keep my thumb pressed below the level of my opened palm.

With the benefit of hindsight slapping young children sounds somewhat barbaric, but in truth the anticipation of the stick was more painful than the reality, except on the really cold days when the zing in the sting could bring tears. Shedding tears was to risk being called a sissy and the playground in Clongorey school was no place to be called a sissy.

The highlights of the school day were the two breaks when we were all let out to play. Adjacent to the playground, where boys played marbles and girls hopscotch, was the field.

The bottom part was for boys from 'her' room to play football. The game would start on a Monday morning and finish on Friday evening. We used to pick different teams each week but invariably PJ Earley and I ended up on one team with Vincent and Laddie Earley on the other. We developed amazing skills whereby each of us could solo a small handball from one end of the pitch to the other at full speed. Occasionally disputes would develop into rows but generally fiercely competitive games were won and lost without any need for supervision.

I spent two years in 'her' classroom. When I left it, I could read, write and do my sums. I say this because over the years I haven't heard too many of her former pupils sing the praises of Mrs Partridge. For long periods each day she'd cocoon herself between her desk and the potbellied stove which threw out a lovely heat. Then she'd rock herself back and forth; more often than not smiling to herself and rhythmically punching the fist of her right hand into the waiting open palm of the left. This carry-on could last for what seemed hours but then she'd spring to life and if we didn't know or do what she asked she'd look for the stick, which sometimes she couldn't find because we'd hidden it. Initiative and enterprise were practiced early in Clongorey.

Mrs Partridge's husband was the master and he taught in 'his' room. He was elderly, and gave off an aura of quiet authority. He wore a dicky bow in preference to a tie. Each morning he would come in at half past ten to call the roll. I yearned for the day when I would be taught by this gentle man.

It arrived one September when we proudly entered 'his'

My sisters Veronica and Marie were still in Her Room. Shyness personified in his white jumper had just graduated to His room. I remember Mother hand knitting this jumper

room. Pencils and crayons had been used for writing in 'her' room, now we used wooden handled three penny pens for which replacement nibs cost a halfpenny. These were notoriously delicate and, when sprained, had to be discarded and replaced. Small porcelain inkwells contained the ink, and were covered with sliding brass covers to prevent evaporation. I loved the unique smell from the ink as I wrote, but loathed the blots it left on my copy book no matter how careful I was.

The only source of heat in the school was from two turf fires, an open one in 'his' room and the pot bellied stove in 'her's.' Each family was obliged to supply a load of turf to fuel these. My cousin Brennie and Chicky Mills were in charge of the slate which recorded who brought in turf and what it was like. I recall an ass, pony or horse load being written after each name. Note was also taken of the colour; white which gave out little or no heat, brown which was a good deal better and then black turf which was as good as coal. Finally the abbreviations for wet, middling or dry were written after each name.

I remember the time before we built a turf shed when my father hadn't yet got a horse and cart. He arranged with a local man who owned an ass to bring in a load from our rick. The wet white turf which he brought in gave out little or no heat and this led tome having to spend a considerable part of each day for a week foraging with others for dry sticks and timber to tide us over until a decent load of turf arrived. It was so desperately cold that everyone had to wear overcoats in class and then take them off every hour or so to swing our arms across our chests in order get our circulation going. Even with this, everyone would have to hold their pens or pencils in their fists rather than between their thumb and the first two fingers, our teeth chattered violently.

Mr Partridge had a completely different way of teaching which suited me down to the ground. He loved Ireland and the 'One True Catholic Church.' A lot of time was dedicated to teaching us catechism from a green covered book with a really nice smell, which at one point I knew off by heart. He had definite views but gentle ways and taught mostly by telling stories. Fourth, Fifth and Sixth class were also taught in 'his' room. I developed a good ear and a precocious knowledge from listening in on what was being taught to senior classes, when I was supposed to be concentrating on exercises he'd given us. He held the 1916 signatories of the Proclamation, particularly Padraig Pearse in the highest esteem. He loved teaching us the Irish language text 'Iosagain' written by Pearse, which extolled the virtuous qualities of piety, Irish culture and purity of spirit, all of which he advocated with his quiet disposition.

I became his most enthusiastic pupil and along with Robbie

Curley came to be thought of as one of the brightest in the class. At this time there were various visits from priests and nuns from different religious orders. These would extol the pursuit of a life of fulfilment for those with a vocation to 'the glorification of the Lord.' I fancied I had a vocation. This was reinforced by reading missionary magazines such as Africa, Divine Word and The Far East which he encouraged us to sell.

As time went by the feeling that I had a vocation grew in my head, but I never mentioned this to anyone. I think Mr Partridge may have become aware of what was happening to me and I became his favourite pupil or 'teacher's pet' as other's in the class weren't slow about calling it. Mary Coffey, Michael's sister, had entered a convent but I had the distinct impression that he saw in me his best hope of realising his great ambition to have a past pupil enter a seminary. The vocation thing did not sit comfortably with me but I couldn't get it to go away. On the one hand I was very much influenced by the faith of the master and the allure of the exotic missionary life as published in the religious magazines, not to mention the dulcet talk from visiting priests. On the other hand, I loved my mother and father and I saw this vocation thing as a betrayal of their way of life. Hard physical work was the ethic they espoused, as did every other family in Blacktrench and Clongorey. Even so my mind was in turmoil. Two roads faced me but I knew that I could take only one.

I was speaking to Mr Partridge one day, when I was in Fifth class. His eyes started to roll most peculiarly in their sockets. Everyone in the room instantly became transfixed. Then he started to splutter as he turned reddish blue in the face. There was an instant scramble for the door by the thirty or so pupils, my legs weakened so that I nearly collapsed, but the momentum of the rush carried me along. Once outside I ran to the adjoining site where bicycles were kept. I hurt myself as I jumped astride one of these but pedalled as hard as I could the five hundred yards or so to my home. I then ran into the porch where the only telephone for miles around had been newly installed only the previous week. I frantically twisted the handle and when a lady spoke I shouted into the mouthpiece for her to send an ambulance as quickly as possible. She did too, it was there within a very short time to save our master's life.

There was talk of Mister Partridge never being able to teach again but the following September he was there to greet us at the end of our summer holidays. He was now so thin that I could see down his chest because his shirt collar was loose. He didn't say much about his heart attack nor did he acknowledge my role in getting the ambulance to arrive so quickly. However I knew that he knew from the extra kindness in his eyes anytime he looked at me.

I was now in Sixth class and the important Primary Cert exam beckoned at the end of the year. Regardless of homework there were jobs that had to be done around the farm and around the house. One of these involved bringing in turf from the newly built shed. It was this task I was performing one particular October evening around dusk when my father came out to me.

'There'll be no more of that for you from now on.' His voice full of emotion.

'What do you mean?' I looked at him closely to see if he had drink taken.

'I want you to have an education and chances in life that I never had.' He threw his strong arms around me and held me so close that I could easily smell him.

'I've enrolled you in Newbridge College and you're to start in the morning.'

My Confirmation Photo taken outside Clongorey School

We finished off loading the barrow and he wheeled it into the house, grinning at me all the way. I walked in beside him not knowing what to say or do but loving the closeness. I intuitively knew that my life was about to change significantly as I sat down beside the range. My mother half lilted, half sang *The Ould Lammas Fair* as she plugged out the iron and laid out my white shirt for the following morning.

'DOMINUS, DOMINE, DOMINUM...'

The others in the class had a nine day start on me. They were on page five of the Latin Textbook, with its six cases of the second declension singular, to be learned off by heart. White robed Father Clandillon noticed the new boy and raised his hand to interrupt the recital in order to welcome me to First Year in Newbridge College. I joined with the others as we resumed in unison:

…'Domini, Domino, Domino.'

We spent the rest of the class writing out sentences with the correct use of the Latin word for Lord, with which I was already familiar from hearing 'Dominus Vobiscum' used by the priest in Mass. The bell rang; he gathered up exercise copies and went out the door.

The others then became somewhat apprehensive because Fr Casserly or Hoppy as they called him was next up. He taught Maths. I looked up when I sensed the silence. There, framed in the doorway, stood all five foot nothing of him in his white habit. I couldn't believe that someone so small had caused such apprehension. Over the next few years this cross looking man would teach me Maths and English and earn my total respect as he did so.

Up to this, the College was the place where I went to half nine or twelve o'clock Mass every Sunday. I didn't know anyone who went to school there; yet here I was. I'd heard my father say the fees were thirty pounds. I'm not sure whether this was per term or per annum, but it was a substantial sum for the times that were in it. The understanding was that I had to 'buckle down to the books.' Most of the students

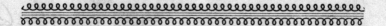

Newbridge College

NEWBRIDGE

CO. KILDARE

Student's Report

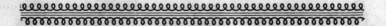

School Year 1964-65

MASTER Noel Heavey

FORM Upper Second

SUBJECT	Percentage in Exam.	Place in 'Class	Number in Class	Application	Progress
Religious Knowledge	50	15	31	3	3
Irish	46	22	30	3	3
English	70	16	31	4	4
History	76	9	31	5	5
Geography	67	8	31	5	5
Mathematics	48	25	31	3	2
Latin	69	15	31	6	6
Greek					
French	46	14	33	3	4
Science					
Drawing					
Commerce					
German					
Elocution					
Music					
Drill and Games					

Pass 40%   *Honours* 60%   1*st Class Honours* 80%

Easter Term

Conduct and Discipline...... Good ....

Health...

6 signifies Excellent, 5 Very Good, 4 Good, 3 Fair,
2 Unsatisfactory, 1 Bad.

REMARKS

As you can see these are moderately

good marks. I feel sure however

that Noel could apply himself

etter in such subjects aw French,

Irish and Maths.

The College re-opens..... *April 30* ....

The strictest punctuality in returning on the opening
day is essential.

...... A. Valkenburg ....Headmaster.

were boarders but the ginger haired boy I found myself sitting beside told me that he too was a dayboy. His name was John Herlihy and I quickly worked out he was our doctor's son.

Another thing I worked out fairly fast was that dayboys were very much regarded as inferior beings in the Newbridge College scheme of things, being referred to as 'day dogs' by the boarders. I never bought into this and consequently never felt anything other than that I was a pioneer operating in a new frontier. Clongorey was less than four miles away but it was literally a different world from what I imagined boarders considered normal. This must've been the case because from early on I was called *Bogman*. I was happy enough to accept this moniker even as I realised it was meant as a 'put down.' I was proud of where I came from and the derogatory aspect of the expression slid from me like water off a duck.

Within a few days I had settled into my new world. When I pulled the chain in the jacks the shit simply disappeared. Never for one second did I let on that this was all new to me but it was. Early on, our dry toilet at home became an issue after I befriended another dayboy and invited him out to our house but I'd made sure he had his 'number two' done before his family's chauffeur drove us out to Clongorey.

My ordinary routine for getting home soon became established; I was to wait around until my father drove home from his work as a house painter in the Curragh. This allowed me stay on in the College until a quarter to six each evening whereupon I started to play rugby. We either had a practice which everyone referred to as 'a strip' or we'd play tip-rugby on the gravel surface of the yard between the millrace of and the brick buildings which housed the junior dormitories adjoining the science labs.

Tip-rugby became the continuation of the football games I used to play the bottom of the hill in Clongorey school. We

The Ellers, 1964-65: Team Of The Year
Back row, l-r, P Murphy, N Burke, T Gannon, P Boylan, T O'Brien, C McInerney, N Heavey
Front row, l-r: M Adamson, K Murphy, G McManus, J Dillon, P McDonagh, R McGrath, J Hall
Sitting: P Horan, F McLenan

started each game on a Monday during the eleven o clock break, then resumed immediately after lunch and continued at every opportunity until Friday evening when a winner would be declared. One evening I looked up and there was my father trying to conceal himself as he watched his son hold his own with the others. We played as if for Ireland in Landsdowne Road. Robbie McGrath and Freddie McLennan would both go on and do precisely that, winning the Triple Crown in the process. I'm sure if I asked either they'd agree that skills they picked up as thirteen year olds on that gravelly quad played no small part in making them the players they became. I knew little about rugby then but the hundreds of hours spent playing our version of Gaelic football stood to me and in no time at all Father 'Dux' Delaney picked me at wing forward for 'The Ellers' and we went on to become the team of the year in 1964-65.

We travelled to the games by train to Kingsbridge Station. Then we'd get the bus to Belvedere, St Paul's in Raheny, Willow

Park or wherever. Invariably we spent an hour or so rambling around O'Connell Street, Abbey Street and the Quays before we'd catch the train home. Dublin without my mother was quite an adventure for the young lad from Clongorey, terrified of becoming lost or missing the train. Chips and a Pepsi poured into a glass by one of the Caffola waitresses was the nearest I'd flown to the sun at this point in my life.

There was one particular game against High School played in a downpour that we won 3-0. They camped on our line for most of the match but we held them out. Dux was emotional after the match as we all were. He singled out myself and Robbie McGrath for special praise and as he spoke I felt a warm glow and I imagined myself as a warrior being praised by the general after the battle.

I tried to assimilate into the life of the College. Dayboys were in the minority. Most of them cycled home immediately after class and consequently were very much on the margins of the school's heartbeat. At some point in the year I managed to get myself into a situation where I had to fight a lad called Harney from Longford in the middle of the gravelly quad. He was smaller but more agile and danced rings around me, making me look and feel awkward. Boarders gathered around to loudly cheer their colleague. This disheartened me but greatly spurred on my opponent who went on to 'beat the living shit out of the daydog.'

The only consolation I had was that I never flinched from one of his punches even though I tasted of my own blood after he cut my lip. Also I never gave him give him the satisfaction of registering even the slightest suggestion of being hurt. In a strange sort of way this seemed to gain me acceptance from the boarders.

Certainly, after this I never felt an outsider during the five and a half further years I was to spend in Newbridge College OP.

A Trip to Sallins

This short horn cow in the long field was the mother of the illfated heifer we drove to Sallins. She is about 14 years old when this photo was taken

'The Heifer' was called this because she was the first heifer calf born on our farm. She held onto the name even after she became a cow. Each of our six cows back then had names – The White One, The Kicker, Katie, The Rogue and The Strawberry were the others. I had a particular attachment to The Heifer because she was one of the first animals I'd helped to rear. A meek calf, she was one of the few not to whoosh the emptied bucket up into my private parts at the end of feeding time. We'd kept her on as a follower and she duly went in calf herself. As a cow she was also a favourite because she never once kicked over the bucket at milking time. However, she was now ill, seriously ill.

Mr Osborne, the vet, had diagnosed blood murraine. He said it was too far gone to save her and that we should try to get something for her in the meat factory while she could still stand. My father became anxious to turn her into money before she died. Every time she passed water it seemed to be getting redder and redder. Along with this there was a horrible stench from the blackish stuff which trickled uncontrollably down her leg. This smelt all the worse because of the heat as it was the height of summer.

The question which now arose was how to get her to the meat factory in Sallins. Father couldn't get anyone with a car and trailer nor could he take time off work himself.

'How do you feel about a trip to Sallins tomorrow?' he asked that evening. I was twelve years old at the time and like most twelve year olds, I was anxious for any bit of responsibility that came my way. I was keen to go but not at all sure I would be able for the job.

'Will you be able to get me help?' I asked hopefully.

'I'll ask Jack Taaffe if he'll let young Marty go with you.'

Marty was a couple of years younger than me but he was a steady sort of chap and on hearing this, I agreed to chance bringing The Heifer to Sallins. There was one further snag; while I was well familiar with the road as far as Halverstown which was about half way, I had but a rough idea of the other three and a half miles to Sallins and hadn't a clue where to go once we got there. My father sensed this.

'Come on, we'll go for a spin,' he said and within minutes we were at the cross roads at Halverstown. 'They're always flying along on this piece of straight road between Caragh and Naas. You'll need to be very careful crossing here.' I said nothing as I was busy drawing a map on the page of a copy book I'd brought along for the purpose. I paid particular attention as we turned left on the canal bridge at Osberstown, just before we came on to another main road where we turned left into Sallins. There were two further bridges before the left turn down the canal towpath to reach the animal entrance into the slaughter house.

At least I now knew the way. We drove home but before we drove up our road we called into Taaffes to make arrangements with Mister Taaffe for Marty to accompany me the following morning.

Marty came down just after eight o'clock. My mother made us eat a huge breakfast of scrambled eggs and toast before we left. She was down in herself, now that it was time for us to start The Heifer's last journey. She tried not to let on that she was concerned but I could tell by the way she sprinkled holy water that she was worried. We hunted The Heifer onto the road. It was around nine o'clock when I turned to get my hug from her. We then plodded on down the road, past the Gurteen field which had been her usual grazing pasture. She put up a bit of a battle to break in here but we were alert for this, and a poke of the stick into the ribs persuaded her to walk straight on to Tooles Cross and the Blacktrench Road.

Huge yellow Roadstone lorries now trundled past every few minutes on their way to and from the quarry in Allen. There was a grass margin between the road and the hedge and it was along here we drove her on towards Paddy's Bridge, I at her flank and Marty cycling ahead on my mother's bicycle to spot any open gates or gaps. The Heifer was uneasy as she wouldn't ever have seen these lorries before. Even for Marty and I they were disconcerting enough as they drove past within a few feet of us.

Before we came to Paddy's Bridge I had decided that the road was far too busy and that we'd be better off to travel down The Double Ditch – a long narrow road with a ditch on either side which would take us to Halverstown via Caragh. It was a little bit longer than going by Flood's Cross but there would be a good deal less traffic. We 'sailed down' the Double

Ditch without meeting a vehicle of any description.

We met a couple of people cycling along the road in Raheens who stopped to talk to us. At this stage the sun was getting higher in the sky and flies appeared from nowhere and began to hover over The Heifer. I was embarrassed and ashamed to talk to anyone, particularly when they were from Caragh and recognised me. Caragh people back then weren't slow about passing remarks, especially disparaging ones, about anything or anyone from Clongorey.

We passed Mrs Reddy's house on the Back Road. She saw us through her open door and called us back to have a drink from a can of water she brought out to the gate. We told her about our journey and she said to us: 'Yez are great little men.' The railway bridge on The Back Road is quite steep and I was afraid The Heifer wouldn't be able for it, but by dint of the stick and a few shouts we got her into a sort of a trot which duly brought her to the top. It was with considerable difficulty we made it up the next hill on which was built the new church. We were now on the main road and I began to have doubts that we could make it to Sallins at all, where my father had her booked in for 'around dinner time.'

We carried on past Coffey's shop and the school. The road was busy enough but we had settled into a certain rhythm by this stage. Nonetheless I was relieved that it was all downhill. When we were on the narrow Liffey bridge she had slowed down so much that several cars held up behind us began to beep their horns. After this there was a grass margin on the side of the road and we felt it necessary to let her take another rest.

Her hind quarters more or less collapsed at this stage and as they did so, she slid into the ditch at the side of the margin. I became desperately concerned and close to tears but within minutes a man stopped as he cycled by. I recognised him to be one of the Campbell's.

'Are yez in trouble?'

'We sure are.'

'Jaysus, there's wicked smell off her, isn't there?'

'She has blood murraine and we're bringing her to the factory.' He looked at me for a few moments.

'You'll have your work cut out young fellah, but let's get you out of here anyway.' He left down his bicycle and stopped a car which happened to be passing by. The driver had a passenger and between us all we pulled the cow out of the ditch and stood her up onto her feet.

'Now, keep her moving, If she goes down again you mightn't be able to get her back up.'

'Thanks very much, Mister Campbell.'

'No bother at all, the best of luck to you lads.'

Another man on a bicycle told us it was half eleven after we had turned left at Halverstown Cross. I knew we were just past half way and I prayed to God that there would be no more mishaps. The two of us also knew we were up against it, but The Heifer seemed now to have regained her rhythm, it wasn't a trot or anything like it but it was certainly more than a plod. There is a bend before Osberstown where a house in a yard separates the Liffey from the road. I had sent Marty ahead to ask the woman of the house if we could let the cow have a drink from the river. Instead, there were three buckets of water lined up by the time we guided her into the yard. She drank them all and another one as well. I was relieved we didn't have to let her down to the Liffey.

We resumed our journey, but now we were moving very slowly and when we came to the left turn across the canal bridge I had to give her a good few whacks of the stick to get her over the top. I fully realised I was being cruel but at the time I felt I had no choice.

Immediately after this was the railway bridge where she tried to maintain the extra bit of momentum she had acquired from coming down the previous hill, but we both had to push with all our might to get her over the top.

After this we were on the main road into Sallins. I now became gravely concerned because of the final two bridges confronting us in the heart of the village itself. The Heifer was literally on her last legs. Somehow she mounted the Railway bridge and as we pushed her over the hump-backed canal bridge I became conscious of the curious looks we attracted from passers-by. However, the meat factory now stood before us. We turned down the canal towpath which lead into the cattle holding area. Marty leaned against her flank as I pushed her behind into the chute.

There is a heavy overpowering stench of death that I associate with meat factories. It was particularly strong in Sallins that day. I presume it was this that had the other cattle lowing loudly in their pens. The Heifer now became agitated even with her in the lowly state she was in. Marty and I became extremely uneasy, then:

'Where the fuck are you going with that animal?' came a loud agitated roar from behind us. We turned to face a fat black-haired man with a red face. He wore a beige work coat that was splattered with dung. He had a clipboard.

'My Daddy has her booked in.' He looked at the clipboard.

'You should have been here at one o'clock. She's missed her slot. She can barely stand up. They won't take her here, you may bring her home.' I was dumbstruck and once again close to tears but I wasn't going to cry in front of this horrible man.

'I'll ring home to see what we'll do.'

'Hurry up, I don't want her dying here.'

We went to the front of the factory where I knew there was a phone booth. On the way Marty and I had a quick chat and both of us agreed that there was no way the cow could be walked home. I tapped out the number so I didn't have to put any money into the slot on top of the coinbox. My mother answered the phone. I told her the situation but she was as nonplussed as I was myself, and told me to ring my father on the Curragh. This I did but could only get through to an operator who was a bit snooty at first, but I told him it was an emergency and could he please get 'my daddy'. He agreed to look for him and having taken the number he told me to hang up, that he'd get my father to ring back. I waited for what seemed ages in the booth fearful that someone would come along and look to use the phone. After a while the phone rang.

'They won't take The Heifer.' I blurted out. There was a pause at the other end, I sensed what was coming.

'The dirty fuckers.' He went on a good bit more in the same vein. I had to interrupt him.

'Daddy, what am I going to do?'

'Listen son, you've done really well. Ask them will they slaughter her on compassionate grounds. They needn't pay us but ask them to allow me to come down for a leg of meat off her for the greyhounds. Tell them I'll be down before six.'

I went back and put this proposition to the man. He shook his head as he looked at me without saying a word, and went over to a small office in the corner. We could see him talking on the phone through a grimy window. When he was finished he came over to us.

'We're going to slaughter her but there'll be no money paid for her and under no circumstances is your father to come down here looking for a leg for greyhounds. He's lucky we're doing what we're doing for him.'

I looked at the man and could think of nothing more to say other than a very meek

'Thank You.' I don't think he heard me because he had

81

already turned and walked away. I looked over then at The Heifer. Her hind legs had gone down again and she was struggling to regain her standing. From the corner of my eye I saw men walking towards her.

I looked then at Marty who jerked his head in the direction of the road. My mind became a blank but I followed Marty's lead as he retrieved my mother's bicycle. We walked back up to the top of the canal bridge. There I stood on the pedals and with Marty on the carrier we freewheeled for home.

THE FACTS OF LIFE

I think I was in second Year, when I first heard of 'the facts of life' as an expression. This had been covered in class on one of the very rare days I was absent.

There were smirks and conspiratorial whispers the following day but when I heard someone remark it had to do with birds and bees I wasn't too concerned and quickly lost interest. This was a mistake because as the talk receded I began to realise that there was important information in this but I was now outside the loop. I determined to say nothing as I instinctively knew that to ask questions would be to leave myself open to ridicule. At fourteen years of age I wasn't about to put myself in that position.

I became adept at covering up that I knew nothing of the facts of life or anything about the birds and bees. However, I started to pay particular attention to the words of love songs on Radio Luxembourg which I used to listen to on a transistor under the blankets. The words of a particular song grabbed my interest.

'Let me tell you 'bout the birds and the bees
And the flowers and the trees
And the moon up above
And a thing called love.
When I look into your big blue eyes,
It's so very plain to see
That it's time you learned 'bout the facts of life
Starting from A to Z'

It may have grabbed my interest but it didn't do much to provide me with any answers to questions I wanted to ask but couldn't articulate. Here was I, the son of a farmer from Clongorey totally familiar with boars putting sows in pig, and the way bulls went about their business, but nobody had ever explained to me that girls and women could become pregnant. I knew all about sex and its consequences with animals. I just couldn't relate this to people. Around this time my father and I were alone in our back kitchen one night.

'Do you know about the facts of life?' He asked.

'Of course I do,' I replied blushing like a beetroot.

'Good.'

Thus was the opportunity to make the connection allowed pass. The ongoing thought that everyone in my class, of my age and younger knew all about these facts of life about which I understood nothing, really bothered me. True to form, I never contemplated asking anyone to enlighten me but acted as if I knew all about these things. I focused on rugby and also closely followed the fortunes of Noel Cantwell, Denis Law and George Best of Manchester Utd.

Also In my state of chassis I decided to give girls as wide a berth as possible and grew the thought in my head that I probably had a vocation to the priesthood, which I also never spoke about to anyone, as this possibility also made me very uneasy. To make matters worse I was constantly arguing and fighting with my sister Marie. All in all I wasn't the happiest boy in the world but I never let on, not for a minute.

Recently I'd taken to wrestling with Chrissie, anytime we were alone. Chrissie was the young woman who worked for my mother and slept upstairs in the girl's room. She was part of the family, a great worker and full of devilment but our recent wrestling took on a new dimension which I didn't understand. I became aware of a stimulation somewhere below my belly button during these encounters which was rather exciting. My mother caught us one night and even though nothing further developed between Chrissie and I, things were different between us.

In her wisdom Mother made arrangements with my aunt, her sister Annie, for me to go alone on holidays to Portstewart, County Derry. I was met off the train in Belfast after the longest journey I'd ever made on my own. Around this time I'd bought a James Bond book called *Thunderball* and had a good bit of it read by the time I was met off the train by my auntie. Somewhere between Dundalk and Belfast the hardness in my trousers returned as I dallied on page seventy eight.

That night I had my first ever wet dream, on my Aunt Annie's sheets. The following morning, after she made the bed she found the book and threatened to:

'Tell your mammy about the dirty book you've been reading in my house.'

I was mortified but in my hour of need God provided me with an ally from an unlikely quarter. My cousin Anne was slightly older, and had over the years teased and fought with me, even worse than my sister, but she now became my best friend.

Anne brought me out and around Portstewart. She was a pupil of the local Dominican convent and seemed to know everyone. She went out of her way to introduce her classmates to her cousin who 'went to that college in Newbridge.' She had a particular friend, also called Anne, who along with beautiful big eyes had a big smile for me anytime we met. After she gave me the other half of the *Bounty* bar she'd bought on the Promenade I instinctively knew that there was something between us. Trouble was I knew nothing of what to do next. I came to realise that ignorance is a terrible handicap, but also things were definitely on the up.

At the time there was a programme on BBC called *Top of The Pops* which I saw for the first time in the company of the two Anne's in my aunt's sitting room. We were surprised when *Help* by the Beatles could only get to Number Three in the Top Ten. *Can't get no Satisfaction* by the Rolling Stones was

Number Two while *I Got You, Babe* by Sonny and Cher held Number One over the two weeks I saw the programme. Cher, with her big eyes, reminded me of the girl sitting on the floor beside me. Suddenly there was more to life than rugby and Manchester United. Before I worked out a way to way to make the breakthrough into romance, my two weeks came to an end. It was with a heavy heart I left the town of Portstewart.

ALF TUPPER'S PROTÉGÉ

M y father and I often visited his mother and stepfather Jay. They lived in Gingerstown, next door
to Byrnes who were our cousins. There were
four lads in this family, to all of whom I could relate: Liam,
John Joe, Tommy and Noel. I often slipped out to play football with them if I thought Father was settling in for a long
visit. Their mother Kathleen inadvertently sowed an idea in
my head one afternoon, during my school holidays. She had
called us in for tea and was taking down cups from the dresser when she caught my eye looking at the large silver trophy
on the top of it.

'That's the Odlum Cup' she said. 'Liam won it for winning the
mile race last summer at the Sallins sports. He'll win it again in
three weeks time.'

I was most impressed by the size of the cup and the look
of pride in her eyes, as she told how her son came to win it.
Most evenings, no matter what we'd been doing during the
day we gathered up in the field behind Earley's house to play
football. Occasionally we'd mount our bicycles and go for a
cycle, maybe as far as Caragh or Allen. From the evening after
I came home from Gingerstown this changed.

I had a stack of *Victor* comics that I'd been reluctant to swap
or let go. It was to these I now referred, to draw on the wisdom
and inspiration of *Alf Tupper - The Tough of The Track*. Alf
was my comic strip hero and the main reason I bought and
held on to *The Victor* each week. He was always winning cups
against cocky lads. If Liam Byrne and Alf Tupper could win
cups, then why couldn't I? And what would be wrong with
making my father and mother proud courtesy of Alf and his
training methods?

Every evening thereafter for the next fortnight or so, football was suspended. Three of us, PJ and Laddie Earley and I trained for running. We stuck sticks in the ground to mark out a track around Scott's field at the back of Earleys. Also we trained on the road, the distance marked by electricity poles. Always we'd take it easy at the start, and then 'go hell for leather' when the finish was in sight. For some reason, probably to do with us not knowing what our parents would say, we decided to keep it a secret that we were going to race for the Odlum Cup.

Around midday we set off on an array of bicycles for Sallins. We had togs on, inside our trousers. Vincent and Coffey came along for the spin. I had a slight problem as my mother's bicycle had neither front nor back brakes, and also had a broken cotter pin, necessitating an extra little effort with every revolution of the pedals. I looked on this as an ill omen for the task in hand. We actually arrived way too early, so to fill the time we explored the empty railway carriages parked in a siding beside the sports field. Watching us was a beautiful looking girl of about our age who followed us from a distance. She smiled a lot without speaking. I tried my best to get her to talk but she wasn't interested and I ended up blushing like a beetroot instead.

Within an hour the field filled up with people. Eventually, the man with a loudhailer called for entries to: 'the main event – The One Mile Open Race for the Odlum Cup.' I remember feeling a huge surge of excitement as thirty or so lined up at the start. PJ, Laddie and Liam Byrne who didn't speak to us were the only ones I knew. Most wore football boots, a few wore spikes. Taking inspiration from my mentor *Alf Tupper – the Tough of the Track*, I had decided to run in my bare feet.

The Starter explained there were six laps to be completed. Then: 'Ready, Set.... ' he fired the pistol which he'd pointed into the air.

There was a ferocious rush at the start. I was swept along in the middle of the pack, giddy with the excitement of it all. After a lap or so things settled, I found myself running alongside a big strong runner, wearing a black singlet and spikes. I ran slightly behind him on his outside. He passed people, so did I. He started to sprint, so did I. I knew there was a lap to go but I was willing to die rather than let him away from me. When we came to what I thought would be the Finish the next time around, he threw himself over the line and collapsed. Maybe it was the finish I thought and if so we had dead heated.

I was very confused and stopped running hard. I looked around, people were gesticulating and cheering on the others who were now right behind me. When I saw this, I started to run hard again. I regained my rhythm and ran like 'the hammers of hell' down the back straight. People were clapping and cheering. At one point I looked around, I was twenty or thirty yards in front.

I couldn't believe it, I was out on my own and winning the Odlum Cup. I silently thanked God and experienced a feeling of total elation as I ran through a white ribbon held across the line.

Afterwards people were looking at and talking about me. I was exultant but became slightly embarrassed with all the attention. However this quickly waned after I was presented with the cup, as everyone's focus switched to the next event.

I then went looking for the girl with the blonde hair. When I found her, she had eyes only for my cousin Vincent, with whom she headed for the empty rail carriages without as much as a smile for the boy with the big cup.

I was looking for my other friends when I heard the loud hailer announce that entries were being taken for the half mile race and the Corbett Cup. It didn't occur to me to enter this until I saw the same fellahs as had ran the previous race queue up to receive their numbers along with the pair of safety pins. I asked a man I recognised to hold the Odlum Cup for me and went to enter. There was much less hubbub about this race and I detected a palpable resentment as I pinned the number to my vest. The other runners were watching me closely. This time I didn't track anyone. I went to the front from the very start and over the first couple of hundred yards the runners that were trying to track me fell off one by one. For most of the last lap I was on my own.

The difference this time was an eerie lack of excitement both from myself and from the spectators who barely clapped when I was presented with the second cup which was identical in every way to the Odlum.

People began to drift away home. I looked around but there was no sign of the blonde girl or my cousin. By this stage I'd met up with Laddie and PJ, we decided to go home. We went over to recover our bicycles which we'd hidden in the ditch at the corner of the field. We wheeled them out of the field and pointed them for home. It was a more than a little awkward with the two cups but I was reluctant to let either out of my grasp. I held one in each hand each by a handle clasped to the handlebars.

The previous occasion I'd cycled the same bicycle out of Sallins was three years before with Marty Taafe on the carrier with his legs spread-eagled to avoid the spokes after we'd surrendered a sick cow to the meat factory.

That was then, this was now. I had exceeded my wildest dreams in winning two races, and yet I was left with a curiously empty feeling after the hullaballoo of winning the Odlum Cup. We arrived home within the hour where my mother's eyes opened wide with disbelief when she saw me with the two cups.

Alf Tupper's protégé had done well.

MY FIRST HOP

July 1967. It was my second year of going to Hops. I am 16 and have just won Mr. Teen Newbridge at the TEEN hop. Stephanie Walshe is Miss Teen

All my friends, even my sister who was a year younger than me, had been going to the *TEEN* hops held weekly in the Supper Room behind the town hall in Newbridge. They all told me about it too and I suspected I was the best informed fifteen years old who'd never been to a hop in all of Clongorey and Newbridge. But the day duly dawned when I knew that this void in my life was finally to be addressed. I made arrangements to cycle into the town that evening along with my cousin Vincent and Anthony Conlon. I milked the cows early that evening and did myself up by rubbing a good daub of my father's Brylcreem into my hair.

When I eventually made it inside the door of the Supper Room, I tried to take in the music and spectacle in front of me. The first thing that assailed me was an invisible wall of perfume, sweat and other smells which I couldn't quite identify. My ears pricked up when 'Get Offa my Cloud' by the Rolling Stones boomed out. I recognised individual faces in the crowd but they were too focused on their crazy dancing to notice me.

I was mesmerised and just stood there with my mouth agape, staring at the spectacle in front of my eyes. Everyone seemed to have distinctly different moves, yet somehow the whole thing gelled into a unified sway at one with the music. Shyness evaporated as I slipped into the middle of the crowd. Suddenly I too was dancing wildly to the tempo of 'Can't get no Satisfaction.' As it reached a crescendo, I felt the floorboards move gently up and down beneath my feet. I became exhilarated with a sublime joy, and I felt at one with all that was around me.

Thoughts about priesthood took a backward step after this. As far as girls were concerned, I was 'the new kid on the block' and became a sort of a curiosity for some of them. 'I got off' with a girl called Roisin that night and left her home. She held my hand as we walked and talked until we arrived close to her house. We stood there under a street light, up against a hedge about fifty yards from her house and then I put my arms around her and kissed her on the lips. My eyes were open until she opened hers to have a look. She very nicely suggested our eyes should be closed. After I arrived home that night, I practiced my kissing technique on my open palm, with my eyes gently closed. I think I may have cycled into Newbridge every night that week to meet my girlfriend.

We'd hold hands as we talked and walked about the place and every so often we'd stop to kiss. Roisin told me I'd become a good kisser. As far as I was concerned this was confirmed when one night the girl with the torch at the pictures came down and shone it on top of us; we were supposed to be watching the film. Whatever about Roisin I was more proud than embarrassed over this and I now developed the habit of looking people in the eye as I met them.

One sunny Holy Day when we were on a day off school,

Roisin came out to Clongorey for a visit. We met and dallied on the Baune Lane. Time ran into the evening so I offered to give her a lift back into Newbridge on the bar of my bicycle. Somewhere between O'Gradys's farm and my aunt's shop in Roseberry I met my father driving home from work.

He drove past with no sign of recognition but slowed down without stopping after he drove past us. I left Roisin off, and then cycled home as fast as I could.

I arrived home slightly out of breath and feeling rather sheepish. My father was waiting. He caught my cheek in a pinch and threw me onto the armchair in the front room.

'How dare you, you little fucker? In broad daylight as brazen as you like.' His face was as red as a turkey's neck.

'Wha?' I asked, pretending not to know what he was talking about.

'Me payin for your education and you riding around the country with a young one on the bar of a bike.'

I thought he was going to hit me then but my mother had moved in close and I knew he wouldn't.

'You are to stop seeing that young one and concentrate on your books.'

This line sounded so pathetic to my ears that I nearly laughed into his face but I daren't and I didn't. However I now became more angry than afraid.

'She's my girlfriend and I was only giving her a lift home.' The anger had drained from him by this stage but it nearly welled up again after I said this but he let it pass.

'You've had your warning, don't let me catch you again.' He went outside.

My mother made a face at me and went out to the back kitchen. Shortly after this Roisin found herself a boyfriend with a less vigilant father and thus ended a most significant chapter in a life now changed forever.

ANGST

'Out the window with him' someone shouted. Someone else opened the latch and pushed up the sash. Before you could say 'defenestration', Wally was deposited onto the ledge, ten feet directly above three concrete steps.

The window was then slammed shut. The steps led down to the water of the Liffey as it waited calmly before tumbling over the weir, on that stretch of river between Junior House and the Millrace that flows through Newbridge College. Wally, or Peter Sloane to give him his real name, had just upbraided some of his Upper Fourth colleagues for unruly behaviour in History class. He may even have used the word 'boors.'

Unfortunately for Wally we had just covered the Defenestration of Prague in European History and were so taken by it, that his consequent eviction through the window seemed wholly appropriate to us hormonal teenagers, coming to terms with the vagaries of growing up.

'Ah Lads, open the window and stop messin,' pleaded Wally through the window from his precarious ledge. We hooted and jeered, oblivious to the danger. We were reluctant about to readmit him when Fr Flanagan or *Coote* as he was called by the students threw open our door, stood there and glared at us like the paradigm of doom I thought him to be.

'What's going on here?' His cheeks reddened as he pulled a bamboo cane from the folds of the white habit worn by Dominicans, and swished it through the air with the flick of his wrist in the fashion of *The Three Musketeers*. Unbelievably he didn't spot Wally perched precariously on the window sill, as he concentrated on facing us down one by one. During these thirty or so seconds our demeanour switched from

94

near riotous to total subservience. Simultaneously I began to realise the danger to Wally out on the ledge but also the dire consequences for us all if *Coote* switched his eyes even just a fraction to his left. I was to his right as he looked at us and when his eyes met mine, I knew I had to take the situation in hand.

'We're sorry Father, there won't be any further noise from us,' I said as I stood up.

'There had better not.' He glared at me in the derisory fashion as was his wont in this type of situation. The silence was such that noises from another class up the hall could now plainly be heard He turned, luckily for us in the same direction he was facing, and went back up the corridor from whence he came to carry on his mission of converting savages into gentlemen. The fastening was unlatched and Wally slipped back into the classroom just before Fr Osborne, or *Dracula* as we called him, sauntered in to conduct his English class.

We had been together as a class for three years and the Inter Cert exams beckoned.

Being in Upper Fourth we were regarded as the brightest of the bright as we had been streamed since Second Year. But my brightness was far from evident to me, more to the point it was far from evident to my father, who had become increasingly dismayed after reading the formal reports on my lack of progress in academic studies.

'Has ability but needs to apply himself more' was the gist of the remarks on the report sheet. After the arrival of a report at the end of each term there would always be tension between us. He'd start on me from the moment I'd sit into the car or if he was feeling under the weather, he would strongly admonish me anytime he laid eyes on me for not availing of the opportunities provided through being educated in Newbridge College.

Unfortunately these admonitions bounced off me like hailstones off a duck's back.

There were many contradictions in my life at this time. I loved my father, even the very smell of him I revered, but lately it seemed that everything I liked seemed to elicit only his disapproval.

One Sunday morning I was thrilled to see my name printed in the Young Persons' section of the *Sunday Independent*. In a column *Seeking Pen Pals* I had listed my hobbies and stated that I was a fun loving boy anxious to hear from boys or girls with similar interests. Unfortunately that very week, one of my classmates had won some sort of national essay competition and a photo of John Herlihy, with a mention of his proud parents, was published in the very same issue. My father saw this before my name jumped out at him from the back pages. He immediately lit into me about 'fuckin pen pals' and my spurning of the opportunity he'd worked so hard to provide. I knew he had a point but the more he said this type of thing, the more I resisted. These admonitions became a wedge between us and a pain for me to listen to. They had no effect whatsoever at getting me to improve my 'application to study.' In fact I started to do things specifically to displease him. Like, he hated 'that rotten loud pop music' which I had started to listen to on the transistor at every opportunity, even as I milked the cows. That was until one evening when I was in a hurry to get the job finished and realised that pop music made them give more milk, so I immediately switched off the radio.

It all came to a head one night, as I held a whitehead weanling in the calf shed for him to inject. I wasn't concentrating properly and the animal lashed out at my father and broke free with the needle still stuck in its rump. My father became enraged and hit me a wallop to the side of the head that knocked me to the ground.

'I fuckin hate you,' I cried as I jumped to my feet.

'You fuckin waster, throwing away every opportunity myself and your mother are breaking our arses for to provide you with an education.' I thought he was going to hit me again but instead he roared his head off at the ungrateful git who never listened.

I roared back and within seconds my mother and sisters were out from the house, looking on disconsolately. My brain flipped and I strode into the house to throw my clothes and Post Office savings book into a duffel bag. I would hitch to Dublin and from there sail to Holyhead to catch the train to London.

In the event my younger sister Veronica, who had a loving nature, grabbed me and wouldn't let go. There were lots of tears and sobs, as my father and I, with my sister holding onto to me for dear life stood facing each other in the space between the greyhound run and the calf shed, as rain drizzled through darkness barely lit up by the yard light atop the big shed. The anger slowly drained from us and we were left at the lowest ebb of our relationship. Afterwards we both seemed to resolve that things between us should never come to this again and in fairness, I don't think they did.

The relationship with my mother was entirely different. All this time we kept cows which had to be milked and calves that had to be bucket fed. Father had to be at work on the Curragh by half eight in the morning and so most of this work fell to Mother and I. While I was never in love with farm work, I loved helping her and when we were left to it, both of us would sing to ourselves as we went about our chores. She rarely gave out to me about studying or anything else and while I had long since passed the 'getting hugs from my mother' stage, I loved being close to her and I knew she loved having me around.

At the time we had eight cows whose milk we strained into twelve-gallon churns to be collected by the creamery lorry. Feeding the calves added a further twenty minutes or so to what had to be done before I cycled in to school. This was no big deal but it meant that more often than not I was late, especially when Religious Education was the first class on two or three days a week. Fr O'Hanlon, or Birdie as we called him on account of his beak, didn't seem to mind on the occasions I'd arrive in late, so long as I had a good excuse. I had plenty of these without ever having to disclose my business to boarders. One day after heavy rain, the Liffey seemed rather full.

'I'm sorry Father but the flood was across the road and I had to take a detour.'

'I see Noel, well that's too bad and are you alright?'

'Yes Father, I'm grand.' Another one I can remember was:

'I'm sorry Father, but there were cattle on the road and I had to give the farmer a hand to hunt them back into the field.' If I couldn't think of something original, I'd sometimes rub my hands along the bicycle chain then announce on joining class twenty or so minutes after the first bell:

'I'm sorry Father, but my chain kept coming off.'

'Very well Noel, sit down there and compose yourself. We'll just carry on here.'

After a while I came to realise that there seemed to be a conspiracy afoot between Birdie and the smiley boarders; so I put a stop to this charade by making sure I was on time, cows to be milked or no cows to be milked. Years later John Conway, a classmate, confirmed my suspicions when he told me how they all used to wait in thrall to hear what excuse I was going to come in with.

My mock exam results that Easter were poor and I now became very anxious.

Mugshot of a part-time soldier in the FCA c1968

Even though I belatedly started to study in earnest, there was too much ground to make up.

I resigned myself to failure but determined to do the best I could. Alas after each exam my worst fears were realised to such an extent that I was convinced I had indeed failed every single subject. I was in the FCA* and now had two weeks of playing soldier to look forward to but after that there was the turf and the hay to be saved. Before I departed for Gormanston

An Roinn Oideacais
DEPARTMENT OF EDUCATION

Brainse An Meán-Oideacais
SECONDARY EDUCATION BRANCH

Meán-Teistiméireact Onóraca
HONOURS INTERMEDIATE CERTIFICATE

Bronnad an Teistiméireact seo ar
THIS CERTIFICATE WAS AWARDED TO

Noel J. Heavey

as uct Pas le hOnóraca a fnótú sa Scrúdú
WHO PASSED THE INTERMEDIATE CERTIFICATE EXAMINATION WITH

Meán-Teistiméireacta, 1964. Fnótaif sé
HONOURS IN 1964. HE/SHE PASSED WITH HONOURS

Onóraca sna hábair seo :-
IN THE FOLLOWING SUBJECTS:-

Licriioct an Déarla	Stair 7 Tíreolaíoct	Matematic
English Literature	History and Geography	Mathematics

Laroin	Frainair	Eolaíoct
Latin	French	Science

agus Pas sna hábair seo :-
AND PASSED IN THE FOLLOWING SUBJECTS:-

Licriioct na Saeilse
Irish Literature

J. Ó Raifeartaigh

SCR ....

3788
Uim. Scrúd.
EXAM. NO.

Rúnaí

Inter Cert Results

I told my father that while the exams hadn't gone well, I had seen the error of my ways and would make it up to him.

On the day I knew the results were due out I went down the Baune Lane to intercept the postman. I met him at the culvert where he gave me the letters to bring home. I immediately opened the one white envelope and was stunned by what I read. Six honours and a pass in Irish. My first and enduring thought was that somehow my results had become mixed up with someone else's but I kept this to myself after I ran home to share the news with my mother, she threw her arms around me and hugged 'til it hurt.

That evening when my father read the results he smiled a grin from one ear to the other and then pulled me in close. I remember feeling the bristles of his beard on my cheeks as he too hugged me and told me how proud he was. Sleep didn't come easily that night. That letter changed things. It made me consider and ultimately choose a road no Clongorey boy had trod before. I would go on to receive results of many exams in the Years to come, but never again would I experience anything close to the sheer relief and elation I felt on opening that white envelope on the Baune lane.

*FCA. Forsai Cosanta Aithiuil. Irish for Local (Reserve) Defence Forces

BALL GAMES

Only once can I recall hearing screams of pleasure from young women over something I've done. A precious memory it is too. I was playing for Sarsfields in the semi-final of the minor championship and I'd just out jumped two Carbury players in the middle of the field. I knew, without looking, that the screams had come from three girls standing at the railing on the Kilcullen side of the stand in the county grounds, Newbridge. I knew also that I shouldn't have noticed them but there was something about the bearing of the girl in the middle which was difficult to ignore.

Anytime I recall that summer of football, that passage of play flashes into my brain.

Philly Duane runs to the corner flag, his arm raised looking for the pass. Ray O'Sullivan and Bernie Geraghty break forward and will support him when he gets it. My midfield partner Aidan Comerford blocks off a would-be tackler while behind me John Dempsey and Mick Sammon are roaring out instructions to cover off. Vinnie O'Hanlon and Nicky Leahy await developments as they loiter with deadly intent on the edge of the square. I feel the excitement as the whole team moves like a pack of wolves on the scent of a kill. I see surprise, then fear, in the eyes of our opponents. I feel enormous satisfaction as we go about our business. Above all I hear the piercing screams of the three young ladies, which thrilled me to the core.

Anytime this scene plays in my head it does my heart good, even after all these years. Carbury were a fine team that included seven players from the county team but on that particular day we were winged Gods as we recorded a memorable victory. We went on to easily beat Devoys in the

MINOR TITLE GOES TO SARSFIELDS

SARSFIELDS 4-4   **DEVOYS 1-6**

DROICHEAD NUA side, Sarsfields, added the Minor Football Championship title to their earlier Juvenile title when at Naas on Sunday they scored a seven-points win over a spirited Devoys selection who tried valiantly until the very end.

This win not only has ended a ten-years spell in the wilderness for the minor teams but fully bears out the wisdom of a policy that has seen a full concentration on the under-age players over the past few years.

The winners, with thorough preparation and a more impressive earlier round record, were favourites but what a battle they got from a game fifteen who in a thrilling first twenty minutes looked as if they were about to score a shock win.

During that spell, of first rate football, the Devoys matched their opponents in every sector. However, towards the end Sarsfields got through for two goals and a point to leave them a flattering four points in front at the interval.

It was again top class football in the second half but with Sarsfields now in command the tempo slackened and long before the end, the title was obviously on the way to Droichead Nua.

The winners deserved their win. All round they were the superior side. Full-back John Dempsey was the outstanding defender, with Ray Sullivan Mick Sammon and Ray Loakman also in top form. Aidan Comerford and Noel Heavey played their part at midfield, while Vincent Hanlon at full-forward was the star in attack. He scored one goal and two points at very vital periods. Nick Leahy and Phil Duane were others to impress here.

The losers had a few outstanding individuals with Richard Donoghue, always a real danger in attack, scoring 1-3. Right full John Carr, with Leonard Cullen were best in defence. Eamonn Donoghue starred at midfield and best of the forwards were Michael J o h n s o n, and Peter McGreevy.

Scorers: For Sarsfields — Vincent Hanlon 1-2, B. Geraghty 1-0, N. Leahy 2-0, P. Duane 0-2.

For Devoys — R. Donoghue 1-3, E. Donoghue 0-2, M. Sheerin 0-1.

Sarsfields — M. Dunne, M. Keogh, J. Dempsey, D. O'Hanlon, R. Sullivan, M. Sammon, N. Loakman, A. Comerford, N. Heavey, P. Duane, B. Geraghty, P. Dunne, N. Leahy, V. Hanlon, N. Loftus. Sub.: Dunne for Comerford.

Devoys — L. Blanchfield, J. Carr, D. Dalton, J. Maguire, L. Cullen, M. Birmingham, A. Dalton, E. Donoghue, B. Corr, R. Donoghue, M. Sheerin, M. Johnson, P. McGreevy, J. McGarr, B. Whelan.

Referee: M. Curtis, Naas.

Factory   **Appointed**

August 1967 Leinster Leader

county minor final. It was our time and I enjoyed every second of it. Tommy O'Hanlon was the man who moulded us into the team we became. He'd heard of the young rugby player in the college and he came over to me one afternoon as I walked uptown to meet with friends. He asked me out straight if I'd play for Sarsfields for the one year I'd left to play minor and assured me that this wouldn't affect my eligibility to play for my own parish team, Raheens, in other grades. I agreed there and then, even though I'd played mostly rugby for the previous four years.

I was very fit and after a few games I found that skills

developed years before at the back of Earley's and in the Clongorey school field came back to me. I was able to hold my own, more than hold my own. One evening Tommy brought me up to the Curragh where the final trials for the Kildare Minor team were being held. I was nervous but I played well when I came on. About a week after this, one of the county selectors, a man called Ray O Malley, came to my house, one very wet evening, to collect and bring me to Trim. I lined out as a half forward against Cavan and I scored three goals and two points. It was only a challenge game but I felt a huge affirmation as I lapped up the praise and enjoyed the respect, communicated by nods and winks from strangers, as we trooped off the sodden pitch when it was all over.

The next game was the first round of the Championship, against Carlow, in their fancy coloured jerseys. We won easily enough but I ended up in a fracas with my marker, whom I'd knocked to the ground because of his persistent pulling and dragging out of me for the whole game. This little episode cost me my place in the next game against Laois. I focused on the performance of my replacement and while people would have observed me cheering and encouraging his every move, in my heart of hearts I wished him to make a mess of every ball that came his way, so that I'd be brought on to replace him. This eventually happened but it was too late for me to have any influence of the game. Steak and chips in a fancy hotel with all the tomato ketchup in the world did little to appease the empty feeling of defeat. Thankfully my county medal win with Sarsfields was more than a consolation as was making the acquaintance of the young lady by the railing, the one in the middle with the bearing.

All these Gaelic football experiences were well behind me in October when I was approached by Fr Heffernan, our rugby trainer, in my final year of Newbridge College. I was the blindside wing forward on the senior team and was walking out to take my place for a training session, or strip as it was called at the time. We were a strong side and had commenced our training programme, in preparation for the Leinster Schools Senior Cup,which has always been the Holy Grail of schools rugby.

We were being talked about as the best team that had ever come through the College and were favoured by many to win the Cup. Essentially we were the same bunch of lads that had been playing together over the previous four years. I was proud to be the only day boy on the team. If we were to be successful each of us fully appreciated that we would be regarded as legends forever. My main job as a wing forward was to stay on our side of the ball as it trickled back through our opponents' scrum or ruck and to tackle their scrum half before he could mount an attack. Another primary duty was to track back behind our backs to form a second line of defence. All of us on the team had an inherent understanding of what each of us would do in any given situation based on our experience of playing together for so long.

'Hey Mister, do you not want to be on this team at all?'

'Of course I do, Father, why are you asking me a question like that?' I replied as I looked Fr Heffernan directly in the eye, having being startled to be asked such a question.

'Well then you'd better give up playing this Gaelic football. I'm not going to have you become an integral part of this team, only to lose you to injury because you want to play Gaelic.' I felt my cheeks redden, a sure sign that my mouth was about to work faster than my brain.

'I'll never miss a strip or a game. You have my word on that but let me tell you this; I won't be giving up Gaelic football. My father played for Kildare and it's a huge honour for me to do the same.' Now it was his turn to redden and look me directly in the eye.

'Well that's just not good enough Mister.' He said, as we walked onto the field where he bid us to complete our few warm up exercises.

He then called us together and made a point of telling everyone why I was being dropped from the Firsts, then I was made to walk across to the Seconds to swap places with their wing forward. I was incandescent with anger to have been treated like this. No sooner had the game started when fists and boots began to fly from two of the Firsts, former team mates who never liked me anyway. I immediately went to retaliate but someone had locked me in a bear hug, thus pinning my arms to my side. My assailant, whom I always detested, seized this opportunity to wham his fist into my face. Instantly I felt my eyebrow droop. Heffernan was over in a flash, literally frothing at the mouth. 'You,' he said pointing at me as blood poured down my face, 'are nothing but trouble. You are off the panel. Go.' He blew his whistle there and then to signal the end of the practice game.

I was distraught at what I perceived to have been a conspiracy to get me off the team which would now consist exclusively of boarders. My best friend on the team, scrum-half Robbie McGrath, tried to console me as we trudged off and offered to intercede.

I told him not to bother. I could and should have said to Heffernan when he first came on to me that the Gaelic football season was over but youth, pride and stubbornness are not good bedfellows.

As one door closed, another opened; I now immersed myself in the more cerebral aspect of school life and gravitated towards friends who had a complete disregard for all things

Paul Cullen, Eoin McBennett and myself representing Newbridge College in *Mark Time*

rugby. I made the debating team and also represented my school on Teilefís Éireann school quiz show *Mark Time* for which mother bought me a new shirt. Karl McDonagh loaned me his school blazer as I'd outgrown my own. Appearing on the telly allowed me a certain notoriety among the senior girls of the Cross and Passion College in Kilcullen which I wasn't slow to exploit.

In sport I concentrated on cross country and came to know 'the loneliness of the long distance runner.' I enjoyed running and went on to win silver medals in the Leinster cross country championships and later in the three mile event in the track and field championships. These were considerable achievements that made me feel really good about myself but they cut little ice in Newbridge College at that time. The Senior rugby team became the main focus of everyone in the school and duly went on to defeat Roscrea and then Belvedere in the quarter-final of The Cup. I was very much of the opinion that I was better than the captain's brother who had 'taken' my place that fateful day but I kept this to myself as everyone else had most definitely moved on.

The semi-final against St Mary's College was a closely fought affair. Newbridge were the better team but led by just two points going into the final play. Then disaster struck. We were defending resolutely when the chap who had replaced me on the team went offside. The referee awarded a penalty on the stroke of full time. Disbelief and despair registered on the faces and in the hearts of every Newbridge player and supporter. The total silence in which Andrucetti ran up to take his kick contrasted eerily with the cacophony of noise that erupted from the St Marys' supporters even before the ball rocketed over the bar. Their delirium was understandable but was difficult to stomach when set against the utter desolation felt in the hearts of every Newbridge player and supporter including me.

We had dared to dream and lost when we were within a hair's breadth of reaching the final, which St Marys' subsequently won easily. For some of us, desolation came accompanied by anger, jealously and maybe even guilt. It has taken more years than it should have for all this to dissipate but in the words of a line from a song from that bittersweet era long ago – 'it's alright now.'

BELFIELD

It was mother who decided I should stay in digs with her friend Lily Holohan for my first year in University. I'd spent the summer living with Lily's family in Chanel Avenue, Artane. My summer job had been on a building site just down the road, but now I would have to make my way right across the city. Lily's husband Paddy organised a lift into town and then, as he said:

'All you have to do is hop on the 46A and you'll be out there in no time.'

It was an old type bus with an open platform at the back, onto which I often jumped after an all out sprint, to grasp the chrome bar as the bus pulled away. It was the one route I knew south of the Liffey from being a competitor in the Leinster and All-Ireland Schools Cross Country events which were held in the Belfield grounds. The Dean in my old school had been explicit: 'Catch the 46A at the railings at Trinity College and ask to be let off at the Montrose Hotel'. He was spot on.

The Cross Country experience meant I was one of the very few who knew anything about Belfield that first morning, when hundreds of us crammed into the Science Block for our first day in Belfield. I was lucky to be there at all. An escapade in a Newbridge bar nearly cost me my academic career before it even started. To get into UCD one had to have two honours in the Leaving Certificate. English and History were my two bankers. The History exam wasn't until a week after the others and the handful of us sitting this exam were bored beyond belief. It was the hottest day of the year, with the sun at its highest when four history candidates decided in our wisdom to 'go up town for just the one, as the exam isn't 'til two o'clock.' We were nursing our lovely cold pint ready to go when four more pints of Harp appeared in front of us.

'There you are now boys, enjoy them and thanks very much for coming in,' said Joe McTernan, the proprietor, who just that week had opened his refurbished bar.

We were so impressed by this generous gesture that we felt honour bound to order four more pints, so we did. Coming up to two o'clock we had to press gang Mr McTernan to drive us down to the College. We more or less fell out of the car and barely made it up the stairs to the Study Hall to sit our final exam. The supervisor looked at us severely and refused to let any of us out to the toilet until a half hour had elapsed and then only one at a time, under supervision. The History exam did not go well. Luckily for me, when the results came out, Latin had saved the day.

'Shake hands and say hello to the person sitting either side of you,' said Doctor Scott, our Physics and first ever lecturer. One hundred and twenty students enjoyed the moment.

'Now just remember this; Apart from you, there are about thirty repeat students studying on their own, who will also be sitting the exams in summer. But there are only fifty places available in the Veterinary College in Ballsbridge. The reality is that two out of every three of you won't make it. Welcome ladies and gentlemen to first year Veterinary Medicine.'

The Science block was the only one inhabited by students. A huge Arts block was built but stood empty because of some dispute or other. So that first year we had the whole of Belfield to ourselves. We were the Freshers – first year students of Science, Veterinary Science, Agricultural Science, Medicine and also the notorious Engineers who seemed always to be on the brink of a riot.

For the first time since national school, I found myself sitting beside girls, the most gorgeous girls. After a while I became used to this and gradually came to regard them as colleagues and friends rather than objects of awe and desire; there were a couple of near exceptions.

I had come through second level in Newbridge College with a bit of a complex about 'coming from the bog' and hadn't yet developed the social skills to turn this to my advantage. Most of my peers were solidly middle class and projected an aura of confidence that I certainly didn't feel. Outwardly I was 'one of the lads' but I envied fellows like Declan who exuded confidence, played firsts rugby for one of the senior clubs and was boyfriend to Dara; the most beautiful erudite girl in Belfield, with her soft blonde hair and piercing blue eyes. Both were medical students but I was in their circle and delighted to accept Dara's invitation to her house party in Sandycove. It was a fabulous house with a large carpeted room in which a guy with well groomed long hair held centre stage. He strummed a guitar and led out a dreamy slow song as we all sat cross legged on the floor; 'I loved you in the morning, our kisses deep and warm Your hair upon the pillow like a sleepy golden storm. Yes many loved before us…'

I sat on the edge of the crowd in my bawneen jumper feeling just a little bit uncomfortable. I slipped out and found myself alone in another room. I looked around and there stood Dara. We were alone now and I became very nervous. She took my hand smiled softly into my face and for a few fleeting seconds it seemed the most natural thing in the world that I should kiss her. But I baulked and the opportunity was gone. For years I blushed with embarrassment any time the memory of this incident surfaced in my consciousness and silently regretted the things that made me feel so awkward and inadequate in the presence of that beautiful girl.

As the year progressed, the thousand or so freshers settled down in that large green-glassed building. We became familiar with the workings of things like Krebs Cycle, oscilloscopes, vascular bundles and benzene rings. I never considered myself studious, but I was careful enough to attend every lecture, practical and tutorial. I joined the Freshers gaelic football squad. Kevin Kilmurray who had played in that year's All Ireland final with Offaly was the star. I discovered that if I trained hard, I could compete with the best of them. I made the team and enjoyed long overnight trips to Cork, Galway and Belfast to take on our counterparts. We played hard, drank hard and had great fun. In time Kilmurray and I became good friends. I had also befriended John Byrne, a rugby player and a fellow Kildare man in the first tumultuous days of college.

During the zoology practicals I shared a bench with a very good looking girl by the name of Jo Brennan. We became good friends and good friends only, as both of us had begun 'to go steady' but this hadn't been written in stone. Professor Carmel Humphries declared early on 'no matter how well you perform in other exams, nobody enters Second Vet unless they pass the zoology practical.'

Jo was a top class student and very helpful to me as I grappled with the intricacies of dissecting the organs of earthworms, snails and rabbits. Any romantic spark that may have been fanned by our physical closeness in the lab was well and truly smothered by the pervasive fumes from the formalin used to preserve the specimens. Jo's love life had become quite problematic and I became her willing confidant during a particular practical. That day we had been assigned the dissection of the urino-genital system of a male rabbit. We went through the motions of dissection but talking and listening to the issues of a troubled romance took precedence.

The year flew by and before long the examinations were upon us. I felt they had gone well enough for me, until the very last one which was the Zoology practical. My worst fears were realised when I flipped the exam paper to discover that the major part of my assignment was the dissection of the urino-genital system of a male rabbit. All the responsibility and guilt of letting my parents and myself down descended onto my shoulders and induced a sort of helplessness in me. At every turn, bits of *vas deferens* and scrotal sac seemed to disintegrate under my heavy hand. I floundered to pin bits together but I was in despair. After the best part of an hour, I gradually came to the realisation that there was a different type of acrid smell from the bottom end of my rabbit cadaver. I shot up my hand as soon as the penny dropped.

'This rabbit is rotten.' I was close to panic and my voice and tone to the supervisor was louder than intended. All heads in the vicinity turned in my direction.

'Lower your voice please, what seems to be the problem?' asked the bemused supervisor.

'There's no smell of formalin off this part of him, he's red rotten and every tissue I dissect is coming apart in front of my eyes.'

In fairness the supervisor discerned the import of the situation and called the attendant who confirmed that the tissues were in decay. He had a new rabbit in front of me within two minutes. It was too late; I'd lost the best part of an hour and even Doctor Barnard the eminent surgeon couldn't have completed the task in the time remaining. I was aghast and afterwards went to see the professor.

'Can I take the exam again?' I asked after she was appraised of what had happened.

'You should have detected tissue decay in your specimen immediately and asked for a replacement. This is a highly competitive exam and there is nothing to be done.'

Emphatically unsympathetic was an understatement of her

attitude. I stood before that professor and inwardly raged how authority figures always had an answer to get themselves off the hook.

When the results came through I was adjudged to have 'passed'. Fifty six was the number opposite my name under the heading 'POSITION'. Fifty five candidates were accepted into the Veterinary College that year. I was informed that I had the choice of repeating the year or proceeding into second year Science or Agricultural Science. I was even advised there was the possibility of a place being available for me in the Dental College in Cork.

My mind flew back in time to nights spent in Clongorey school when PJ Keenan, the agricultural advisor brought knowledge and wonder to a handful of bog men and a ten year old boy. I hesitated for no more than a minute, before visions of working with country people to modernise farming in Ireland drew me into the Agricultural Faculty and I bade goodbye to Veterinary Medicine.

NEW YORK
1. FINDING MY FEET

Oliver Kilmurray and I walking across the tarmac having
arrived in New York in 1971

I was totally unprepared for New York. Searing heat enveloped every crevice of my body. I opened my passport on the J1 visa page and stepped off the passenger stairs onto the tarmac. I was glad to be out of that narrow aluminium tube packed with fellow students, each of us seeking adventure and fortune. A haze rose up from the concrete as we walked the short distance to the terminal building. We were drenched in our own sweat by the time we reached it. Inside people chewed gum, none of them smiled and the policemen wore guns on their hips. The large sign read:

Welcome to Kennedy International Airport.

'Scrambled eggs and rashers please,' I ordered in Bickford's Fast Food on Pennsylvania Avenue after we had checked into our huge hotel beside the train station. 'Scrambled and what?'

The middle aged waitress made a big deal about the word 'rashers'. She made me point to the little picture on the menu card. She was the first American I'd seen smile and I smiled back. The rashers were shrivelled to nearly nothing but they tasted so good.

I was awe struck by the never-ending snake of humanity, eight or nine people deep that shuffled past our window. Out on the street I became light-headed when I looked up and tried to come to terms with the height and splendour of the buildings. This was in contrast with the roads which were pot-holed beyond belief. Some of them were on a par with the Baune Lane. Then I went up and down in the high speed hotel lift a couple of times, just to experience my ears popping and the same sensation in my stomach I used to experience when my dad drove fast over the canal bridges on the way to Allenwood. We were a long way from Allenwood now.

The next evening, Tom Stanley, who originally lived down the road from me at home, but had emigrated to New York years earlier, called into the hotel to collect John Byrne and myself as pre-arranged. We 'caught the subway' and within twenty minutes we were outside his Apartment, 167 Sherman Avenue off Broadway at the top of The Bronx. We climbed three flights of stairs 'til we reached a green door with the sign *Home Sweet Home*. Tom's brother, Watty was tending pots when we walked in, he was grinning from ear to ear and didn't say much. The smell from the pots said it all. After forty-eight hours of nonstop new experiences, the prospect of potatoes, bacon and cabbage was more than welcome. They were jokers, my friend John was somewhat reserved but the four of us struck it off well from that first dinner. The Sunday after this, we went for a drive to Rockaway Beach. The expressways and turnpikes were as wide as football fields. Everything and everyone seemed to be gigantic and hot, it was so unbelievably hot and heavy with humidity. The waves lapping onto a half empty beach of soft sand seemed the perfect antidote to it all. That night we discovered the pain of severe sunburn but we weren't too bothered.

The following Sunday John and I caught a bus to Orchard Beach which was only a short distance from the apartment. The small beach was tightly packed, mostly with black and Hispanic people. They seemed uninterested in the water, content just to sit on the sand and look out at the sea. We hadn't a ghetto blaster or a cold box of beer, so we decided to take a plunge. As we walked into the water, I became conscious that all eyes on the beach seemed to be focused on us. I determined to carry on, but then a soft brown object brushed against my right cheek. I looked and couldn't believe a piece of shit had touched my face. Suddenly I realised why we were the only ones in the water as hundreds of bobbing shits floated on a gentle wave. I resisted the urge to tear the flesh from my cheek and headed in utter disgust for the shore. A sea of gleaming white teeth in black mouths seemed to vibrate in harmony as a whole beach full of people celebrated the moment with animated laughter. We waded onto the beach, changed and caught the bus home.

I was anxious to tie down a job as soon as possible and tried every personal connection I knew. This generated lots of talk but no job. We'd been warned on our orientation course that summer jobs in New York were very scarce. Now I developed a knot in my stomach and became really anxious. Tom and Watty were generous to a fault but the money my father had given me had all but run out. I was close to despair and took to walking the streets, even in the unbearable heat as the noise and the unnatural coldness of ubiquitous air conditioners indoors was even worse. Ten days after we moved into Sherman Avenue, a kid called me a 'motherfucker' after I caught his handball as it bounced off a wall. I'd never heard this expression before and it traumatised me. I continued walking up Broadway until I came to a nondescript opening into a park, which I hadn't noticed before. I went in and climbed a hill overgrown with trees and shrubs, until I came to an old brown building on the top. It was open but there was nobody about that I could see. There were old paintings and artifacts in room after room. Intrigued, I explored the place for what must have been a couple hours without meeting a single soul. Eventually I came to a courtyard in the middle of the building. Mystified I went back the way I had come. At the bottom of the hill the dark cloud that had been enveloping me seemed to lift, as if by magic. Years later I discovered this wonderful old place was a museum called The Cloisters.

Later that very afternoon, my friend Kevin, who had been flown out to play football with the Leix* club as a condition for him having a union job as a carpenter, rang to tell me of a trial game being held that very evening in Flushing Meadows, near La Guardia Airport.

'Listen, the guys in charge of the clubs have the giving out of any jobs that are going. They are all going to be there. If you play well, chances are one of them will sign you up and offer you a job.' He added it was time 'to shite or get off the pot.'

There were some serious players there that evening. I found myself marking Colm McAlarney the County Down midfielder. The backdrop was surreal, planes landing and taking off every minute. It must have suited me because I played as if for my life and I felt I did more than okay.

After the trial-game Kevin told me that his mentor Joe McCabe, boss of the carpenter's union wanted to sign me for his club but there were no carpenter jobs at the moment. Another man called Jimmy French walked over to me and

We needed to work fast together as we excavated the Sewer.
I was the only Irishman on the job

Frankie was my partner. We worked well together

offered a job at one dollar ninety cents an hour as a cleaner in a school if I'd play for his team, Waterford. My heart gave a jump on hearing this. Suddenly New York was a wonderful place. He told me training was in Van Cortland Park on Tuesdays and Thursdays and that they were due to play their championship against Leix a fortnight later in Gaelic Park.

I started work in PS 28 in the middle of the Bronx the following day. This was a big old building with at least three floors. Inside, the brown linoleum floors reeked of polish. I washed and scrubbed school furniture as if there was no tomorrow. The permanent guy who worked there was from Leitrim and much older than me. He now became uneasy with all this productivity. He told me to slow down a bit and never to bother looking for him between twelve and two. I was rooting around under the stairs in the basement a few days later when I discovered the reason for his odd request. There he was fast asleep in his hideaway bed.

The evening before the championship match in Gaelic Park, word came through that a timberman job had come up and that Joe McCabe said it was mine if I switched clubs back to Leix. I signed the papers on the Saturday and phoned Jimmy to tell him. He wasn't at all pleased. I didn't feel great about it myself but the pay was seven bucks an hour, over three times what I could earn as a cleaner.

I came on as a sub in Gaelic Park that Sunday against the guys I had trained with on the previous Thursday evening. It was unbelievably hot and humid. I ingested a handful of salt tablets, ended up wearing a white bandana to stop sweat running into my eyes and managed to score a couple of points. I shipped a fair few belts from angry Waterford men. I was glad when it was all over.

Gaelic Park is at the northern tip of the Bronx was a somewhat dilapidated place at this time. It's small bumpy pitch was rock hard, devoid of grass in the goal areas and enclosed by high mesh wire to prevent access to supporters. After the games everyone gathered inside a ramshackle enough hall. Here I had my first taste of Rhinegold beer which was sold in long neck bottles. Tom had told me to watch out for narrowbacks. These were the first generation daughters of Irish immigrants. They were there in droves. I was gobsmacked by the whiteness of their teeth when they smiled, which was a lot. A Céili band struck up. I stood around with Kevin and my new team mates drinking cheap ice cold beer. As I ogled those vivacious ladies with the beautiful teeth that evening in Gaelic Park, I contemplated my construction job the following morning and thought to myself that this was as close to Heaven that I'd come to at this point in my life.

The job was in Queens which seemed to me to be altogether less built up and less intense than either Manhatten or the Bronx. The contractor was Italian and the job consisted of digging up a street to replace an outdated sewage system. A timberman is a cross between a labourer and a carpenter. The work with a jack-hammer entailed me driving timbers into soft New York sand to prevent excavations from collapsing. Union pay was triple that of a school cleaner and five times the going rate for labouring work back home. In other words I had it made.

We needed to work fast and together. I settled in after a few days and became an integral part of the crew. I was the only Irishman on the job. Most of the workers were Italians.

I figured I was the trade for some favour Joe McCabe had performed for the contractor. There were two black guys Frankie and Jimmy and they were good fun. It was with them I shared our lunch breaks. One of the Italians was a most unpleasant guy; he worked opposite me and was a loud foul-

Barman Jarleth Gilroy, Ned Murphy, Pat Diamond and I
having a drink in the Liffey Bar in Woodside, Queens 1970

mouthed braggart who got on my case right from the start. Joey was one huge pain in the ass for everyone but particularly for me. He ranted all day, every day. His favourite rant was about the 'De Stoopid I wish.' I tried to ignore him as best I could.

'Hey, that Italian pain in the ass, he's gone,' my workmate Frankie said to me first thing one Monday morning.

'Yeah,' Jimmy joined in. 'The boss paid him up and told him not to come back here no more.'

I felt so relieved.

Around this time I'd made contact with a distant cousin, who had once visited us in Clongorey He asked me out to his home in Brooklyn that Sunday and I really looked forward to the visit. Bill and his wife were very friendly and laid back. She was Italian and had prepared spaghetti and meatballs for lunch. She told me she had a brother and that he'd be coming over 'to say hullo.' I was delighted to be breaking bread with civilised Italians. When her brother walked in, Joey – the bane of my life, stood before me. Both of us blushed crimson. He was gone from the job but a week.

I silently thanked God for this, but he turned out to be a totally different animal in his sister's home.

We actually managed to nearly enjoy each other's company, as we became mildly sloshed on his sister's red wine.

I settled into the rhythm of life in New York. Danny from North Carolina and Luis from Portugal were workmates whom I also befriended. Luis was newly married and was paid the same rate as me. He always seemed to be broke and used to cadge money from me on Wednesdays to tide him until payday when he would pay me back. The cost of living in New York that time wasn't all that much more expensive than home yet we were receiving over three times the pay that my old landlord Paddy Holohan was being paid as a painter in Bolands Mills. Paddy and Lily reared their family of four children on this meagre wage without complaint or ever leaving their family short of anything. Anytime I was in Dublin for the weekend I used to drink pints of Guinness with Paddy in the Ardlea Inn in Artane. Every time I baled out Luis I would think of Paddy and Lily and indeed my own parents and how they managed to look after their families on such a meagre salary. It wasn't easy for a twenty year old to make sense of it all.

NEW YORK
2. STAR GAZING

I moved in with Kevin and Pat Diamond, who had obtained the use of a second floor apartment in Woodside, quite near my new job in Queens, where I worked as a *timberman*. That first week Kevin and I went up on the roof, one night to check out the stars in the sky. Some people in New York apartments weren't too fond of curtains and within minutes our focus shifted from stars to what was going on in two bedrooms in two blocks opposite ours on opposite sides of our roof. We eventually went downstairs to go to the deli as per our original plan, we returned in less than ten minutes with our groceries in brown paper bags, to find three NYPD cars outside the apartment block. Eager cops with guns drawn were all over the place.

'What's up?' I asked one of the officers after some hesitation.

'Are you guys residents'?

'Yeah, apartment 204,' said Kevin.

'Please go to your apartment and keep the door locked. You've got prowlers on the roof.'

'Fucking hell, I hope you get them,' I said.

'We'll get 'em, go inside and lock your door, Sir.' We walked smartly through the gauntlet and did as we were bid. Inside we went straight to our bedroom and collapsed onto the beds in convulsions of laughter, but there was no more star gazing.

This land is my land, this land is your land,
From California to the New York Islands,
From the Redwood Forests to the Gulf Stream waters
This land was made for you and me.

These are the opening lines of the opening song played

every Saturday night by the resident band in The Red Mill. I loved the excitement of this place in the middle of The Bronx, where lonely Irish students met 'narrowbacks' a slang word at the time for American daughters of Irish parents. Here I developed a taste for Seagram's seven year old whiskey mixed with 7Up called *Seven and Seven* .What a feeling it was to have money in the pocket as one contemplated the finest New York had to offer. However there was one bit of a snag; these otherwise highly intelligent young women were on the prowl for husband material. For some peculiar reason, young Irishmen were reckoned to make ideal husbands.

I thought this a bit bizarre but it was made abundantly clear to me by a vivacious young lady called Mary Paterson that there was 'nothing doing' unless I was open to becoming engaged.

'I'm nineteen and just finished first year in college for Christ's sake,' I exclaimed but Mary stuck to her guns and so did I. Nevertheless we hung out with each other for the rest of the summer. Once she brought me to meet her grandfather who lived in a small apartment off Tremont Avenue. He became emotional when he met his pride and joy's young man with an Irish accent. We listened to his fiddle music for a while; he wanted to play for us the whole night, but I and indeed his granddaughter had other things on our minds. After a decent interlude we withdrew to spend the balmy night until dawn, kissing and chatting each other on a wall overlooking the steady stream of cars that drove all night on the Cross Bronx Expressway.

Over the summer I managed to accumulate fifteen hundred dollars in my bank account in Chase Manhattan, which had a branch in Dublin. I left my job on the same Friday I was due to fly home. The flight wasn't until the evening and I'd been promised a full day's pay for turning up for a couple

Posing with towel and my first pair of sunglasses at Rockaway Beach, July
1970 with Kevin Kilmurray, Pat Diamond and Seamus O'Kane

Kevin Kilmurray and I with Elsie Kehoe, from Kilkenny, who owned
the apartment in Woodside where we stayed for the best part
of Summer of '69, in Queens, New York

Kevin Kilmurray, Ned Murphy and Pat Diamond outside our apartment block where we absconded one night to see if we could Gaze At The Stars

Me and Mary Patterson at The Red Mill Ballroom in the Bronx

of hours and so I arrived with my case fully packed. The job took an early lunch that day and my work buddies brought me down to a bar. By the time a taxi was called to bring me to the airport, I was drunk.

On a whim I bought a present for Tommy –my young brother. It was a two thirds replica of an M1 carbine rifle. It just about fitted into the sleeve of the new coat I had purchased the previous weekend in Macy's department store. This I had to carry through check-in and on board the chartered Aer Lingus plane. It was parked on the same tarmac which had radiated a heat haze only four months previously. The only haze this time was the one in my brain.

There was mayhem on board, as a planeload of students celebrated the summer's achievements and anticipated going home. On a mad impulse, I pressed the light switch to bring the attractive green uniformed hostess scurrying down the narrow aisle as we awaited permission to take off.

'Can I help you?' she beamed.

'I want to go to Cuba,' I said as I uncovered the replica rifle and pointed it directly into her face. For a split second she froze, but then she whipped the gun from me and ran up to the front of the plane. A dark foreboding descended. Within seconds the very stern looking captain stood before me. My fellow passengers now hushed and waited.

'I was only messing. It's only a toy but she whipped it from me before I could take it down.' At this stage the gravity of my situation had well and truly percolated through the inebriation. 'Look I'm very, very sorry. It was only a prank but I see that I was so wrong to do it.' The Captain looked directly at me as he sized up the situation. He seemed to take an age before he spoke in what I took to be a thick Limerick accent.

'You are very lucky that I'm allowing you to stay on this flight and not handing you over to airport police.' I breathed a sigh of relief as normal hilarity slowly returned. The hostess passed by sometime after this. She looked at me very crossly indeed.

'I'm so sorry, it was a stupid prank, but you whipped it from me so quickly, I didn't get the chance to explain. It's only a toy I bought in a huckster shop for my young brother.'

She raised her left eyebrow:

'OK, look, I accept your apology, let's forget about it,' she smiled briefly.

'Do you think, I'll be able to get it back?' I chanced. She nearly cut me in two with a look.

I slept for most of the rest of the journey, but was awoken by cheering and clapping. The green fields of Ireland below us had been spotted and they stimulated an unexpected gush of emotion from every passenger on the plane. My family, Second Year Agricultural Science and a certain demure lady awaited. I was relieved now that things hadn't developed too seriously with my New York Mary. We landed first in Shannon, which was the way with all transatlantic flights at the time. An hour later we touched down in Dublin. As I prepared to disembark, I felt a tap on my shoulder.

'I wouldn't like to deprive your little brother,' she smiled broadly as she handed me the replica rifle.

'Thank you so much,' I had an impulse to give her a hug, but in a rare moment of restraint, I confined myself to returning the smile. It was good to be home.

LOST LOVE
IN TIMES OF FLATLAND

Before the end of our relationship, I used to cringe any time one those sentimental love songs came on the radio. After our break up, I'd listen for any insight or comfort for the broken-hearted. I even began to sing the damned things.

'Those were the days my friend, I thought they'd
never end,
We'd sing and dance forever and a day.
We'd live the life we chose, we'd fight and never lose
For we were young and sure to have our way'

At the outset we were no different from the dozens of other couples all around us at the time. We ducked and dived along the trajectory our young lives took us. It was no big deal. Sure, people recognised us as going steady, but for that first part of our journey neither of us attached too much import to this. We had exchanged letters with each other while I was working for the summer in New York but I had no compunction about going out with others while I was there.

I'm sure it was the same for you here after you completed your Leaving Cert exams. You didn't say and I never asked. On my return we had taken things up where we'd left off. I loved the unique Charleston-like dance steps you had developed over the summer. I tried to emulate them when we danced together but succeeded only in looking and feeling like a drunken ostrich. However, I recall a straw in the wind – the night I refused the lift from Ollie Delaney in order to walk you home.

The Ardenode was the epicentre of our scene back then. There was a discoteque on every Sunday night. The rugby crowd from Naas, Kilcullen, Newbridge and other places I'd never heard of, danced to the sounds of DJ, Willy Kiernan, and drank themselves silly as they sought love or whatever passed for it in the back of a Mini or a Morris Minor. Usually I had a lift there and back with Ollie or any friend who had the use of his father's car, except for that night when the frost lifted me out of it as I tramped the sixteen miles to home.

For me, the Rubicon was crossed the night I found out I'd nearly lost you. You were in the phone box in your village at the bottom of the hill. We had just finished speaking on the phone when a runaway lorry trundled downhill and knocked over the phone box with you still in it.

Amazingly you were unhurt but the thought of you being nearly killed catapulted my feelings for you onto a completely different plane.

That October Kevin Kilmurray and I rented a bedsit looking onto Portobello Bridge. It took us three evenings to procure that little room. We'd get the *Evening Press* as early as possible, take over a phone box and start tapping numbers. By the time we'd get to view the room there would be a queue before us or a note on the door *Room Let*. We'd still be looking if we didn't hit on the idea of going to *The Press* offices in O'Connell Street and convincing the lady at the front desk to let us have an advance copy before it hit the streets. She said she wasn't allowed but Kevin had a way with him.

At that stage you commuted to your secretarial course in Dublin each morning by bus. I went home most weekends, but then Kevin and I hit on the idea of hosting a little party one Saturday. It was to be our first party in our first flat, our first whiff of freedom. He had forgotten that Offaly's first match in the League campaign was against Kerry that Sunday, until we copped the article in the paper.

'We'll have to call off the party,' I said to him.

'No way, I'll just have one or two, it'll be over early and I'll go to bed.'

'Hmm.'

You were there that night but you left early, maybe we'd had a row or maybe it was to catch the last bus home. After the pubs closed all hell broke loose. It seemed as if half of Dublin turned up looking for the party. Unseemly acts spontaneously happened on the stairs and any available space in the house. Everyone said the party was brilliant. It ended around four in the morning when a Wexford hurler and his girlfriend initially refused to leave my bed. The lady went quietly enough, but it took three of us to evict the hurler.

The Saturday evening, after the party, you and I went to see *Butch Cassidy and the Sundance Kid* in the Capitol cinema in Abbey Street. Kevin had gone away for the weekend and we had the room to ourselves. We became lovers that night. There were no candles or violins, just a turf fire in the grate, with light from the street lamps and the sound of the city coming in through the big window.

You finished your course shortly after our momentous night, and then commenced a job, working in a bank opposite Stephen's Green. At the same time you leased a flat in Leinster Road along with your friend, Catherine. Whereas my room was brash and cheap, yours was demure and sophisticated. The grabbed moments when we had it to ourselves were not wasted. I felt so proud, happy and content to know I was in love with you and you with me. Around this time a cartoon started to appear in the Irish Independent, called *Love Is*. Even if I was careful to make sure that nobody noticed, this little drawing with the sentence became the first thing I looked for every time I opened the newspaper. I knew this was me being somewhat pathetic but I couldn't help it.

I never spoke of our being in love with anyone, not even Kevin, but people weren't stupid and it would have been obvious to those who knew us. It was no big deal to anyone, with one exception – your mother. I came to know that she knew we were lovers and while she never said anything directly to me, I could see she was concerned for you. Life was becoming complicated.

I sometimes wonder what if you hadn't fallen for the guy with the motor-bike? Back then, I was naive and never read the signs or saw the danger. It started with you going for 'a spin with a work colleague' one Sunday while I was off playing a football game. Raheen's junior team had a run in the Championship that year and I had a game down home most Sundays. Catherine dropped hints once or twice that I should watch out but I was oblivious and never saw it coming.

You didn't beat around the bush when you realised you weren't in love with me anymore but you were as gentle as you could be. At first I didn't believe you and when I did, I couldn't accept the new situation. It was as if my whole heart and stomach had been ripped out of my body. I could think of nothing but you being with someone else and not with me.

As days slipped into weeks, things became worse for me rather than better. I couldn't bring myself to discuss this new situation with anyone. My friends knew and were concerned but were flummoxed as to what to say to me. I went off food and started to smoke cigarettes. One Saturday around this time Second Ags were playing Second Arts in the Duke Cup, an interfaculty football competition. A bit of a melee started in which Mick Barry was head butted in the face. I was never a fighter but that day I ran fifty yards to exact retribution. My first belt smashed the Art guy's nose and my second knocked him to the ground. Thank God others dived in and prevented a serious criminal assault. I saw him walking around Belfield a few times but I was embarrassed and managed to give him a wide berth. It was a small consolation that even his team mates reckoned the couple of belts didn't go astray on him. Truth was his broken nose had more to do with you than his head butting Mick Barry.

It took months for the fog to lift. Slowly but surely, I started to go out with others but was careful not to become too involved with anyone. One night I was sitting alone on a bus going home when I saw you get on. My heart started to race, I blushed and so did you when you saw me. There were very few others on board but you came down to sit opposite me. Your eyes were gentle and you smiled your smile for a while before you spoke.

'Well how are you doing?'

'I'm doing OK. How are you? Are you still seeing the guy with the motor bike?'

You nodded your head in reply which I took to mean that you were. I forget what else we said before your stop came up and we bid each other goodbye, but after this unexpected encounter, I knew I had moved on and I knew you knew it too and were glad.

OFFALY

'I'm sorry lads, it's players only today.' The man at the gate blocked my way.

'Who says so?' My question was a reflex rather than a direct challenge.

'Orders from the top.'

'Oh.'

'Take the car and drive out to my house. I'll get a lift from one of the lads when we're finished training,' said my flatmate Kevin Kilmurray, Offaly's centre forward and the George Best of Gaelic football at the time.

Offaly were still the defending All Ireland champions but now they were in limbo. The All Ireland final against Kerry had ended in a draw the previous fortnight. In exactly a week's time, the players would be running out again onto Croke Park for the replay. No one could remember the last time there had been a draw and the replay was the talk of the country. The newspapers that morning had it that Kerry were now firm favourites but everyone around Edenderry that afternoon thought differently. It occurred to me as it did to most people who were there that Father Gilhooley, the trainer, must have something up his sleeve.

Dermot and *Plumbob* from Rhode were also turned away. They were Kevin's cousins and now they jumped into the car with me. I drove out to Kilmurray's home, ten or so miles out the Daingean road. It was a typical October day, overcast but no sign of rain. Mrs Kilmurray wanted us to come in for tea, but we were as well pleased to stay outside to talk about the upcoming game with Kevin's father. After a while I opened the boot of the car to find a football which I kicked into the field opposite the house. We hopped over the wire and hunted the cattle down near the gate and started a bit of a kick around. The grass was well grazed down except for the tufts that had grown around the older cowpats. At this stage a few local lads had joined us and we had enough for three a side. We were all wearing shoes, rather than football boots and Sunday clothes, we were loathe to get dirty but I threw my suede jacket down to help make one of the goals.

We were just getting into it when Mick Wright and Liam O'Hanlon showed up and demanded to be let come on.

'Why aren't you training in Edenderry?' someone asked.

'He only wanted the players who'll be starting. Pass the ball, quick,' said Liam O Hanlon.

Both of these were local lads who played for Daingean. Both were subs on the Offaly panel and I wondered to myself why they weren't in on whatever was being hatched in Edenderry. Their addition to our little game raised the stakes somewhat. What had been a leisurely friendly kick about suddenly was a little less friendly and became even less so when Mick Wright nearly knocked me into a fresh cow dung. Another car pulled up shortly after this and I was surprised when Kilmurray emerged out of the passenger side. When he saw what was going on, he shouted out at his two fellow panellists.

'Wright , O'Hanlon, come in here before you get hurt.'

'Fuck off Kilmurray, go on into your Mammy, she'll give you a cup of tea.' Mick Wright winked at me as he shouted back. The next thing Kevin had the jacket off and he and John Smith, the Offaly full forward were tucking the bottom of their trousers into their socks. Within minutes All Stars Willy Bryan and Eugene Mulligan appeared and when they saw Kilmurray and the others they ordered their fellow players to stop. Further words were exchanged and now the Offaly centre fielder and half back joined us. For some reason half the Offaly

A Fact – Or Sales Talk

Kevin Kilmurray

team seemed to have driven out to Kilmurray's that afternoon and they joined in.

Now we went at it full tilt with no quarter asked or given. All Ireland champion footballers were not prepared to concede an inch, even in their Sunday clothes. It was Willy Bryan who shouted after about a quarter of an hour.

'Stop, Stop for fuck's sake stop before one of us is broke up.'

When he said this and because it was he who said it, we all stopped. I was absolutely out of breath and covered in sweat. All of us knew what had just happened shouldn't have happened and there was an unspoken agreement that it was not to be talked about. Seemingly Father Gilhooley had called the team together for a session that afternoon but decided that the players had played enough football and there was there was to be no more until the Final exactly one week hence. Instead of the training session, there had been a short meeting at which he told the team he wanted them to be 'like a coiled spring.'

The following Sunday the All Ireland replay took place in Croke Park. I watched from the Cusack stand as Kerry played imperious football up to half time. I was worried as Offaly looked leaden footed and that somehow this might have something to do with the aforementioned game in Kilmurrays' field. From the throw at the start of the second half, Willy Bryan plucked the ball from the sky and proceeded to give the best half hour of centre field play ever seen in Croke Park. He was magnificent as was Kevin and the rest of them who had regressed to their boyhoods the previous Sunday. Kerry had been favourites but they were destroyed in that second half as the Offaly players wrote themselves into the history books.

There was a glorious celebration dinner in The Grand Hotel, Malahide that night. Winning the 'two in a row' with that splendid second half performance precipitated an enormous outpouring of joy among the throngs of supporters. The toasts and speeches seemed to go on for ages. At a certain point in the proceedings I slipped out to the toilet, which was surprisingly empty, but I heard someone whistling behind me. It was Willy Bryan. When he recognised me from the previous Sunday, he shook his head and we both burst out laughing. The night belonged to Offaly and their great hearted supporters. Because of my friendship with Kevin I was part of it all one hundred per cent. Even so I wondered if such a thing could ever happen for my own beloved Kildare. Forty years on I'm still wondering but hope springs eternal.

WARRENSTOWN

By the end of second year in UCD, I had opted for Horticulture rather than Agriculture, principally because I thought intensive farming better suited our smallholding at home. Also to be honest, I didn't fancy the idea of being beholden to the authoritarian regime I considered the Agriculture Department of the Faculty to be at this time. In order to progress into Third year I needed to undertake an oral interview to prove my 'practical expertise.' My knowledge of horticultural production was more or less zero, so I decided to do a practical year without offering myself for assessment.

In 1971 there was a choice of two places where this could be undertaken: the Botanic Gardens in Glasnevin, which specialised in amenity horticulture or Warrenstown College in County Meath which had an excellent reputation for food crop production. I applied for and was awarded a scholarship to Warrenstown, to be taken up in late September. I also applied for and was granted my second J1 visa to work and live in America for the summer.

I bought my return ticket and flew to New York in May. I already had a social security number and was a member of the Timberman's Union since the previous summer. The girl in the Union sent me to a job in Brooklyn.

The summer in New York was good to me. The job was hard and in a tough area close to the train station at New Lotts Avenue. I held my own though, had the time of my life and earned so much money, that I briefly contemplated staying on after the summer as 'an illegal'. I had two years invested in my degree course, was enjoying the camaraderie and I was confident I was on a good career path. I had left it as late as possible to fly home on the last Friday in October, knowing

I had to be in Warrenstown by Monday morning in order to retain my scholarship and place in the college.

Salesian College Warrenstown was situated on four hundred and sixty verdant acres near Dunshaughlin, County Meath. That Sunday evening I stood before the principal who welcomed me. He went through the rules of the college, I noted the ones about *'Mass in the mornings and lights out in the dormitory at 11.30'* and thought to myself, how in the name of God am I going to stick this place for a whole year?

There were over a hundred and twenty students learning the theory and practice of Agriculture in a relatively modern building, and about thirty 'Horts' who lived and toiled in the original big house at the bottom of the hill. Our quarters were on a farm within a farm and separate from the modern campus where the chapel and refectory were based. Six students were on a practical year from UCD, most of the others were at least three years younger. On week day mornings there was Mass before breakfast. Each student of the Catholic persuasion was allocated a seat in the chapel so that attendance could be checked from the balcony behind us.

When I became aware of this, I immediately started to think up ways to thwart the system. Before long I had conspired with two of my UCD buddies to sit in different seats each time, resulting in every student now being in a different position. I was delighted with my little victory.

An integral part of our education in Warrenstown was participation in the work on the farm. I found myself on the *Brussels sprout harvesting* roster each frosty morning for the first few weeks. Hands and fingers quickly numbed to develop into chilblains during class in the afternoons. Others were rotated among the warm confines of glass-houses, mushroom tunnels and similar cushy numbers.

I was a marked man and without a word being said I knew the authorities had gotten their own back and that the score was now 'one all.'

Brother O'Hare was the principal of the Horticultural dDepartment and our chief lecturer. He was the most knowledgeable person on crop plants I ever met and it was my misfortune that we didn't see eye to eye with each other in those early days. I had saved in excess of a thousand pounds over the summer but now had little or no opportunity to spend any of it, except at the weekends. On Friday evenings I was usually among the first on the minibus which brought us to Dublin, or civilisation as I liked to think of it at the time. Much of this leisure time was a bit of a blur as much of it was spent in pubs. Bizarrely, one of my clearest memories is of the night I familiarised myself with my Uncle Tom's favourite tipple.

On a Friday evening I found myself in Kirwan House in Leeson Street close to the corner of Stephen's Green. This was 'a home from home' for UCD Gaelic football heads. Here I had a flashback of my Uncle Tom lowering *rum and black*, in Jordan's of Maugherow in County Sligo. I called for one, but ended up drinking over twenty of 'the sweet little bastards.' All was fine until I hit the midnight air outside where I collapsed.

My brain was coherent enough except for the fairly serious issue of being unable to stand. I had to make my way to Castlewood Avenue in Ranelagh, where my friend Karl Roche had his bedsit. He was away that weekend, but had given me the key to his flat. I eventually decided that the only way of getting to Ranelagh was by holding onto the railings and walls along Leeson Street. The problem of crossing the roads and the canal bridge was solved by perambulating monkey-like on all fours. I eventually arrived at the flat and sat on the steps. But my inebriation had now reached the point where I was unable to extricate the key from my pocket and it was becoming very cold. However, I ended up with a pound in my fist and immediately the homing instinct kicked in. Somehow or other I made it to the taxi rank in Rathmines where I asked the taxi man to take as far as a pound would take me in the direction of Newland's Cross in Clondalkin.

He brought me as far as The Red Cow Inn on the Naas Road. My sozzeled brain was now in recovery and I was able to stand sufficiently well to start hitching. There weren't many cars on the road that winter's night and none of them stopped. I staggered on towards Newland's Cross. I hitched for a while, but without success, so I started to walk. Whenever I heard a car coming from behind, I'd turn to raise my thumb but no one stopped until many hours and ten miles later by which stage I had walked to Kill. The man who gave me a lift dropped me off at the Bundle of Sticks junction, just outside Naas. I had to walk the final four miles as there was no traffic at that hour of the morning. I was totally cold sober by the time I reached home, just as the weak winter light began to spread its mantle of grey across the sky. Having climbed onto the flat roof of the back kitchen, I eased up the sash of the landing window and slipped downstairs. I had made it home. I sat there for a while in the back kitchen and savoured a much needed drink of water.

'You're up early, what time did you get in?' my father, who suddenly appeared in his bare feet startled me. He asked me to find his shoes.

'I dunno what time it was, but I've a bad headache and I can't find your shoes," I said rather sheepishly.

'Are you alright? Maybe you should go back up for a while?'
'Maybe I will.'

I went up to bed without finding the shoes and slept for the best part of two days

On a cold Sunday in January we sat in Tracey's lounge bar in Newbridge after a rugby game. None of the hundred or so people in the lounge were particularly interested at first in newsreader Charles Mitchell, or the Six O'Clock News when it came on the television.

I was in the middle of the crowd, well back from the screen when I became aware of a growing silence as people switched focus to the telly. When I turned to look, there on the screen was a bald priest in a sort of a crouch waving a white flag with blood on it. Behind him three or four men carried a body between them. The camera scanned to other bodies lying in the street. The Parachute regiment had opened fire on a demonstration in Derry. The decibel level in the bar immediately trebled and the air thickened with expletives of 'fucking bastards' and the like.

I was in a state of shock and didn't return to Warrenstown College that night. On the Monday, the radio and the newspapers were full of outrage about the 'shootings in Derry.' This fuelled my anger to such a pitch I could neither think nor talk about anything else. I decided to go up to Dublin the following morning. With no particular plan in mind, I made my way towards Belfield on the top deck of a bus. From this vantage point I saw streams of people walking purposefully as if to an important football game. I pressed the bell and clattered down the stairs.

I had stumbled onto a protest outside the British embassy. People were coming in from all directions. There were no speeches or anything other than guttural roars and chants from sections of the crowd which soon numbered a couple of thousand or so. About a dozen Gardai stood on the steps in front of the door. Most of us just milled around, vexed, looking and waiting.

Around lunch time I saw a student colleague of mine pull

in on his Lambretta scooter and park on the footpath beside the railings. He had a plastic drum on the platform between his feet. When I looked again I saw people filling milk bottles from the drum. Rags jammed into the neck of the bottles were set alight and the next thing petrol bombs were flying through the air.

Every time one broke on the wall or door and burst into flame a cheer went up from the crowd. I remember feeling sorry for the Gardai on the steps as the flames erupted behind them and at their feet. Suddenly focus switched to lines of Gardai, three deep, drawn up on the Merrion Street side of the crowd. Within seconds I was swept along as the crowd rushed back into Mount Street. Gardai in full riot gear swung their batons with deadly intent as they charged into us.

Several people beside me were injured and blood streamed from their heads. The atmosphere now became extremely nasty, we were apoplectic with rage.

More Gardai came to stand in front of the embassy. All the time more and more people were arriving and petrol bombs continued to fly through the air. A couple more baton charges happened but after a while a sort of understanding had developed. They charged, we ran; then they went back and we moved back to our original position. Sporadically, the odd petrol bomb flew and broke on the wall or the door.

I had linked up with a couple of student friends among the crowd. Around four o'clock we slipped away and headed back towards Stephen's Green. Opposite the College of Engineering in Merrion Street we came on a film crew with English accents shooting a report. We stopped to check this out. We didn't like what we heard and the film crew didn't like what we said to them. They stopped their filming mid-report, wrapped up their equipment and walked away.

That evening I returned to Warrenstown unsure if I wanted

to be there at all. I had settled in after the first few weeks and found the course to be interesting enough, but I felt I was a square peg in a round hole. Word spread through the dorm that I was back and when I received word that Brother O'Hare wanted to see me in his room, I fully expected to be asked to leave.

'Were you at the British Embassy today, Noel?' he asked.

'I was Brother.' I replied as he looked at me from behind his desk. He had the disconcerting habit of joining the tips of his fingers together when he wanted to say something important, this he did now and I waited in anticipation.

'Take a seat Noel and tell me what it was like.'

There followed the most unexpected conversation as he told me of his abhorrence of British oppression and how it operated where he was from in the North. Instead of being asked to leave the college I was asked to lead the students into Summerhill for noon the following day as part of the national day of protest.

In Dublin that day the British Embassy was burned out and gutted.

It was Spring time in Warrenstown. Sowing and planting became the order of the day. I had knuckled down to learn all about celery, carrots, rhubarb, tomatoes, mushrooms and a myriad of other crops. All in all, I was amazed and delighted at how well I'd grown into the place. A feature of Warrenstown was the range of extracurricular activities organised to burn up any surplus energy. Football training started in March under the guidance of a genial Kerryman called Brother O'Sullivan.

I was confident of getting my place on the team but there was stiff competition as there were county minors and under 21's from all over Ireland vying for places. Tosh Daly and Jack Kennedy were among the best footballers in the place. Both were fellow UCD men and particular friends of mine.

Tosh sidled up to me before breakfast, and spoke to me in a conspiratorial tone.

'Listen, don't say a word about this, but I'm twenty-one today. Will you come out with me for a few scoops tonight to the Warrenstown Arms?'

'Are you serious?' I asked.

'I am.'

'Sure thing. Don't say a word is right. We'll slip out after supper as soon as it gets dark.'

After breakfast I was approached by Jack Kennedy. He had a half grin on him and as usual the eyes danced in his head.

'Hey, can I have a word?'

'What?'

'Are you doing anything this evening?'

'Why do you ask?'

'I'm twenty-one today and I want us to go out for a few pints.'

'Fuck off,' I said to him.

Jack was not at all impressed with my response. I felt I needed to lay my cards on the table.

'Listen, Tosh has just asked me the same question. He says he's twenty-one today as well.'

'Fuck off, are you serious?' Jack was now the incredulous one.

'I am for sure, Jesus this'll be good. Say nothing to anybody, the three of us will slip out immediately after supper.'

No one ever told us directly, but we sort of knew that leaving the college to drink in a pub was strictly forbidden and was probably punishable by suspension, expulsion or maybe even death by hanging. But the way we looked on it was that God had provided us with this occasion for great joy and it ill behoved us to throw it back in His face.

We slipped into the darkness after supper.

Things were quiet that night in 'The Arms' but we livened it up somewhat as we skulled pints and sang a few songs. Around eleven o'clock we said our good nights and made our way back across the orchard field in full song with our arms around each other and the full moon behind us.

The judge said stand up lad and dry up your tears
You're sentenced to Dartmoor for twenty one years
So dry up your tears babe and kiss me goodbye
The best friends must part now, so must you and I.

Suddenly two full moons seemed to spring out of the bushes. These turned out to be two big torch lamps held by Father Harrington, the principal and Brother O'Hare. The two furious soldiers of Christ escorted us down to the parlour where we were briefly interrogated.

'Report to my office, first thing in the morning. Do not go to class or present yourselves for practical work.' Fr Harrington said.

I was convinced that this time it would be the end. Immediately after Mass, Tosh, Jack and I took up position outside the office. We were the talk of the college. Eventually Father Harrington opened his door.

'Step in the three of you.' He resumed his seat and looked at his papers for what seemed a long time before he raised his eyes. 'Leaving the college to drink in a local hostelry is an expellable offence.' His voice trailed and we shifted uneasily in our stance. He looked us in the eye before continuing. 'However we've checked the dates of birth and as you are all legally now entitled to drink, we've considered the circumstances and decided on less drastic punishment. You will not be allowed home for Saint Patrick's Day. And you will be expected to participate in any work that has to be done,' he added gravely.

I have a nervous habit of smirking in the most inappropriate

SALESIAN AGRICULTURAL COLLEGE,

WARRENSTOWN,

DRUMREE,

CO. MEATH.

TELEPHONE:
DUNSANY 7.

Christmas 1971.

R E P O R T   F O R M .

Class : Horticulture I.   Name *Noel Heavey*.....

Subject.	% Mark.	No. in Class.	Place.
Biology & Fruit.	59	32	25
Crop Protection and Vegetables.	*abst.*		
Soils, Manures & Glasshouse Crops.	76	32	5
Building Construction.	58	32	22
Hort. Engineering & Machinery.	78	32	18
Identification of Specimens	75	32	10

Pass Mark = 45%

Conduct *Good* .... Application *Very Good*: .... Work *Very Good*.

Marks Allotted: Excellent. Very Good. Good. Fair. Unsatisfactory.

College re-opens: Tuesday January 18th, 1972.

Signed.. *J. Harrington SDB*

Headmaster.

148

of circumstances. Over the years this has landed me in some tricky situations and nearly did so that morning in the Principal's office.

'Now get out of my sight and report for work,' he said with a face as straight as a ruler. We just about held it together until we were out of the office, whereupon we burst out laughing. At this point the football maestro Brother O'Sullivan materialised out of nowhere. He winked at us, as he passed on down the corridor.

We won the initial All Ireland championship for Agricultural Colleges later that year. I was the full forward on the team, Tosh was the centre forward and Jack was full back. We were presented with small plaques to mark the achievement. I treasure mine to this day.

SEVENTIES LONDON

Aldgate House, in front of Petticoat Lane and just a stone's throw from Tower Bridge on the Thames, is hardly an architectural marvel. Situated on the left as one exits the Underground station, it blends into the city-scape like thousands of similar office blocks scattered all over London. That summer morning in 1973 it was a building site where I was told to: 'Report to the subbie before eight, if you want the start.' The subcontractor's name was Howard. I went over to him and told him who I was.

'Right, climb up that ladder there with the others.' He said. I joined the twenty or so young men who were waiting for the signal to ascend. The shuttering work for the concrete columns and floors was on the sixth floor and the only way to reach this was a single ladder-way, up through the scaffolding at the side of the building. On about the fourth ladder up that Monday morning I had the misfortune to look down. Immediately every muscle and fiber of my being froze as I became paralyzed with fear.

'What's the fuckin' problem?' Boomed a voice which, even in my dysfunctional state I recognised as that of my new boss, but there was nothing I could do. I became aware, but barely aware, of shovel handles being shoved up my ass and my hair being pulled to get me up. But I was stuck to the ladder as if by superglue. My mind went completely blank except for one clear thought that I must not flinch a single muscle or move one inch either up or down that ladder ever. A standoff developed for about a quarter of an hour. During this time my breathing deteriorated into short pants like a frightened dog on a hot summer's day. Eventually, a soft Kerry accent from above cut through the haze.

'Where are you from?'

'Kildare.'

'Right Kildare, look at my heels above you.'

I looked.

'Now look at fuckin' nothing else and think of nothing else,' said the voice. 'The same thing happened me and half the fuckers on this site so don't you worry one bit about this shite. Now take just one step up after me.' He slowly moved his right foot up the ladder.

So did I, then he slowly moved his left foot and I did the same. In less than five minutes I was on the sixth floor where the Kerryman winked at me, shook my hand and was gone. The debacle had delayed the whole job by nearly twenty minutes and while there were wisecracks and jibes aplenty, most of the workers were quick to go about their business. A blur of activity happened in front of me, as men carried and worked with timbers and steel. I stood there beside a pallet of stout steel tubes with square heads on them. I was past feeling embarrassed about the total and abject humiliation. The recurring sentence in my head now was:

'How in the name of Jesus am I ever going to get back onto the ground?'

Then the subbie appeared with another guy who wore a white shirt and had a mop of scraggy hair a la Beatles.

'This is Mick my ganger man. You are his labourer and you're to do as he tells you.'

'Thanks Mister Howard.'

'Don't fuckin call me Mister.'

'Right.'

'Right Kildare, I want you to put a row of acrow up under that beam, over there.' Mick the ganger man said in his thick Limerick accent.

He nodded towards a beam suspended between two

supporting walls. I was determined to recover from my humiliation, but the trouble was I hadn't a clue what an acrow was and I daren't let on.

'So where can I find the acrows?'

He looked at me for a few seconds, then came over and leered right into my face.

'Are you fuckin serious, what are dem there beside you?'

I blushed a deep red and wished to God I was anywhere else. I looked at the stout tubes with the square heads at either end and wondered to myself, what am I supposed to do with these yokes? When I looked up again the ganger man was gone and I was left to my own devices.

An acrow prop was and is a five foot steel tube within a wider steel tube, each tube has a foot or head attached at the extremity, and each also has holes that need to be aligned with a steel pin when it's set at the desired height. The final height is tweaked by screwing a steel band up against the pin. I was delighted with myself for figuring all this out on my own and proceeded to erect five or six acrow props under the beam. Unfortunately I screwed one of the bands too much and the props already in place became loose. One of them toppled over and hit me a fair whack on the head. I was stunned and so very nearly started to cry. But I was twenty one years old and a seasoned construction worker having held my own with 'hombres' in New York and Dublin and I wasn't going to disgrace myself on my first job in London.

The Kerryman came to the rescue again, he told me his name was Patsy and pointed out the holes in the head of the acrow which needed to be secured by nailing to the beam, he then helped me to re-erect them. A hooter sounded, It was the ten o'clock break. All work ceased and there was a rush to the ladder. It was all I could do to keep the fast moving pair of boots immediately above me from clattering into my mouth.

I was ravenous after the drama of the morning, having only smoked a cigarette and downed a glass of water for my breakfast much earlier. I devoured everything put in front of me by Patsy, who treated me in that temporary little cafe on the fourth floor. I can still recall the taste and sizzle of those fat brown sausages all these years later and anytime this happens I silently thank God for the kindness of a young Kerryman that Monday morning. The main preoccupation at breakfast was a 'twenty five' card game that seemed to generate a fair degree of controversy. When I resumed work on the top floor I realised that my paralyzing fear of heights was no more.

Over the next few days I gradually became proficient at anything I was asked to do, most of which was menial enough as I fetched and carried for a gang of carpenters, none of whom were much older than myself. These were Howard's men and mostly from Erris in North Mayo, an area I was to get to know very well, a little later in life. They were a hard working, friendly group of lads but it took a while for me to understand their accents. Meanwhile Mick the ganger man was still on my case. At every opportunity he bawled me out and tried to make out I was a complete idiot. He was an asshole of the highest calibre and everyone on the job knew it, it was my misfortune that he had zeroed in on me and wouldn't let it go.

About a week into the job, he ordered me down to the fifth floor to strike or take down sheets of plywood and acrows a few days after a pour. This was a tricky assignment as the height of the plywood sheets was ten or twelve feet and these didn't always immediately fall after the props were removed. It was dangerous work and I was careful enough. He started his usual abuse the instant he saw me, as was his wont. The hateful fucker roared as he walked the whole length of the floor, I blushed my usual deep colour but at the same time became aware that the two of us were the only people on the floor. I was working near the edge from which I could see the safety net far below on which were timbers and other bits and pieces that had fallen or been thrown off the various floors. This time he came right up to me, so close his spittle landed on my face as he ranted and raved. This tipped my equanimity and I felt the blood drain from my cheeks. In the split second before I grabbed him he realised that this time he'd gone too far. He stopped but it was too late. I grabbed him, pulling loose two buttons from his white shirt.

'You fuckin cunt, I've had enough of you,' I trundled him over to the edge and held him at arm's length by his shirt. His eyes nearly bulged out of his sockets with sheer terror.

'Kildare, Kildare don't do it. I'll never bother you again, I swear to God.'

I slowly pulled him back from the ledge. Two human beings looked into each other's eyes and realised that a really dangerous moment had passed. He walked back the way that he came. In fairness to Mick the ganger man, I cannot remember him even speaking to me again, but that was okay by me. I was troubled by what had happened but didn't say a word of it to anyone and as far as I know neither did he.

About a month or so into the job, one of the carpenters had reported that a job down the road was offering 'sixteen into the hand.' Howard was paying them fourteen. I was a labourer who was on nine pounds a day. Five of the guys said they were going. Five, being an odd number was a problem because shuttering carpenters worked in pairs. The odd man out was Steve, a young Scottish carpenter who went around the job and came back with a saw, a level, a hammer and a nail-bag. He put them in a plastic bag and handed them to me.

'Right Kildare, it's time you became a carpenter, are you on? 'Sure thing, let's go.'

The job was down the street. Steve and I were assigned to a job which involved putting in place shuttering for what they said was to be a ramp. I was handed a blueprint and immediately knew I was in trouble because I hadn't a clue how to read it. I kept a sheet of half inch plywood at hand and anytime a foreman or engineer came around I measured, marked and sawed like a top class tradesman but each day was long, very long. On the Friday afternoon, I noticed three boss men in fancy donkey jackets, leaning over a wall watching me. They followed my every move for what seemed ages as I sweated and inwardly raged at the humiliation of not having a clue of what I was supposed to be doing. One of them came over to me.

'I have to let you go.'

'This isn't my line of work at all. I'm a cabinet maker back home.'

'I don't believe that for a second, but you'll probably make out eventually.'

'I hope you're right.' I was actually relieved that the charade was over.

I was now out of a job but had tools and was determined to make it as a carpenter.

I spent two days the following week going from site to site but there were no vacancies for a young Irishman on his own. The awful worry and loneliness of being out of work, the humiliation of rejection after rejection was a very difficult experience. I then remembered that my football mentor Jimmy Divine from Longford was 'a subbie' and I asked him at training on Tuesday evening if there was 'any chance of the start?' He said he'd see. The following Thursday he said he had a job for me at £15 per day. I worked with Jimmy and played football for St Pats for the rest of the summer. That in-between week was to be the last time in my life that I experienced being out

Measuring with a tape was a very important part of looking
busy as a carpenter in London

of work. I was a student 'chancing my arm,' but even so it was
a desperate feeling that I've never forgotten to this day.

My cousin Anne and her husband Eamon ran a busy pub known
as the Olde Plough, on Kilburn Lane, just off the Harrow Road
in North London. Anne gave me a room on the third floor, my
dinner each evening and two pounds for every part time shift
as a barman. Eamon was from Geesala in County Mayo. He
had a great personality for the pub business and the lounge
was packed with Erris people at the weekends. There was also
a steady enough trade of casual drinkers during the week.

The first evening I worked behind the bar was terrifying. I
was well used to bars but not from the inside looking out. I felt
like a monkey in a cage with every eye in the place following
my every movement. I was just getting used to this when I

served a Connemara man in the public bar. He paid with what I took to be a five pound note. When I gave him his change he just stared at it. Next he reached over the counter, grabbed and pulled me towards him.

'I'll have you, you little fucker,' he shouted.

'Take your hands off me.' I pleaded.

Eamon separated us, but had quite a job to pacify him. The Connemara man had paid for his drink with an English twenty pound note which I mistook for a fiver as I'd never come across a twenty before. I was desolated by my mistake. Above all things, I hated thieving barmen but the more I apologised, the more he thought I was trying to rob him. He had to be barred, but Eamon was not well pleased. I had to be careful anytime I left the premises as I had learned in Dublin and New York that a Connemara man with a grudge against you was not a good idea.

About a month into my stay I decided it was time to make myself available to the discerning ladies of London. I made my way to the Gresham Ballroom on the Holloway Road which I'd been told was where 'the best looking women' were. I yearned for the company of girls and I was looking forward to the night. By the time I arrived, the place was packed. I waited until the dancing had started, before walking across the floor to the best looking girl still sitting after the initial rush.

'Would you like to dance?'

'No thanks.

I went to the opposite end of the hall to chance my luck with someone else, only to get the same response. When the third lady refused me, all the old doubts flew home to roost. I waited for the next dance but my head was now in a tizzy and I could see eyes trying to avoid me as I approached girls to ask them out. I was cold sober and bitterly disappointed.

I retired to the packed bar upstairs and took comfort in a few pints of Guinness. I ruminated over the debacle and couldn't decide whether to blame the clothes, my sobriety or that I was just trying too hard. Towards the end of the night, I struck up a conversation with a Dublin lady which ended with me asking to leave her home. This she agreed, but a look passed between her and her friend that alerted me that something was not quite right .However I found myself in her sitting room somewhere in the middle of London. We were just getting down to business when there was the sound of someone outside.

'That's my husband, get to fuck out of here.'

'What?'

'I'm sorry but you must leave now. The back door, quickly.' She had jumped up and I could see by the panic in her eyes that I needed to be out of there fast. Without further ado I removed myself to a tiny back garden and had to scale a wall to find myself in a dark lane. I eventually managed to hail a taxi and then had the dubious pleasure of watching the meter click away the best part of a day's wages, as I made my way across London back to the Olde Plough. My mind, not to mention my 'physical apparatus' was in absolute turmoil. I never again tried my luck in a London ballroom.

The public bar in The Olde Plough was frequented mostly by Caribbean people and locals. One such character was Bob, who hailed from Jamaica. He was a friendly sort of chap who never stopped yapping. For some time he had been asking me to accompany him to a party and after my Gresham ballroom experience I said: 'Why the hell not?' I arranged to have the Saturday night free. When we arrived I was somewhat surprised but secretly pleased to discover I was the only white person in a room of thirty or more people. I was well into the reggae music but there were very few females at the party. The only overt action consisted of serious looking dudes gambling at a card game. However there was one stunning Caribbean lady, dressed in a bright red and yellow dress that clung to her figure in a most revealing way. I found it difficult to keep my eyes off her. Unfortunately she seemed to be with one of the guys playing cards. I caught her looking at me a couple of times but in the circumstance there was nothing doing.

Bob handed me a rolled up cigarette which I knew wasn't a cigarette, but I had a couple of puffs on it anyway with absolutely no effect. Bob was disappointed with this, but not as much as he was when I laughed at his suggestion that I sleep over at his place. He became somewhat upset when I told him I wasn't his type. I left the party and hailed a taxi. London was not a happy hunting ground for a horny young Kildare man.

Brian Grogan and Dermot his friend from Clare were young professional men who drank in the lounge of The Olde Plough. Brian invited me to play football with his team Saint Patrick's who were based in Luton. The main driving force here was Jimmy Divine, who had bailed me out by giving me a job after I was sacked. The football standard wasn't great and I enjoyed being their star turn. Brian had a good way with him and we became great friends.

Later that August, he brought me down to Sunbury to play rugby for London Irish. Saturday after Saturday we travelled around London playing teams from Wasps, Saracens and London Welsh. There were attractive women there aplenty in these places after games but exigencies of time not to mention the proximity of boyfriends and partners meant that one never got beyond exchanging glances across a club room of raucous children running wild.

However we enjoyed our rugby for the 'B Specials' under the captaincy of a genial Corkman Gerry Holland, whom I met many years later when he told me that this team's record of winning all its matches in a season has never been matched and still stands alone in London Irish.

The summer simmered with tension and daily slaughter in Northern Ireland. One day I went to work on the train to be met by a sea of headlines with the words IRISH SCUM looking back at me. I became cautious about where I'd speak in front of strangers, lest my accent trigger some unpleasantness, particularly after hours in takeaways or the like. This had the effect of entrenching my anti-English views inherited from national school. My mother, who lived in London during the war, loved to speak in glowing terms of Cockney humour and wit but her son went through that whole summer in London without having a single decent conversation with an English person. Thanks be to God, I've had many chats and acquired many English friends since.

October meant homecoming. Just before this I went down to Carnaby Street and brought myself a sharp looking suit and a black hat which set me apart. I arranged with my sister Marie to be collected at the airport, and entreated her not to tell any other family member. That Saturday I walked into the back kitchen, just as my mother and father were about to sit down for a late breakfast. Dressed in my fine garb*, I managed a fair imitation of an English accent, to put my father under severe pressure for a few minutes, until I relented. We had a great laugh about this but tears of joy flowed down our cheeks as we hugged each other. Marie put on a record of Strauss Waltzes on the radiogram in the sitting room. She turned up the volume when the strains of 'The Blue Danube' came on and we all started to dance at eleven o'clock on a misty Saturday morning in Clongorey. It was so good to be home.

* The 'fine garb' is contained in the bags I'm carrying on the photo on the front cover of this book.

AFTER EIGHT
YEARS DANCING

I was never one for the mad rush across the floor in order to bag a dance with a flashy looking lady. Ray Lynham and his Hillbillies had finished the first song of their set by the time I noticed her sitting quietly in an alcove near the doors of the Olympic Ballroom, just off Camden Street. She wore a bright yellow blouse and a red tartan skirt with a giant silver pin holding it closed half way up her thigh. She looked absolutely stunning. I could hardly believe she hadn't been snapped up in 'the rush.' 'Would you like to dance with me?' I asked.

I'd always been a prowler of the backwaters. This may have had something to do with being a late starter and being possessed of an innate shyness, which wasn't always obvious. I was fifteen and a half and nearly a year behind my peers before I plucked up the courage to venture into my first hop in the Supper Room behind the Town Hall in Newbridge. I stood there that night and tried to take it all in, having walked into an invisible wall of smells from the hundred or so dancers who seemed in perfect balance even as each dancer moved with crazily different rhythms. The music of the Rolling Stones drew me in that evening and I took off like a young bull calf released for the first time into the haggard on a sunny day in Spring.

I became a busy little boy that summer after Roisin sent word that it was 'all off' after Father took exception to me giving her a lift on the bar of my bicycle. There was a hop on every Wednesday night organised by the TEEN Youth Club in The Supper Room. At some point of the proceedings the chairman would attempt to address us, but we weren't interested in speeches, we just wanted to dance to the hits of The Beachboys, The Beatles, The Monkees and others, who we otherwise only heard on Radio Luxembourg via the tinny sounds of transistor radios under blankets.

Joe Barnes was a big middle-aged man with cross eyes. He always wore a filthy cap and walked with a limp. He was there in case there was 'any messin.' I knew Joe Barnes from the time Paddy Donnelly brought him out from Newbridge to break down walls with his sledge-hammer when we were doing up the house. I used to laugh to myself every time the DJ, Liam Kett, introduced Percy Sledge's record 'When a Man Loves a Woman' – my favourite slow song at the time – because I couldn't imagine a more incongruous pairing than Percy singing his sexy song and Joe swinging his sledge. Yet they are forever linked in my mind. When I'd hear the riffs of this song, I'd head straight for Angela, a quiet, good looking girl I really fancied. She asked me one night why was I smirking. She wasn't impressed with my explanation of the sledge connection and that was that.

I branched out to *Macra Na Feirme* socials in Donore Hall which is on the Prosperous side of Caragh. After this there were carnivals with marquee dances in places like Kilcullen, Clane and Robertstown. These places had a completely different ambiance from the Supper Room. Now I had to weave my way through drunk lads looking for fight and ladies looking for action, while pretending to be totally disinterested. Somehow or other I'd always find a girl to dance with. I couldn't jive at the time which was a big disadvantage in these places but I loved to dance. Sometimes I'd get off with someone, which meant I could leave my hand on her hip at the end of the song, then hold hands and maybe go outside for a 'breath of fresh air.' It was all fairly harmless. As the years melted into each other during the late sixties and early seventies the awkwardness all but disappeared and it became easier for me to be my natural self around girls.

There was the odd setback along the way, particularly at the beginning; like the night I went with three friends from Clongorey to a carnival dance at The Fairgreen in Naas. Here I encountered two lads dancing together. This was a spectacle I'd never witnessed before and I must say I was quite intrigued. The smaller of the dancers saw me looking at him. He had a Beatles-style hair cut and came right up to me, smiling the biggest smile I'd ever seen. A split second later I felt a fuzzy warm sensation around my nose. When I touched it, I realised I was bleeding profusely. I was deeply puzzled. My friend Michael Coffey rushed over when he saw all the blood.

'What's goin on here?' asked Michael in a strident voice, looking at the Ringo Starr lookalike.

BUP. The head butt was so fast I nearly didn't see it. Two seconds later, blood started to flow from Michael's nose. There were now two country noses bleeding profusely inside the marquee in Naas. I had never before either seen or heard of a head butt, and was quite incredulous at what had just happened. A crowd gathered around us in an instant. I quickly realised then we were being contemplated by the notorious *Spike Island Gang*. Their reputation was such, it terrorised young lads who weren't from Naas as well as a fair few who were. We became afraid, very afraid.

'Why are ye little bog fuckers coming in here, for to cause trouble?' asked one of the three bouncers, who materialised out of nowhere.

'I was only looking at two lads dancing together, when one of them came up and did this to me,' I said, as I tried to stem the flow from my nose.

'Yeah, well you'll know fuckin better the next time. We're going to escort you as far as far as Murtagh's Corner. After that, you're on your own.'

We were then marched out, all four of us deathly pale at the imminence of a really severe hiding or worse. True to their word, the bouncers escorted us to the corner where the Kilcullen road intersected with the Limerick road. The trouble was the *Spike Island Gang* were in tow, twenty or more, some of them brandishing steel combs with handles filed down to resemble knives. They roared and hollered like how I imagined cannibals danced around a boiling cauldron of dinner on the edge of the jungle.

'We're going to be fucking slaughtered, ' moaned one of my *compadres*.

'Alright lads, I hope ye are good runners,' said the talking bouncer.

Silently, I thanked God for all those evenings spent training for The Odlum Cup. We bolted like scalded hares, with what seemed the whole of Naas in hot pursuit. At the Fire Station I glanced back to see that most of our pursuers had given up. By the time we reached Swan Dowling's there were only three of them still chasing four of us. It took only a few seconds to realise the odds were now reversed. Fear gave way to anger, and a certain amount of cunning. We deliberately slowed down and started shouting insults to lead them on. Suddenly, the four of us turned on the three 'out of breath' former would be assailants. With thumps and kicks, we exacted a modicum of retribution for the two bloody noses and the bejaysus that had been frightened out of us. However, it was quite a while before any of us again ventured to a dance in Naas.

My dancing career developed further afield to bring me to such edifying spots as Rathcoffey Hall, The Red Mill in the Bronx, The Ardenode Hotel in Ballymore Eustace, The

Gresham on Holloway Road and a very interesting little hall in the middle of the country near Kenmare in County Kerry.

With the benefit of hindsight I can see that all these experiences were part of an apprenticeship to prepare me for a single moment as Ray Lynham crooned his gentle country song that night at the Ags Dance in the Olympic Ballroom. I took the lady's hands to get into the swing of the music. I'd only recently learned to how to jive properly and had surprised myself by how much I liked it.

'I can't jive,' she said, but she didn't pull her hands away.

'It's easy, just twirl when I wink at you,' I smiled. She laughed.

She looked into my eyes intently, laughing all the time. I winked, she twirled. We both laughed.

'My name is Noel, what's yours?

'Bernadette,' she smiled. We both laughed some more as Ray Lynham carried on singing. The earth didn't shake nor did the crowd start to cheer. Maybe they should have. The boy from Clongorey had just met his match.

A Strange Night
on the Town

Most Fridays I went home but lately I'd met a girl called Bernadette at the Ags dance, in the Olympic ballroom, located just off Wexford Street, where I went each Wednesday night. I thought it would be nice for us to spend time together over a weekend in Dublin and was none too pleased to discover she had made her own arrangements to go home to Mayo. All wasn't lost, as someone had told me of a party to be held in a hotel on Pearse Street that very night. When I got there I found the hotel closed up and from the appearance of the place, it had been closed up for quite some time. I tried to remember who had told me of the party because retribution would have to be exacted but that was for another time. Meanwhile there I was on my own outside a derelict hotel on a Friday night with nowhere to go.

In times of need inspiration sometimes comes, and on this occasion I remembered the Zhivago Club, off Baggot Street. I had been one of its first members, back in the summer of '69. It had been quite a while since I'd been there but now I seized the moment and walked up Westland Row. There were very few people on the street that night and when I heard a desperate scream at the junction with Lincoln Place at the back of Trinity College, I stopped in my tracks. So too did two other men. Each of us had been on our separate journeys but now the three of us converged on the source of the screams. There was no one else about that I could see.

A man and a woman were struggling in a doorway. He held her by the hair with one hand while boxing her with his full force into her face with the other. He was so intent on his business that he never noticed us advancing towards them until I shouted:

'Hold up there'.

Another man now materialised from the shadows. He wore a grubby white overcoat with a belt.

'Fuck off you boys, this is nothing to do with you,' he said.

We ignored him but suddenly we were looking into the barrel of a pistol which he'd pulled from his pocket. An appallingly empty feeling now took hold of the lower part of my body. I went weak at the knees and nearly collapsed. Each of the three of us now slowly backed off, never taking our eyes off the man as he continued to point the gun at us. Not one word had been exchanged between us since we'd heard that first scream and now we quickly and quietly resumed our separate journeys. I had been frightened, very frightened but livid at the same time. I continued up Merrion Street until I came to a lone youngish Garda standing alone outside the gates of Dail Eireann.

'Guard, there's a woman being battered in a doorway down at Lincoln Place. Three of us went to stop it but another guy pulled a gun on us.'

'That type of thing goes on around here every weekend.'

I was incredulous at the blasé nature of his response. I looked at the Garda and spoke sharply.

'So what the fuck are you going to do about it?'

'That's none of your concern, and if I were you, I'd be very careful about using that language to a Garda.' He stared into my eyes and I thought for a second he might actually arrest me.

I shook my head and moved off in the direction of Baggot Street .

I hadn't been to the Zhivago Club in two years and I was

hardly in the mood for romance, but I strode on. When I reached it, there were a few people in front of me on the stairs. I recognised the security man on the landing. He was a giant of a man by the name of 'Lugs' Brannigan who'd headed up the Garda *Riot Squad* in his day.

'Hullo Mister Brannigan.'

'How do you know my name, son?' he smiled back at me.

'I was one of the first members to sign up here.' He examined the old membership card, I had produced from my wallet.

'You were indeed, it's nice to see you back.'

It was nice to feel welcomed, especially with the way the night had gone so far. Zhivago's was buzzing, the music was wall to wall and there was a heady smell of perfume and a whiff of imminent action. I let it all soak in as I paid for my drink and headed for the only available seat that I could see. I didn't have to wait long. Within a few minutes I was approached by a small stocky guy in a blue pin striped suit with two flashy blonde ladies in tow. He made a rapid lateral motion with his greasy head pointing towards the door.

'Up!'

'What did' ya say?' I said as I jumped up.

'This is my table.' He pointed his finger at me and immediately clicked his fingers and within seconds two right hardy looking gents appeared by his side. The blonde ladies tittered at my discomfiture. I rapidly considered my options as the two moved in to grab me.

'Ok I'm going.' I moved towards the door.

I felt humiliated and as vexed as I'd ever been in my life. I walked towards my flat in Glasnevin. I thought of my new girlfriend who at that moment was probably sitting up with her family having the craic in Mayo. I thought about what might have happened the unfortunate girl in the alcove and indeed for days afterwards I scanned the newspapers to see if there were any reported assaults or worse in Dublin that night. There wasn't. The attitude of the Garda outside the Dail was a mystery to me, though I'd come across something similar, late one night a few years before when I was interrupted by a middle aged jack-ass in uniform as I went about courting a young lady on a bench in the middle of Ranelagh.

Most of all I thought about Mister Pinstripes in the Zhivago Club. What I wouldn't have given to be in the company of Dinny O'Connor and a couple of other Agricultural students to sort him out along with his two gorillas. I actually did meet two colleagues at the bottom end of Grafton Street, but they were on their way to the Television Club in Harcourt Street, both were on a mission, as they called it, and could not be persuaded to come back with me to *The Zhivago Club*.

Over the years I've spent many fabulous nights on the town in Dublin. Whenever I pass near any of the places I walked that night my mind flies back and a small sigh escapes me but even after all these years I become somewhat twitchy, whenever I come across blue pinstriped suits mooching about after sunset.

A Chance Encounter

The Albert College in Glasnevin* was our Alma Mater for the final two years of the B.AgSc(Hort) degree course. Its old dowdy buildings were no longer fit for purpose and for years they had been earmarked for decommissioning. It somehow seemed inappropriate to even laugh within its precincts. Its only saving grace as far as I was concerned was the toilet bowl in the men's jacks. A tall blue willow patterned affair with a graceful profile, yet perfectly proportioned, to receive even the stoutest of bottoms. I often wondered what became of it after the place was demolished.

To add to the decrepitude, some of the lectures were boring beyond belief. One lecturer in particular was so uninspiring that we used to chat openly among ourselves or do whatever we felt like while he droned uselessly, remorselessly on. One particular day he challenged Tosh, who was actually being discreet as he tried to complete the crossword in *The Irish Independent*.

'Ah Mister Daly, can I help you with your crossword?'

'I don't think so, it's a bit hard today.' Tosh had the grace to blush, as he didn't really mean to be smart but our man hadn't the wit to recognise the irony.

By this stage, a few of us had developed a routine that more or less guaranteed good exam results. Anything we didn't understand we'd clarify with the lecturer as soon as possible, regardless of how poor he was. We'd then leave it until shortly before the exams. At this point, we would form into small interchangeable study groups. Brennan, Galavan, John McDonnell and Tony Harte were usually my compadres. Each of us would then study a particular aspect and impart this to the others in the group. Mostly this took place in the Great Hall* in Earlsfort Terrace, where there were tables and spaces aplenty and where we could talk freely albeit lowly among ourselves, without being told to 'shush.' We had finished one of these all day study sessions and were coming out that night when I discerned highly unusual activity in one of the adjoining rooms. Black trousered, white shirted waiters scuttled hither and thither armed with silver trays, from which they served peculiarly shaped glasses, filled to the brim with amber liquid, to people in formal dress as they chatted in small groups. We held back for a few seconds.

'It's sherry.' Brennan said. Between us we managed to purloin about twenty glasses of sherry and in no time at all we were the life and soul of the reception.

I noticed a small, kind man smiling in our direction. He seemed vaguely familiar and when I said hello, he came over. After a few seconds I realised we were speaking with Erskine Childers, recently elected President of Ireland. He asked us what we were studying and seemed impressed when we told him we were third year horticultural students. He said he was from Wicklow, the garden of Ireland and asked if we were familiar with Mount Usher? I said it was one of my favourite gardens and he seemed delighted with this. I didn't know whether or not to shake his hand as I had become conscious we were interlopers and were now the centre of attention. I told him I had hitched home to vote in the recent presidential election. He seemed quite impressed with this. He didn't ask nor did I say that I had in fact voted for him. None of us in the room could have known that within a few months he was to experience a heart attack and die. He was a gentle man with laughing eyes but I discerned an inner strength and integrity in the minute or two of our little interaction, which I think he too enjoyed.

* The Albert College in Glasnevin has largely been demolished and is now the site for Dublin University more popularly called DCU
*The Great Hall was refurbished and established as The National Concert Hall in 1981

THE AGS AND THE MIAMI

The Troubles in the North were the backdrop for my student days in the seventies. I used to read newspapers and listen to the news. For the most part I avoided any great connection to the grief and awfulness up there, apart from the protests around Bloody Sunday. This disconnect was much the same for most people I knew and was somewhat similar to how the present young generation regard gangster killings in Limerick and Dublin.

Occasionally someone I knew was maimed or killed and then it was different. Such an occasion was when Fran O'Toole and two other members of the Miami Showband were murdered on the side of a road as they travelled home after performing at a dance in Banbridge County Down, in July 1975. This was an appalling atrocity that shocked me to the core, as it did many others. It wasn't that they were personal friends or anything but there was an unforgettable night, just a year or so before, when the Miami played *The Ags Dance* in the Olympic Ballroom* just off Camden Street.

Baby faced Fran O'Toole was their new front man and he winked at me, as he handed me the microphone. Both of us were incredulous at the huge crowd in the Olympic that night. Someone said it was the biggest crowd ever. I was on stage because I was the public relations officer for *The Ags Dance* committee and had to make a few announcements. My friend Ger O'Donnell was the chairman and another horticultural student, Gerry Byrne, looked after the money. Our job was to run dances every Wednesday night to make enough money to fund an educational tour at the end of our final year studying Agricultural Science.

OLYMPIC BALLROOM

DUBLIN'S MOST POPULAR BALLROOM

AGS DANCING EVERY
WEDNESDAY NIGHT
10 - 1.30 : TOP BANDS : SELECT CROWDS

● WEDNESDAY, 10th OCTOBER—
FABULOUS **MIAMI**

● WEDNESDAY, 17th OCTOBER—
BILL RYAN & BUCKSHOT

● WEDNESDAY, 24th OCTOBER—
NONE OTHER THAN . . .
Big Tom AND THE **Mainliners**

● WEDNESDAY, 31st OCTOBER—
THE **TIMES**
HALLOWEEN SPECIAL

Your November attractions include :
JOHNNY McEVOY and his COUNTRY BAND, INDIANS,
DANNY DOYLE, MAXI and the MUSIC BOX,
BRIAN COLL and the BUCKAROOS

ADMISSION : : : : **50p**

CONCESSIONS TO STUDENTS AND NURSES 30p

Printed by Abbey Printers (Cavan) Ltd., Cavan

The Ags Dance in the Olympic Ballroom had been on the go for forty nine years but the fiftieth anniversary nearly didn't happen. We'd heard on the grapevine that Mick Quinn, the new owner, was a mogul who wanted nothing to do with 'meddlesome amateurs'. We arranged to meet him one Saturday evening in his house in Castleknock. I remember being awe struck by the splendour of his home and the glamour and friendliness of his wife, who made us dainty little tomato sandwiches. He'd had to leave a wedding reception earlier to keep our appointment. We hit it off straightaway but before long we'd come to an impasse in our negotiations. However by this stage, both sides saw how we could work to our mutual benefit and, even though it was way past midnight, we threshed around looking for the win:win solution both parties wanted. I was delighted with myself after I came up with the 'breakthrough.'

We agreed to let his people look after all the bookings and paying the bands. The first seven hundred pounds was to be his and anything after this was to be split with sixty per cent going to us. Into the bargain we secured a nixer for our friends Eamon Galavan and Tony Harte to look after his garden.

The first rabbit I pulled out of my 'public relations hat' was to commission a special anniversary page in the *Evening Press*. For some obscure reason I came up with the idea of a pyjama race around St Stephen's Green as a publicity stunt. It worked; photos of me winning the race were carried in the evening newspapers. Free passes and posters became the currency of my life and I loved nothing better than going into busy offices with 'my materials'. I'd ogle the ladies and occasionally they'd ogle me right back.

My girlfriend Bernadette worked on the sixth floor of the Revenue Commisioners office block opposite the university building in Earlsfort Terrace. Our chairman Ger O Donnell and a friend, Dick Ahearne, knew this and challenged me to bring

The first publicity stunt I organised was a Pyjama Race around St Stephen's Green, which I won. Peter Rafftery looks very comfortable in second place

them up to the sixth floor to promote *The Ags Dance* with the myriad of female civil servants we knew to be there.

I was a little bit in trepidation as I knew she had a very cross boss. Nevertheless I donned my cowboy hat, reserved for these opportunities, led the lads in and pressed the button to summon a lift to the sixth floor. We were ascending with speed when the lift stopped at the fourth floor. The doors opened. There in front of us stood Bernadette with a file in her hand. She had an incredulous look on her face but immediately twigged what was afoot. She stepped into the lift and pressed the ground floor button to bring us back to Earth, and then escorted us to the front door. I knew what was good for me and there were no further attempts at promoting our wonderful dance in *Teach Earlsfort*.

Danny Doyle, Roly Daniels were just two of the acts in Mick Quinn's stable, and they featured regularly at 'The Ags'.

The Indians were one of our favourite bands at the Ags and always drew a terrific crowd.
Here I am making announcements on stage

These were middle of the road bands that suited our clientele and would attract somewhere between six to eight hundred dancers. Our big hitters were bands such as the Indians and Red Hurley, twho always brought in around twice that number. The Miami Showband we thought 'would do about seven hundred or so' as we hopped off the bus just after eight o'clock. Our main job on Wednesday nights was to 'meet and greet' the punters as they came in the door. As usual we slipped into The Sword* on Camden Street to gulp down a couple of pints before taking up our posts.

When we emerged, we were astounded to realise that a queue of over two hundred yards long had formed, as people waited patiently for us to open up. We kept our heads down and quickly walked up to the door to commence our duties. We had to open a second box office; even so it took over an hour and a half for close on three thousand punters to crush into the Olympic. Every available foot of floor space on both floors was taken up. We literally made buckets of money that night. There was hardly room to breathe as the condensation poured back down from the ceiling on top of the dancers coincidentally keeping them cool.

Each Tuesday after lectures, we used to hold class meetings to give an account of the previous Wednesday and to thrash out issues that arose from time to time. At one such meeting, our chairman Ger O'Donnell came up with the suggestion that we take a fresh look at what constituted an educational tour. Someone in jest said that we should check out goat farming on a tropical island. The following week we committed ourselves to just that by voting for the Corfu Sun option. Most of us had been abroad before but if we were, it was to work in America, England or wherever during our long summer vacations. Many of us didn't even know what a Sun holiday was, much less having been on one, but all of us to a man looked forward intensely to our Greek idyll.

*The Olympic Ballroom is now The Olympic Office complex on the same site on Mountpleasant Street, off Camden Street.
* The Sword on Camden Street is now called Anseo, but is otherwise largely unchanged from what it was when we drank there.

GARDENS OF IRELAND

Mount Usher in Ashford was the last stop on our grand tour of the great gardens of Ireland which we'd completed over three days in May 1973. Organised by Pat Dempsey, our Amenity lecturer, this turned out to be memorable for more reasons than the obvious. A minibus and two carloads of 'horts' had set out for Kerry at the beginning of May to visit the great gardens of Ireland. When we landed that first evening, at a seaside caravan park somewhere near Kenmare, we immediately repaired to a local hostelry. There was a dance on after the bar closed, at which we represented the horticultural wing of the faculty as best we could. Some of us were taken advantage of by giggling young ones, but we let them have their way.

The following day Ger O'Donnell brought a few of us to his home in Fenit, outside Tralee. There is a fine pier there from which I jumped into the deep green water of the Atlantic Ocean. I wasn't at all sure if I could swim while out of my depth, and there was an interesting few seconds until I levelled out and swam to the steps. This was also the occasion I discovered that the Gulf Stream wasn't as warm as it was made out to be.

Guinness featured heavily on our menu, which was hardly a surprise. However, a few days into the tour, my worst fears became a reality when I ran out of money . The first time this happened, I bet five pounds which I didn't have, that I'd run a mile inside six minutes. The boys in Galavan's Hillman Minx measured out the mile, timed the run and paid me the fiver, but this only lasted one night and by this stage, funds within our group had run alarmingly low.

Resilience is bred of necessity and in fairness to us, we came up with a plan to solve our problem.

Myself and Tom Daly (Tosh) try out our posing skills on the Kerry section of our tour of the gardens of Ireland

Seven of us pooled whatever money we had left. Between us, this amounted to close on thirty pounds. We decided to speculate twenty, a not inconsiderable sum back in the day when a pound could buy three pints. Tosh, Tony and Eamon stopped off at a well known hostelry on the outskirts of Cork city. They then initiated a conversation about pint drinking which culminated in one of the boys losing a pound bet in a pint sprint against the local 'big gullet.'

A few minutes later, the other car arrived and the four of us walked into the midst of a ferment of 'pint talk' about how the young fellahs from Dublin had been put in their place. Within ten minutes, I squared up to the big bellied Murphy drinker and told him I was prepared to bet any money that I'd drink a pint faster than him. He had no trouble finding backers to cover my twenty pounds that I'd left on the counter. 'Big Belly' never stood a chance. I had my emptied pint glass down on the counter a full two seconds before him. His friends started to roar out vexations. Our 'treasurer' pocketed the money and we left as graciously as we could, albeit in a hurry. We visited a couple of gardens in Cork and Waterford the next day before we headed up the east coast.

Our final stopover was in New Ross where we were booked into the Five Counties Hotel.* We had been downtown and on our way back that night we came across a large piebald horse. He was quiet and seemed lonely. Some of us thought it a good idea at the time to bring him on down to the hotel, which we did, but the night porter told us sternly that we couldn't bring him up to our rooms and he refused to give the horse a room of his own so we had to leave him go. We cast him loose and hoped he'd find his way back up the hill where we'd found him. We were a sheepish enough group of young men the following morning at breakfast, thankful that no great harm had come to pass as we boarded our vehicles to head back to Dublin.

*Five Counties Hotel is now known as The Brandon Hotel

CORFU

Forty years later, I can still recall the exhilaration of that first evening in Corfu. We are sitting outside a white taverna with my friends, enveloped in a wonderful heat as the scent of orange blossom wafts down from groves on the hill behind us. We sit around tables as we enjoy a smoke and guzzle wine. All but one of the wine bottles on our table are empty. The ashtrays are full and there are red stains on the blue and white check table cloth, but we are not one bit bothered. The waiter brings out a dish of black olives. A black shirted bouzouki player with a moustache has just finished with a flourish the theme from *Zorba the Greek*. Waves lap up against the white wall across the road, which seems to be holding back the whole Mediterranean stretched out in front of us.

The wine must have gone to Brennan's head because next thing he jumped up, ran across the road and dived straight into the sea. When he emerged he had a huge gash over his eye from which his bright red blood flowed freely. Someone brought him to a hospital where they stitched him up but he was back drinking wine before the night was done.

We had a total disregard for safety, rather like weanling calves let loose from their shed into the haggart on the first sunny day in Spring. Our tails were up and we went ballistic, especially when we discovered we could hire mopeds for next to nothing. These glorified bicycles had a little engine in front and could reach fifty miles an hour going downhill and there were plenty of hills to go down. Truth to tell we were lucky some of us weren't seriously hurt or worse. Into the bargain I had discovered Ouzo – which fascinated me as it turned milky white when water was added, also it tasted of liquorice but there was more to it than these curiosities and it had me 'under the weather' for a couple of days. By the third day we had all more or less settled.

Most evenings we would treat all and sundry to a feast of Irish songs. My flatmate John McDonnell did a memorable rendition of 'McAlpine's Fusiliers.' Micky Fitz had a really sweet version of 'Skibereen' but every so often our proletariat section would drown all the sweet stuff with the opening bars of our anthem, then the whole of final year, there were close on a hundred of us, would join in to joyously proclaim:

'Hear, hear; the Ags are here!
What the fuck do we care?
What the fuck do we care?
Hear hear..........

This refrain could go on for three or four minutes and even longer. After one such rendition I found myself in convivial conversation with an impressed American, dressed in white shirt and shorts. He told me he was a commander on the USS Forrestal. I didn't attach too much import to this until he offered to:

'Bring you guys out to see our ship for yourselves.'

Five or six of us found ourselves on board a launch taking us out to a giant aircraft carrier anchored offshore. Mick Connolly wouldn't come as he said to do so would be an act of support for 'imperial war mongering.'

The scale of The Forrestal was beyond my comprehension. Croke Park would have fitted inside it, no bother. I think there were fifteen levels below deck and five thousand men served on board. Why such a gargantuan carrier was anchored in the waters off Corfu I have no idea. If it was there merely to impress a representative sample of Agricultural Science undergraduates well then, it succeeded handsomely.

Talking propels one into all sorts of situations. There weren't many locals who spoke English but there was one and he told me he was the manager of the local soccer team which played in the Greek League. I told him we were a famous team in our country and challenged him to a game. Word spread through the little town and its surrounds and at the appointed hour, hundreds of people turned up to see 'Corfu take on Ireland.' The Corfucians were feisty, tricky and passionate but they had never taken on anything like *The Ags* before. Micky Fitz and Johnny O Sullivan were handy enough soccer players. Most of the rest of us of us were Gaelic players of moderate enough ability, but the locals just could not handle the fifteen stones of aggressive Cork muscle that was Dinny O'Connor and our star man, Kevin Kilmurray, who insisted on playing even though he was due to fly home to play for Offaly against Dublin in the quarter final of the Leinster championship that very weekend. We beat them 2-1. They were not one bit happy.

The following Monday, I remember going into Kerika airport on a moped to collect Kevin from his flight back, following the quarter final in Croke Park. Offaly were the defending All Ireland champions and I was astonished when he told me that Dublin, who up to this had been useless had beaten them by a point. Under Kevin Heffernan they would go on to win the All Ireland later that year and two more after that.

We became very proficient on the mopeds. On one particular day, close on two dozen of us traversed the island. We were on the lookout for a nudist beach we'd been told about but we weren't too bothered when we didn't find it. The truth of the matter was that each of realised that our student days were coming to an end. We'd had the time of our lives over the previous five years and we knew it. Sex and the pursuit of it was put aside for the fortnight as we enjoyed the sun and the exuberance of being young men together for the last time before we took on the world.

For the second week, a large group of us moved up coast to Camp Ipsos. This was a young person's campsite on a beach just across the sea from Albania which was notoriously inaccessible under a communist dictatorship at the time. I wondered what life must be like for Albanians living less than ten miles across the sea.

The international nature of the campsite was an eye opener for me. There seemed to be young people, fellahs and girls from every corner of the world. Most of our days were taken up playing volleyball – Ireland versus the Rest of the World. There were three lads from Glasgow, who had set out to go to the World Cup being held in Germany, but they'd caught the wrong train, or so they said.

One night towards the end of our holiday, we all went down to the beach to sing and to drink. Mickey Fitz had just sang *Skibereen* which was my cue to sing *Do Wah Diddy Diddy* for which I was famous in my own head. Just as I hit the climactic note in the song, I felt the temporary filling in my front tooth explode out of my mouth into the warm night but I never faltered. Actually I caught the filling in my hand but never got the chance to put it back to hide the spike which I instantly knew was now protruding from my gum.

Just as I finished to rapturous applause I received an almighty blow on the back of my head. I saw stars. Everyone scattered in front of me. My spontaneous reaction was to whip off my belt which had a heavy brass buckle. My assailant was in dark clothes wielding a big stick. I quickly realised that he was a policeman and the stick was a truncheon but by that stage, the buckle and I were past the point of no return. Then I felt a force of nature grab me from behind, a Kiwi accent in my ear entreated me to 'run man run.' I didn't need too much persuasion. We 'ran like fuck' until both of us dived into a sort of dry ditch behind some scrub plants across the road. We lay there totally silent and frightened until the incensed prattling policemen went away.

A New Zealand chap called Terry Baker had been my guardian angel that night. It was a dangerous time. Corfu was governed by Greece which was quite unstable, being a right wing police state run by an unpopular military junta, which relied on 'ruthless violence' to keep themselves in power. There was a discernable tension the following day as the police came into the campsite 'to investigate the serious assault on their colleague, by a man with a buckle.' They never did find the man they were looking for.

I visited New Zealand thirty years after these things happened. All that time, I'd retained a piece of paper with Terry Baker's contact details at the time. These led me to his mother who put me in touch with her son. So I made my way to Parua Bay in Northland where he was a well known school teacher. We rekindled a friendship forged in 'the heat of battle' many years before. Seemingly that night the police had received a complaint about loud singing on the beach. Two officers had gone down to check things out. When they were told by big Jim O'Dwyer from Tipperary that we were all from Albania, they'd 'lost the plot' and waded into us. Terry had spotted a policeman on the road lining up his pistol to have a shot at me as my comrades fled. I had chosen to battle with the 'black shape' that had battered me from behind on the back of the neck with his big stick.

Some day soon I might return to Corfu, seek out my assailant and apologise for hitting him with the buckle, then again 'Corfucian goats might fly.'

EUREKA

I n the final year of my degree course in UCD, I became impressed with the gardens of David Robinson, a prominent horticulturist of the day and our occasional guest lecturer. He was a great believer in the chemical control of weeds. Simizene was his passion. When applied in the right conditions, this herbicide prevented weed seeds from germinating. A by-product of its usage was the proliferation of different types of mosses in his large garden.

I was intrigued with the concept of moss lawns as an alternative to grass and I was seriously considering staying on in UCD to undertake research on this for Irish conditions and to pursue a Master's degree. However coming to the end of my fifth year of third level study, my enthusiasm for student life and its attendant penury was beginning to wane. The question of what career path to pursue now confronted me.

As part of our final examination I had to make an oral presentation to the class. Professor Eddie Clarke sat in during my presentation on the workings of a Howard Rotavator, an implement which performed the operations of ploughing and tilling in the one pass. After it, I was happy that I'd gotten my points across. The professor called me back as I walked from the room.

'Have you decided what to do with yourself after your finals?'

'I haven't Professor, have you any ideas for me?'

'I think you'd make an excellent teacher. The degree qualifies you to teach Rural Science, you know it's taught in vocational schools?' he put his hand on my shoulder, smiled as he nodded his head in the manner of a sparrow, then turned and was gone.

For twenty years I'd been taught by a long litany of teachers.

Mother most proud leads her B.Ag.Sc Hort (Hons) graduate son and his girlfriend Bernadette, Earlsfort Terrace, November 1974

Sister Philomena, Sister Benignus, Cooney, Joe Partridge, Clangers, Hoppy, Heffo, Manley, Spike, Birdie, Dux, Talty, Ghostie, Paddy Byrne, Dracula, Screwie, Coote, Satch, Willie Walshe, Bog Walshe, Timmy Ryan, Seamus O'Muire and our PE man John Curley. This was before I started in UCD where an even longer list of academics imparted supposedly state-of-the art knowledge to us. Never once over the twenty years of being a student had it occurred to me that I should become a teacher until that kindly old professor said what he said to me.

I had enjoyed imparting knowledge on an implement with which I had no experience, I enjoyed the way my fellow-students followed what I was saying. Most of all I'd enjoyed the feeling of knowing 'I'd hit the nail on the head.' The more I thought about it the more I knew he was right. The following week, I made it my business to see Jimmy O'Loughlin, who had recently been elected a county councillor, and also our TD Paddy Power. They both suggested that I have a chat with Mr Commins, the CEO of County Kildare Vocational Education Committee. His office was upstairs in the vocational school,* Naas. I went in there one day and stood at the front counter, from where I could see several ladies working at their desks.

'Can I see Mister Commins, please?' I asked the lady who had looked up from her work.

'Have you an appointment, Noel?' I hadn't recognised her at first but as she spoke, I could see she was the sister of a friend.

'No, but I only want to see him for a minute.'

'I'm not sure if it's possible.'

'Will you ask him? ...Please.' At this everyone in the office looked up.

'Can I help you?' A small grey haired man with glasses and a quizzical scowl appeared at the half open door of an inner office. The rest of the office staff immediately resumed their work.

'Are you Mister Commins?

'I am.'

'Mister Commins, my name is Noel Heavey and I'm inquiring if there are vacancies for teachers of Rural Science?'

'I see, well you had better come into my office.'

When we were seated and the door closed he proceeded to tell me how inappropriate it was to burst into a busy office without an appointment. He finished with a question: 'and if there were a post available, what qualifications and experience have you got?'

'I'll have my B. Ag Sc. (Hort).'

'A fine degree, yes a fine degree but you are not yet qualified. It's preposterous to think you'd be suitable for a permanent post without experience. You should apply for a temporary position in Leitrim or Donegal or somewhere down the country to gain experience.'

'Mister Commins, I've worked in America, England and Dublin. I want now to work in Kildare as a teacher. If that's not possible, I'll work at whatever is available when my exams are done.' He inclined his head and looked at me directly, over his glasses for a few seconds.

'I see, well if you want to be a teacher, you'll need a teaching qualification as well as your degree, presuming you get your degree. My staff will help if you're interested. Good day to you.' He looked now at the door.

'Thanks very much Mister Commins.'

A very nice lady with deep red lipstick filled me in on the details of The Crawford Institute in Cork which ran a two week training course for science graduates who wanted to teach Rural Science. She happened to have an application form on file and she offered it to me. I took it, thanked her and filled it out there and then. She said she'd include it in that day's post. She also advised me that a Rural Science vacancy would be advertised shortly and that I should apply in due course. When the 'ad' appeared in the Sunday Independent, I applied for the position of *Teacher of Rural Science* for County Kildare VEC.

When I came home from our 'educational tour of Corfu,' there were two letters waiting for me on the dresser. The first one was that a place had been for reserved me the following month on the teaching course in Cork. The second was to the effect I had been appointed as whole time permanent teacher of Rural Science in Prosperous Vocational School, pending being fully qualified with a primary science degree, a teaching certificate and a thing called the *Ceard Teastas*. My mother gave her particular little whinny of a laugh which happened only when she was truly delighted about something. We hugged together in the back kitchen and she loved me with her eyes.

The first Monday in September was when I was instructed to report to the Principal in Prosperous. It was also the first day of my final exam. I dashed off a letter to the effect that I would take up the position as soon as my finals were over and that in the meantime I would have completed the course in Cork. To add to this maelstrom of excitement I asked our neighbour Robbie Curley, who knew all about cars, to see if he could buy me one for under a hundred pounds. Within the week I was the proud, very proud, owner of a six year old turquoise Opel Kadett. He asked for ninety pounds but he gave me a fiver back for luck.

My first long spin was up the dual carriageway, and then to Churchtown where my girlfriend Bernadette lived with her sister Mary and her small family. It was Sunday and the sun shone on the side of the Dublin mountains up by Lamb Doyles, overlooking the city. We sang the *Chuck Berry song* as I drove.

'Riding along in my automobile,
My baby beside at the wheel
Acruising and playing the radio
With no particular place to go...'

We wound down the windows, the wind blew Bernadette's long black hair across my cheek. It smelt of Loxene shampoo. I looked across at her, she smiled. I smiled back. We were going out together now for over a year, but I think this was the first moment, I realised I was falling in love.

My final exams came on rapidly but I was ready for them and breezed through without any trauma. I was early that first morning as I drove down to Prosperous. I had driven down the Saturday before, just to make sure I knew the way. It was the third Monday of September. Ray O'Malley, the principal, was there before me with a big welcoming smile. He turned out to be the same Ray O Malley who had called to my house to bring me to a county minor game in Trim six years before. The school was busy with students and teachers hurrying to class on this momentous day for me. Ray brought me into his office. All our talk was of the team that I'd been part of should have won the Leinster championship and the previous day's All Ireland final in which Dublin announced themselves under Kevin Heffernan by beating Galway. Eventually he handed me a text book and told me that my class awaited next door. This was the moment, I was about to start the rest of my life. I looked down and hesitated.

'What's wrong?' he asked.

'This is a maths textbook.'

'Exactly. Half your hours will be science, the rest will be made up by teaching maths.'

'But the last time I studied maths was for my Leaving Cert,' I answered nervously, very nervously.

'And isn't that why I've given you a textbook?' He laughed and I knew things would work out OK. I went next door to be confronted by a sea of open young faces. I stepped up onto the slightly raised platform and went behind the large desk at the front of the class room.

'How are ye? I'm Mister Heavey, your new maths teacher.'

*The old Naas Vocational School now serves as 'Mean Scoil Cill Dara.'

PROSPEROUS
1. A STUDENT'S RECOLLECTION

He stepped through the doorway into our classroom that Monday morning and said:

'I'm Mister Heavey, your new Maths teacher.'

Because he wasn't wearing a tie and looked so young we thought he was one of the senior students messing. Even so, there was something about him that drew us to listen intently to what he was saying. I was in first year, still coming to terms with being in a new school. He said he was from Clongorey which was in the same parish as Prosperous. I told him I was from Allenwood which was in the same parish as Allen. He asked us about ourselves until some of the boys started to talk amongst themselves, he just glared at them. They stopped after a few seconds.

He told us he had just finished college and it was a long time since he'd studied Maths but that we'd get through it together. We did too. His classes didn't really seem like classes at all, as he conducted surveys and analyzed the results, using things called venn diagrams and set notation. One day he came up with the idea that if we got through the work we'd spend the last ten minutes of the class singing. He took down the set square from the blackboard and pretended it was a guitar. We sang 'Paper Roses' and 'Nobody's Child.' After this we got to sing in class if he felt we'd worked well. It was blackmail of a sort, but it worked. We all got good results at Christmas, by which time we had learned three new songs.

At lunch hour that first day, he burst around the corner of the playground and insisted he be allowed play basketball with the students. Senior students Connie Malone and Tony Moore were both better than him but he made more noise. Before Christmas he went around all the classes looking for students to train for cross-country across the road in Costelloe's field. The boys were in one group, the girls in another. He togged out as well and he roared at us to take small steps up the hill and to lengthen our strides coming down. He was quite mad.

However, It wasn't all fun and games. If you were a lad and got the wrong side of him you were given a choice between writing out one hundred lines of a sentence with 'great big words' in it or they could opt for his specially concocted 'Chinese tortures.' The girls had no such choice and had to do the lines.

Each class lasted forty minutes and then we had to change rooms and move to another classroom. Some of us would have our schoolbags packed and be ready to run out the door but if he copped this he would empty out the books on the floor and mix up everybody's so that we'd be late for the next class.

It was very interesting one day when he caught a girl chewing gum in class:

'Imelda, empty that gum out of your mouth, please.'

'No.'

'What did you just say?'

'I said no.'

'Imelda, please, it's a filthy habit.'

She set her jaw even as she continued chewing. Everyone became so excruciatingly silent we could actually hear her chewing.

'I'm not doing any harm to anyone, anyway it's no worse than you smoking in class.'

He now blushed and didn't say anything further. Some of the boys weren't at all impressed with this and weren't slow about letting him know. He looked at them sternly and warned them to be quiet. When the class was over he called Imelda up to have a private chat. After this she never chewed gum in class again nor, so far as I can remember, did he ever smoke in front of us.

He also had us for Science and sometimes he used to let us do experiments. I remember the slimy feel of a set of lungs he'd got from the village butchers who used to kill sheep every Tuesday morning. He'd then dissect them. I remember when he told us that lungs were like a train station but that instead of people getting on and off the carriages of a train, gases diffused into and out things called red blood corpuscles. I told him I'd never been on a train in my life. He responded by calling me a country yokel and said we were to use our imaginations.

One day, a boy brought in a dead rabbit. Mr Heavey gathered us around the table and dissected the innards. I was amazed at the length of the small intestine, although the thing I remember most was the smell which was disgusting. One of the boys asked to have a go. He handed him the scalpel but the lad cut himself and had to be brought to the hospital for two stitches and a tetanus injection. That was the end of student surgeons.

In Chemistry, my favourite experiment was mixing acid with zinc to manufacture hydrogen, which we collected by displacing water in jars, and he allowed us to light the hydrogen which used to burn with a loud pop. I was always a bit wary when he was performing an experiment because you'd never quite be sure that it would turn out the way it was supposed to. He was very fussy about how we had to write up the report of the experiments.

If the weather was good, he'd sometimes bring us on a nature walk down to the canal during a double class. I should say a nature run because the canal was a mile away and to get down and back took the guts of a class. He'd break an ash stick from a tree and threaten all sorts of damnation on us if we didn't keep in front of his brisk walk.

Sometimes we'd run together but when someone couldn't keep up the pace he'd let them fall behind but usually we stuck together in front of him.

PROSPEROUS
2. MY FIRST YEAR AS A TEACHER

From the first time I stepped into the Vocational School in Prosperous I knew I had chosen correctly. There was a bit of a spark about the pupils and that first morning I enjoyed the interaction between us. I had finished my exams the previous Friday and so after twenty years of being a student it felt a little strange to be on the other side of a teacher's desk.

I have never been a person for formality and whether someone was a lowly student or a senior teacher made no difference to me as to how I thought or talked of them. If I thought a person genuine he or she got my respect, if I thought otherwise, they didn't. As time slipped by I slotted onto the wavelengths of both students and staff. Some of the longer established teachers weren't all that impressed with my informal disposition but this didn't worry me unduly.

There were up to twenty eight pupils in some classes and as few as ten in others. There were boys' classes, girls' classes and mixed which I preferred. Every forty minutes the bell would ring and then a different set of students would present themselves in front of me. Occasionally I mused how ironic it was, that I was now a science teacher, as this was one of my weakest subjects all through Newbridge College. I became conscious of how boring it must be for students to have to sit through a class, listening to the likes of me read things from a book which they didn't understand and that they probably saw as irrelevant to their lives. I determined to make the subject matter as interesting to them as I possibly could and that they should enjoy my classes.

Ray O'Malley was the Principal of Prosperous Vocational School. Here he has the megaphone at a School Sports Day

Ray O'Malley was the school principal. He had a warm bright personality. Also he had an encyclopaedic insight and knowledge of the circumstances of his students and their families.

Looking back now on how it was then, I'd say the vast majority of students enjoyed their schooling in Prosperous and this had much to do with the compassionate disposition of the Principal or 'Priomh Oide' as he liked to refer to his position. He had strong views on many things and I was lucky that by and large we were in agreement on most of them. The obvious one was sport of all kinds, which he loved, as I did myself. His door was always open for the young teacher that he remembered from his time as selector of the county Minors when his entreaties had got 'the lad from Newbridge College' onto the team.

I loved teaching but it was intense enough, so I quickly learned to appreciate free classes when they presented themselves on my timetable. Then I would retire to the tiny staffroom to gather myself and luxuriate in the sheer pleasure of doing nothing for forty minutes. However there was a snag, as most of my free classes were immediately before the eleven o clock break. I was the only one free to go down to the village for the biscuits. No bother, I thought at first, but as time passed this began to grate on my nerves. The anticipated pleasure of the free class became negated by the obligation to run this particular errand. In truth, I began to suspect that it might not be a coincidence and that I was in fact a timetabled 'biscuit runner.'

A plan came into my head. I chose to buy plain Marietta biscuits instead of Kimberly and Fig Rolls. Sure enough after about a week of this there began a rumbling of discontent in the staffroom. This seemed to be particularly strong amongst a few of the ladies who were not impressed with my assurances that there was nothing to beat 'a buttered Marietta especially when dunked in the tea.' There followed a coup d'état shortly afterwards. Anne O'Neill offered to bring the biscuits in with her each morning from her mother's shop. That was that, I was off the biscuit run.

Within a short enough time of starting in Prosperous, I introduced cross-country running, after I obtained permission from local farmer John Costelloe to allow students train on his land. Cross-country running had been a huge and important sport for me when I was sixteen, even when no one else in my school had the remotest interest in it. Dozens of students answered my call and many of them took to the sport like ducks to water. Seamus Cross from Allenwood was a particularly courageous young runner and I derived great satisfaction from watching him battle his way up the field whenever he ran. Before long I was a fairly regular visitor to his home where I was made enormously welcome by his parents, Jim and Maura and their large family.

Maura was a great woman to put up 'honest-to-God' food that demanded to be eaten whether or not you were hungry. Jim was an inspiring man the way he went about anything he put his mind to. Having been in the house a few times, I was invited over one night to play *Twenty Five* for a turkey. I was a handy enough card player, or so I thought.

Playing *Twenty Five* in Allenwood was daunting enough as mistakes at the card table were not appreciated and people were not slow to communicate this. Reneging (not playing a card of the same suit that had been led) was unthinkable. Eventually it became somewhat of a comfort for me to know that I was accepted as someone who 'played for the table' which was to play knowledgeably to stretch out a game for as long as possible to the satisfaction of all. I played there many nights and I remember being within a trick 'for out' on at least two occasions but I never managed to come home with a turkey.

That first spring Jim introduced me to his brother Dick and also his friend Mick Jacob, who lived and had a small farm in the Pulleachs, as the land area behind the Scew bridge was called by the locals, rather than it's official name of Allenwood South. All three worked in the ESB power station. Each also had developed great skill and a pioneering spirit for growing crops on reclaimed peatland. We became friendly and I found their enthusiasm absolutely infectious, mind you they were pushing an open door because more than anything else, I wanted to use my horticultural degree.

CELERY

I had helped harvest celery when I was a student in Warrenstown and had attended lectures on it there and in UCD, but I had little knowledge or interest in it until I came to know the 'Allenwood Growers' who stimulated my desire to grow a crop I knew so little about. Jim Cross was one of these and a parent, whose children were students in the school where I taught. We had grown a crop under contract with a food processing firm in the North. It had been harvested and dispatched.

One particular evening I stood, with Jim and two others, outside the house of Aidan, the Managing Director of the processing firm that had taken our celery. It was behind the Montrose Hotel, opposite Belfield, late October and I noticed how our shadows were thrown up against the front of the house by the street lights.

'Hullo, is Aidan in please?' I asked in as neutral a tone as I could muster.

It had taken ages for us to find the house and now it seemed ages before I heard someone come to the door. We stepped back as we hadn't expected to be confronted by a woman with a baby on her shoulder. There was genuine fear in the lady's eyes, and she hesitated before beginning to answer, but this became irrelevant as Aidan appeared behind her in the hallway. He was closely followed by Michael Greene who had gone to the back door as per our plan, hatched out on the way up to Dublin. Jim Cross, and his brother, along with my father and I, were invited into the front room. Greene wasn't invited but he came in anyway.

'Aidan, when are we going to get paid for our celery?' I asked.

There was a lot of work involved in Celery. Transplanting seedlings into a soon to be erected plastic tunnel. Students Dermot Doyle, Thomas McKenna and Kevin Doyle

Even as I was organising the building of our house, a good part of my summer had been spent at the celery. I had recruited a great little gang of workers from Allenwood, who were my students. In a short space of time, we managed to develop an enlightened cooperative approach which involved growers, pupils and our families. The main challenge with growing celery, a plant native to temperate climates, is its sensitivity to frost. It just happens that Bog of Allen soil is notoriously prone to frosts. So we worked out a plan to propagate seeds in March using a paraffin oil heater. We then transplanted the seedlings from seed trays to a poly tunnel especially constructed for the job. In mid-June we planted the eighty thousand or so plants in the bog field which had been prepared assiduously from the previous spring.

There was a particular day in July I'll not forget as long as I live. The day I had to spray the celery with a knapsack. It was one of those humid days when to walk the field, even with nothing on your back, was to become bathed in sweat. Conditions were ideal for the spread of leafspot which threatened to destroy the crop. Walking the field with a half hundredweight of spray strapped to my back caused rivulets of salty sweat to run into my eyes. There was nothing to be done about this, the field had to be sprayed that day before it rained or all would be lost.

To make matters worse fifty million midges waiting in ambush for me knew it as well. To knapsack an acre with the recommended dilution takes a full day, and is a truly daunting task. That day I had daubed myself with insect repellent but the tiny bastards ignored this and swarms of them attacked their only living target within miles, drawn by the smell of my sweat. All day I stuck to the task. When I'd come to the headland, I'd stop to light the pipe which I smoked at the time in an effort to keep them away from me but this proved useless. When my work was done I was dizzy with delirium and covered in lumps from ravenous bites.

Whatever about the hardships associated with it, the celery turned out to be a fabulous crop and word of it circulated through the tightly knit community of professional horticulturalists. People came from far and wide to see it for themselves. When it was ready I brought a few bags of it into Sean O'Keefe, who owned a supermarket in Newbridge. I wanted to test the waters.

'Would you be interested in selling a bit of celery for me?'

'Have you much of it?'

'Eighty thousand heads or so.'

'Oh right.' He looked at me with a curious eye. 'Shure leave in a couple of dozen and we'll see how we get on. I'll charge the same and pay you the same as for a head of cabbage. Is that ok?'

'Yeah, that sounds about right, thanks very much.'

The following evening I called in to collect my money, and to leave in some more celery. Sean was busy and I had no choice but to wait around the vegetable section until he was free. I didn't count the number of heads but the celery section was still pretty full compared to the one beside it which was all but empty except for a few heads of cabbage, which had seen better days. Two ladies stood there, each with celery in hand.

'Isn't there a grand smell off it, what is it?'

'Celery, they use it in soup.'

'Oh, I must try it sometime.'

With that, they both left the magnificent celery back on the shelf and instead moved forward to the checkout with the two remaining wizened heads of cabbage. This little incident became emblazoned in my brain, and ever after I was slow enough to introduce new food lines to customers who know what they want.

That was all by the way as we stood now in the man's sitting room in the presence of his frightened wife and child.

'How dare you come into my home like this?' said Aidan.

We glared back at him. Then Michael, who had confronted and turned him at his back door, went at him for a full ten minutes. Word had come down the horticultural grapevine that the processing company of which Aidan was MD and which had taken delivery of our celery six weeks before was about to go under. The producers were to be left high and dry. I faced losing the equivalent of a year's salary. I thought of the day with the knapsack and became so enraged that the only sentence I could squeak out was: 'All we want is to be paid what we are due, we're dealing with you as a man, not the MD of a company that's not going to pay us.'

Each of us made our point, except for my father, who spoke

not a word, but remained by the door with his right hand buried deep in the pocket of his none too clean 'Colombo style' overcoat. A rancorous atmosphere pervaded the house by the time we left. Father was the last to leave but as he did so I saw him gently pull Aidan close as he whispered something in his ear. None of us had felt all that comfortable in that man's front room as his child screamed and his wife sobbed loudly in the kitchen.

We drove home without too much conversation.

'What did you say to him, on the way out?' I asked my father when we were alone.

'I told him, I hope these men don't have to bring me back up here again!'

'With your hand in the pocket all the time ..... Jesus, Christ, Almighty!' I exclaimed.

Three days later, each of us received cheques in the post drawn on a private account and signed by Aidan's father, whom we knew all along to be a wealthy man. A short time after this, I read in the *Farmer's Journal* that a liquidator had been appointed to Aidan's food processing company and that it was unlikely that suppliers would be paid.

THE CEARD TEASTAS

I only became aware of it sometime after taking up the position of wholetime teacher of Rural Science in Prosperous. There was a caveat. In order for the position to be permanent, I had to have all the necessary qualifications. This meant I needed to pass a thing called the 'Ceard Teastas.' Everyone on the staff told me not to worry. It was only an oral exam to test the candidate's proficiency to teach through the medium of Irish. I was concerned about having to 'do an oral' but any time I mentioned this, I was reassured by all and sundry that it was a mere formality, 'retained only to stop Greeks and the likes of them from taking up teaching posts in the vocational sector.'

The oral exam was held in the VEC office in Naas during my first Easter holidays. A red faced, reddish haired 'cigire' called O'Muire was my examiner. He grilled in a way that reminded me of the chickens I used to watch revolving in the rotisserie in Fusciardi's chip shop on the main street in Newbridge. When we were done, he told me that my Irish was very weak and that I'd failed. He advised me to go to the Gaeltacht for the summer and that the Department would hold off from re-advertising my post until after the next oral exam, about which I 'would be informed' in due course. I told him that my girl friend was a native Irish speaker and that it would be a pleasure for me to spend time in her home in the Erris Gaeltacht for a few weeks. I have a feeling I may even have thanked him but I'm not sure about this.

The summer holidays flew by and between growing the acre of celery, working myself up to proposing and becoming engaged I never got to utter even a single word of Irish in Bernadette's Gaeltacht or anywhere else. Before I realised it, the holidays were over and I was back teaching in Prosperous. A lively discussion developed as I sat with a few of the other teachers in the little staffroom. Seemingly there had been two 'Rural Science' vacancies the previous summer and I had been the sole applicant. So much for my 'political pull' I thought to myself. The job had been re advertised over the summer and there had been the unprecedented response of seventeen applicants for the one job in Rathangan; thus the liveliness of the discussion.

Suddenly I realised the implications of my failure in the accursed Ceard Teastas. If I was not fully qualified they would be forced to re advertise my job. The inspector had said 'The Department' would contact me in due course about the repeats but I hadn't heard anything from this quarter. I became concerned, very concerned, as I had grown to love teaching in Prosperous. I slipped out and went across the corridor to the Principal's office. I asked Ray if I could make an urgent phone call.

I phoned Bernadette and told her of my unease at not hearing anything. She offered to ring The Department of Education and to phone me back, which she did within a few minutes. I was shocked to be told that the oral exams were being conducted that very day. She had argued with them and they had agreed for me to be allowed to sit the exam at ten o'clock the following morning in Hatch Street in Dublin, where the orals were being conducted. I was appalled at the prospects of this, for the truth was I hadn't thought of the 'Ceard Teastas' since I'd failed it the previous Easter. My declared intention of interacting with Bernadette through Irish and spending time in the Gaeltacht was an example of the self delusion into which I often allowed myself slip. I now became so stressed out, that I seriously considered asking a friend to sit in and do the oral for me. Instead I phoned my girlfriend again.

Bernadette offered to meet me at seven o'clock outside her office in Earlsfort Terrace the following morning to 'converse in Irish for three hours.' Once more did the windows of the little Kadett fog up as the cadence of my fiancée's gentle Irish began to coax my brain to 'smaoineamh tri gaeilge'*. It was excruciatingly difficult at first, but Bernadette was insistent and by ten o'clock the thoughts through Irish were beginning to flow.

'Tú féin aris'* said the same red faced, red haired cigire when he saw me come through the door.. This time, we got on much better. After a while the inspector said to me:

'Tá feabhas mór ar do cuid Gaeilge.'* I had passed 'The Ceard Teastas.' I silently thanked God and my fiancée. I was a now a fully qualified permanent wholetime teacher. The future beckoned.

*'smaoineamh tri gaeilge' 'think through Irish'
*'Tu fein aris?' 'Is it yourself again?'
*'Tá feabhas mór ar do cuid Gaeilge.' 'Your Irish is much improved'

THE BIG QUESTION

Around this time, I came to the full realisation that I was in love with Bernadette. She worked in the Revenue Commissioner's office beside Earlsfort Terrace and lived with her sister Mary's family in Churchtown. We drifted into the routine of Bernadette coming down to Clongorey at the weekends and me going up to Mary's home each Wednesday night. As time slipped by, we relished each others' company more and more until it made no sense to me for us not to be together forever. The question arose in my head of how best to bring this about? I'd never thought too much about marriage before this, now I thought about little else. I waited for the perfect moment to ask the perfect question to get the perfect answer; I waited and waited and waited.

Then one night in June we drove up to the foothills of the Dublin mountains, into a car park on the edge of a forest overlooking the city. I loved Bernadette and I knew that she knew this. I also knew that she loved me but while I was good at humorous repartee and the like, I was genuinely stuck as to how to ask this beautiful woman to be my wife. We sat there in the car park looking at the lights of Dublin spread out before us. The windows of the car were fogged up as usual.

'Bernadette?' There followed a pregnant pause as she looked at me.

'Would you like to be the mother of my children?'

Even as I asked this, I became mortified at the question that had slipped out of my mouth. Bernadette looked into my eyes for a few seconds before she nodded her head up and down. It was hardly the most romantic proposal, but tears of happiness and relief flowed and mixed on our cheeks. A

Charlie and Bessie O'Malley, around the time I asked for Bernadette's hand

palpable lightness and sureness came over me.

I was never great at protocols and I felt I wanted to tell everyone our news and to skip the formality of 'getting engaged' but Bernadette thought differently, so the following weekend we set out on the two hundred mile drive to Mayo. Her father, Charlie O'Malley, was a gentle kind man of whom I was genuinely fond.

I had been to his home a few times over the eighteen months or so since I'd first met his daughter. The only trouble was I found his accent difficult to understand. Bernadette assured me that he found my Kildare accent equally incomprehensible so a fair bit of 'yessing' and nodding would go on whenever we talked. I was a little nervous but felt strong enough in myself as the two of us sat together in that small room in front of the fire. We talked small talk for a while. Both of us spoke slowly. Charlie sensed I was on a mission.

'Myself and Bernadette were thinking of getting married. Would that be ok with you Charlie?' He looked at me for a few seconds before his face broadened into a warm smile.

He then reached over and shook my hand.

'I wish ye both the very best of luck.'

His eyes danced in his head. The two of us laughed easily as the nervousness evaporated up the chimney. He went out of the room and came back with a bottle of poitin that was three quarters full and two small glasses. He filled them to the brim and handed me one. Then he looked me in the eye, tipped my glass as he smiled again and said simply: 'Good health.' We drained the glasses and went back out to the women in the kitchen.

A short time after this I accompanied Bernadette to a jeweller's store in Wicklow Street to hand over seventy pounds for a silver ring with raised diamonds on it. We went outside, I slipped the ring onto the third finger of her left hand and just like that we became engaged.

As often happens to me in the most inappropriate of circumstances I now started to giggle but Bernadette didn't seem to mind. I was deliriously happy and felt like shouting out our news to everyone that passed along the busy Dublin street and probably would have, had I not spotted Tommy Byrne at that very instant. Tommy was the man who'd recruited me to play rugby for Old Kilcullen one chilly morning, after he'd stopped to give me a lift home on the road from Athy. Nothing would do for him but to bring us into the Wicklow

Bernadette and I at a dress dance, The Burlington Hotel 1975

Back, l-r: Tommy Byrne, Frank Conlon, Pat Gleeson, Damien O'Flynn, James Doody, Dermot Cox, Tom Cox, John Doyle, ---------,Noel Heavey. Front, l-r: Dick Burke, Niall Burke, Niall McDonell, Brian McGynn, Hugh O'Rourke, George Fitzpatrick, Peter O'Connell, Bobby Brennan, Stan Orford. Tommy Byrne was the main man behind Old Kilcullen RFC. We are about to take on North Kildare RFC in the Town's Cup, Rosetown, 1973

Hotel and to regale us with his inimitable bonhomie. He bought a bottle of champagne for the three of us and two Havana Cigars. I looked at my fiancée as I exhaled blue smoke and quaffed the finest champagne the Wicklow had to offer. This was the first time in my life I knew what it was like to 'feel like a million dollars.'

After this we drove home to Clongorey to tell my mother and father. When we drove into the yard, we dallied for a few moments before alighting from the car. The pigeons cooed from the big beech tree at the bottom of the garden. It felt like we'd taken a huge step in our lives.

From A Jack to a King

We walked in the door that July afternoon. Mother must have been expecting something because her eyes went straight to Bernadette's left hand and nearly jumped out of her head when she saw the ring on her finger. Our announcement that we were engaged could hardly have been a surprise as we'd been going steady now for over two years. Father grinned broadly from ear to ear then the two of them started to giggle with delight when they heard what they'd been waiting to hear for quite some time. He gave me a huge hug which nearly took my breath away. I looked over at my mother whose cheeks were now smudged with the trickle of tears. For weeks afterwards both of them seemed to smile every time I looked at them.

Before becoming engaged I was a light hearted young teacher without a care in the world. Now I became focused on providing a home for a family, but the question that now preoccupied me was what form this was to take? There was a house on thirty acres up the road which was for sale by public auction. It was owned by Kevin Donohoe who had recently moved to Newbridge and I considered that it would suit us nicely. The manager of the local ACC branch in Naas led me to believe they would finance my bid for the place, but the evening before the auction he rang to inform me that the bank were withdrawing their support for my bid in favour of someone else.

I went to the auction but I was powerless in the circumstances and very angry with the ACC man. However, a few days after this my father offered me the two acre 'field in front of Scotts to build yourselves a home.'

I bought a copy of Bungalow Bliss, studied every plan,

and pored over every one of the seventy three pages at the back which explained in plain language the issues involved in building a home for reasonable money on one's own land. In short time I came to regard myself an expert on matters such as planning permission, loans, grants, thermal values, fascias, soffits and lots of other stuff to do with building. All I needed to know was there in the back of this little orange covered book. Reading about it was one thing, building our home was another story, as I soon began to find out.

There were a couple of house designs in the book which we liked but nothing that really excited us. For two or three months we took particular notice of interesting looking houses as we drove around the place. Sometimes we'd drive into the yard of a particular house that had caught our eyes and explain to the owners that we were about to build a home ourselves and would they mind showing us around? Invariably they did. As the weeks passed into months I began to conceive the essential elements of what was to become our home. I had no skill whatsoever at draughtsmanship but now I started to sketch out what was in our heads, often for hours and hours with a pencil and a rubber. Bernie was involved but not too involved; still she kept a watchful eye on things like wall presses and insisted on us having a utility room.

After Christmas I headed into Noel Fagan, an architectural draughtsman in Newbridge. I had a few rough drawings on an old copy book and I used these to explain what we wanted as best I could. Within a couple of weeks he presented us with a blueprint for our new home. I felt a huge thrill as I examined the plans in detail. Next, I asked a few builders to price building it. They came back with prices ranging from thirty thousand pounds upwards, I knew we couldn't afford this and reluctantly went back to the drawing board or rather Fagan's drawing board, to slice four feet off the whole back of the house, as I'd been told that the builder's pricing formula was to multiply the square footage by whatever figure took their fancy. Our kitchen floor was now twelve feet wide, the width of a roll of Gaff floor covering. Our living room was now four feet shorter and we'd left out the original split in the floor level. Also gone was the brick archway at the bottom of the stairway. We submitted this to the County Council and received planning permission in time to start the groundwork by the first of April.

Before ever starting the job, two things happened which were serious setbacks at the time. My annual salary of three thousand, fifty one pounds and forty four pence meant I was fifty one pounds and forty four pence over the limit to obtain a County Council house building loan which was much more attractive than an ordinary mortgage. I asked in the VEC office if they might underpay me by fifty two pounds to secure the loan but the Senior Officer ran me out of her office for even suggesting such a thing and warned me that if I took unauthorised leave I'd be breaking my contract and would be in danger of losing my job. Then, shortly afterwards, it was announced that the state grant of three hundred and fifty pounds for first time house owners was being withdrawn on the day before I was about to apply for it. We had earmarked this to carpet the house. I became apoplectic and vented my rage in no uncertain terms to an unfortunate work colleague who at the time carried the flag for the Labour Party in the coalition government of the day.

Eventually came the day when we burst through the hedge into the site. The smell of earth being broken in that field for the first time is still with me nearly forty years later. Sean Harris was the JCB owner and also owned a quarry in Kilmeague, he had assured me that I wouldn't beat his price for filling or gravel and that his JCB driver was the best in the business.

COISTE GHAIRM OIDEACHAIS CHO. CHILL DARA
(COUNTY KILDARE VOCATIONAL EDUCATION COMMITTEE)

Oifig an Chontae
(County Office)

Scoil na gCeárd
(Technical School)

Nás na Ri .... 11th Feb. 19 76
(Naas)

Gearóid Ó Cuimín, B.Agr.Sc., Príomh Oifigeach
G. J. Commins, B.Agr.Sc., Chief Executive Officer
Gutháin 045-7358-7885

This is to certify that Mr Noel Heavey,
permanent whole-time Teacher of Rural Science
under my Committee, was in receipt of a total
gross salary of £3,051.44 for the year
1st February 1975 to 31st January 1976.

Signed: *Gearóid Ó Cuimín*
Chief Executive Officer.

VEC Certificate of income, 1976

Father and I loading out roof tiles, as hard a days work as I've ever put in

Father, Mother, Cousin Aidan Morrissey, me, Peter Heavey and a smiling
Bertie Watchorn (extreme right) at my parent's 25th Wedding Anniversary
in the sitting room of Woodbine House

Getting the sub floors ready for concrete

He was correct on both counts. I didn't want straight lines and right angles, so I asked Paud Murphy from Blacktrench to come up to give me a hand to mark out the curve of the driveway and align the foundations, to make the best use of the sun as it made its arc in the sky.

I had purchased a mixer for the back of our little red tractor. My father and Tommy, all fourteen and a half years of him, said they'd give me a hand to mix the foundations. When we went up to the site that Saturday at around eight in the morning Jim Cross from Allenwood was there before us, with his two sons and two tractors with mixers attached. My mother appeared up about noon with steaming tea and with egg and scallion sandwiches; she also gave me blessed medals and scapulars and stood over me until I set them into the four corners. Around five o'clock we finished up. The foundations for our new home were in the ground. I was elated and very proud.

Father divined the spot for the well. I watched as he broke off a forked branch from an Ash tree. He inverted this and held it tightly in both hands. He then walked hither and thither until it swung downwards in his hands. He marked this spot. He then inverted the forked twig again and approached the spot from a completely different direction. When he came to the spot, the twig swung down exactly as before.

The next man on the job was John Champ from up the road with his rig. He had the well bored on the spot my father had marked within a couple of days. In the end there was a difference of a hundred pounds or so in what I owed him and what I thought I owed him. It was a Saturday evening and neither of us wanted to be arguing but both of us thought we were right. In the end I paid him the hundred pounds.

He insisted I accompany him into Naas where he introduced me to German *Blue Nun* wine in the newly opened Chinese restaurant, the first to be located outside Dublin. I forget what we ate and the number of pints or where we drank them but I'll never forget how difficult it was to rise my head off the pillow the following morning.

Just before Easter, the McTeagues arrived on site to lay blocks for the rising walls. When these had set we mixed and poured the sub floors. Shortly afterwards they returned and before long a gable facing dormer bungalow began to take shape. Bernie and I felt a tingling in our bellies one Sunday evening as we surveyed the profile of our future home rise into the Clongorey skyline. I had agreed a price with my cousin Dakie Murphy to do the plastering and he arrived with his gang from Newbridge. These had a completely different way of going about their work from the Allen men and tensions arose from time to time but within a short while our skeletal house acquired its layers of skin. All this occurred during the summer holidays at the same time as I'd taken on the celery project. The schedule called for the house to be ready for us to move into on our return from honeymoon at the end of August.

It was all very busy with plenty stress and no shortage of rows, arguments and trepidations between me and most of the people I was dealing with. An exception was Pa Dunne, who was married to my cousin May. They had a builder's yard in Allenwood. I had priced the roof timbers from several businesses but he beat them all hands down. He also became my *go to man*, anytime I needed advice on anything to do with building. Pa was the main reason I brought the whole project to completion for under fourteen thousand pounds, thus saving ourselves a fortune compared to what it would have cost had I taken on a builder.

BACK TO BELFIELD

The fourteenth of August was our date with destiny. Bernadette and I had chosen Belfield as our wedding church, which I found a little disconcerting because I associated it with being stressed out around exam time. I was and continue to be a great believer in lighting candles in my hour of need.

Finding a place for the reception and making countless other arrangements involved a whole range of considerations and detail that I found difficult. This was where Bernie came into her own, I was more than happy to go along with her lead. We had checked out a few hotels and were on the point of choosing one in Killiney when her father Charlie, on holiday with his daughters in Churchtown, suggested we consider The County Club which at that stage was the preeminent cabaret venue in south Dublin, and where my future brother-in-law, Peader Fitzpatrick worked as assistant manager. We went down to meet the chef and concluded a deal to hold our wedding reception there.

Frank Kilcoyne, a teaching colleague, agreed to be my best man. What with building our house and growing celery, time seemed to fly that summer. It came nearly as a shock to contemplate having a stag party, the first one I ever went to, a couple of days before the wedding. Someone had told me of a fellow from Newbridge who'd been ambushed at his stag, stripped and had his scrotum blackened with shoe polish. I couldn't for the life of me envisage anything of this nature occurring to me but, just in case, I had it arranged with Frank that if there were any sudden moves on me he was to knockout the perpetrator there and then, regardless of who it was. In the event, six or seven friends showed up in Coffey's of

Enjoying a cuppa in Woodbine House before leaving for Coffey's of Caragh for my Stag party. Me, Tosh Daly, Danny Challoner and Frank Kilcoyne

Caragh; we drank a few pints, had a chat and that was it.

The big day duly arrived. I was amazed how calm I thought I was, until I went about shaving myself. Within seconds of nicking my lower lip, blood started to ooze and ooze and wouldn't stop. I started to curse and swear which had the effect of turning the ooze into something much heavier. Father came to the rescue with his corner of a newspaper trick which eventually stemmed the flow.

It was a fabulously sunny morning which, for some strange reason, put me in mind of a particular day of my early childhood when Mother gathered all the kids of Artillery Place in the garden of our little house in Moorefield. That day we had a picnic and she showed us how to make daisy chains. Today I was getting married and I felt on top of the world, even as the cut on my lip oozed a little every now and again, just to remind me it was still there.

We were well ahead of schedule and I thought to divert to Meadow Mount in Churchtown just to see that everything was okay and maybe just to see Bernie for a few seconds but I wasn't let 'next nor near her.' My aunt's husband, Willie Carroll was there before me, he was busy tying a light blue ribbon onto the bonnet of his white Citroen that was to drive the bride to her wedding. Frank, Tosh and I drove on.

When I saw our friends and relations gathered outside the church I became nervous. We small talked for a while, but I wasn't really in form for this and went on up to the front of the church. After a while Frank whispered:

'She's outside.'

I glanced around, and when I saw the church was more or less full, a surge of adrenaline flowed through me. The organist started to play *Amazing Grace* and the next thing I knew Bernadette was there beside me, smiling into my eyes. I couldn't keep them off her. Frank had to nudge me as Charlie stood there with his arm stretched out. I shook his hand, then Fr Conlon took control. The photographs seemed to take ages but our photographer was irrepressible and we all just did as we were told.

We drove then in convoy a couple of miles to The County Club in Churchtown. My memory of most of what happened hereafter is blurred but I remember a spontaneous round of applause when I thanked Bernie's Aunt Bridgie for coming all the way from New Jersey. It was her first trip home in fifty years. Bernie and I sang *The Spinning Wheel* which we'd been practicing for weeks whenever we were alone in the car.

Day melted into night and before we realised it we were in the middle of the floor for the last dance as the band played *Congratulations*. Next, the crowd lined up two by two to form a snake like arch, through which we had to pass as we bade and received goodbyes from our friends and loved ones.

Husband and Wife emerging from the church in Belfield at 1.05pm August 14th, 1976

I was caught unawares as copious tears now began to flow. Eventually we were ushered out to our waiting Avenger estate, destroyed with shaving cream and lurid advice written in large letters with thick red lipstick. To cheers and thumps on the roof I pointed the car in the direction of the Montrose Hotel. Tin cans clattered off the tarmac as I drove hard down the road.

SCOTLAND THE BRAVE

Canoeing to the shore on our honeymoon the day before
we canoed on the lake

It was Tuesday evening by the time we drove into Stirling, the gateway to the Highlands. This was to be the centre for our honeymoon. We hardly regarded Scotland as exotic but it was a foreign country, and I was able to drive my own, or rather our own car. Planning the honeymoon was my contribution to the nuptial arrangements. This I had done through leafing through The AA illustrated roadbook of Scotland and paraphernalia from the Scottish Tourist Board. I had chosen a bed and breakfast run by a Mrs Wallace who turned out to be a kind elderly widow, chuffed to have honeymooners stay in her semi detached home on the edge of town. She had given good directions but when we came to a roundabout outside the town late that evening, we couldn't decide which road to take, so we drove around the roundabout a couple of times trying to get our bearings. Within seconds a police car pulled us over, took our details and held us there on the side of the road for ages while they checked us out. Welcome to Scotland.

It was harvest time and the dominant feature in the fields as we drove past were giant round bales, the likes of which I'd never seen before. The sun shone high in the sky and all was well with the world. We stopped one afternoon in a quiet out of the way spot by a river to hire an Indian canoe which we paddled down the perfectly still river. Bees buzzed around wild flowers on the banks but they were busy and didn't bother us. A kingfisher flew across the river just above the waterline. We came to a little strand and pulled over. The following day we came on a similar place and we hired another Indian canoe. Heavenliness was now synonymous for us with paddling and we again experienced it here, for the first half hour. We then came to the mouth of a lake and paddled for the far shore. Suddenly the wind whipped up, the water now became choppy and started coming in over the side of the canoe. We began to paddle for the shore as if our lives depended on it but I could see we were making no progress whatsoever. Out of nowhere now, the chap who had hired out the boat appeared beside us in his kayak. He calmed us and led the way out of the dangerous current back to dry land. There was no further hiring of Indian canoes.

It was late evening in an isolated part of the Highlands, we had camping equipment in the back of the car and weren't adverse to camping out in any of the beautifully scenic little spots all around us. However it was cold, too cold for honeymooners not to be in a nice warm bed. We found ourselves in a small mountain village called Tomintoul, the highest inhabited village in Scotland, so it said in the road book. We looked around and were relieved to find a B&B, which would take us in so late in the evening. The landlady

Taking a break on the mountainside

wasn't especially friendly but we just wanted to get to bed. She led us to the bedroom and left.

'I don't like this place,' was the first thing Bernie said to me, when we were alone. Then she saw the cerise bri-nylon sheets on the bed:

'Jesus, look at those sheets.'

'What's wrong with them?'

In answer I got a look that told me my chances that night had suddenly plummeted. When she threw back the sheets she visibly paled and stood there without saying a word. I went across to have a look. There were three black hairs half way down the bed. They weren't all that short but they were most definitely curly. It was now dark outside and as close to freezing as made no difference. Leaving and pitching our tent in some adjacent meadow was not an option. Inspiration suddenly flew into my brain. I ran out to the car, rummaged around and came back with two sleeping bags which we zipped together. The atmosphere now changed and Cupid smiled.

One of the reasons we'd come to Scotland was because of the music and song which we expected to encounter around every corner, but we never heard traditional music of any description until near the very end. However we sang songs we never even realised we knew as we drove along the small sun drenched roads. The faint perfume of the blooming mountainsides was intoxicating as it wafted through the open windows. I stopped and pulled a sprig of purple heather to place behind my wife's ear and we sang.

> *Oh the summer time is coming, and the trees are sweetly blooming*
> *And the wild mountain thyme grows around the blooming heather.*
> *Will you go lassie go?*
> *And we'll all go together, to pluck wild mountain thyme all around the blooming heather.*
> *Will you go lassie go?*

Another of my favourite songs was Bernadette's version of The Lough Tay Boat Song. This we sang over and over as we drove along the length of the beautiful Lough Tay, mostly I listened, as Bernie sang like a lark fluttering high above Clongorey bog on a glorious summer's day.

> *When I've done my work of day, And I row my boat away,*
> *Doon the waters of Loch Tay, as the evening sun is setting*
> *And I look upon Ben Lawers where the after glory glows;*
> *And I think of two bright eyes and the melting mouth below.*
> *She's my beauteous nighean ruadh, she's my joy and sorrow too;*
> *And although she is untrue, well I cannot live without her,*
> *For my heart's a boat in tow and I'd give the world to know*
> *Why she means to let me go, as I sing horee horo.*

*Nighean ruadh, your lovely hair has more glamour I
   declare*
Than all the tresses rare 'tween Killin and Aberfeldy.
*Be they lint white, brown or gold, be they blacker than
   the sloe*
*They are worth no more to me than the melting flake of
   snow…*

We stopped for a while on the old bridge at Aberfeldy until someone came along and broke the spell with the honk of a horn.

It wasn't until we made our way to Glasgow that we encountered a music performance of any kind. I had spotted a poster for Calum Kennedy who turned out to be a thick-set man in a kilt. He had a huge voice and we enjoyed him and his daughters who performed with him. We moved on to Edinburgh where I couldn't get a beer because it was Sunday even though the famous Arts festival was in full swing. I can still recall the Tattoo, the highlight of which was a squad of American marines rifle drilling with a precision that mesmerised me. In the middle of their display I had a flashback of Willy Kiernan and Peter Flanagan drawing loud howls of derision from our drill sergeant as we strutted our stuff on the FCA parade on the quad of Newbridge College every Saturday afternoon.

Edinburgh is a gray city. That weekend, there were clouds and showers which weren't at all inappropriate as we both knew the honeymoon was coming to its end. We wanted now to be the far side of the Irish Sea, to start the rest of our lives together. It was time to be going home.

ACROSS THE THRESHOLD

Our house was all but finished. The builders had worked hard but on the day of the wedding there were still two weeks work left before we could move into it. On returning from our honeymoon we found everything just as we'd left it. This was a huge disappointment as it meant we couldn't move in. My mother however had made ready the sitting room in Woodbine House while we waited for our new home to be completed. We were thankful for this but on the second Saturday morning we were awoken by a loud banging on the door.

'Are you getting up? It's gone eleven o'clock and the sun is splitting the rocks' My mother wasn't one for mincing words when she'd something on her mind.

She loved her son but loved nothing better than having her new daughter-in-law to herself. The understanding was that the men took care of things outside, leaving issues inside the house to the women.

'We'll be there in a minute,' I shouted instinctively. I looked at my wife who looked right back at me. 'Bernadette, we're going to move into our own house today.'

'What? Everyone knows it isn't ready, moving now will only cause bad feeling.'

'I don't care, we're moving today.'

The smell of raw concrete pervaded the house. There was no floor covering of any description. The kitchen presses were only half finished and there wasn't any skirting in any of the rooms. Most of the internal doors weren't even hung yet, but the walls were beginning to dry out as I'd been lighting a fire each day in the Stanley cooker. The back boiler was connected to the radiators in each of the rooms.

We had electricity and water. We had enough.

That afternoon I installed our bed in our bedroom. I then called Bernie over, grabbed her up into my arms and carried her through our front doorway across our yet to be installed threshold. It wasn't the way I'd planned it but for better or worse, we were now ensconced in our new home. It's a fine house that has been nearly finished now for close on forty years.

As was the way at the time we hadn't lived together before our wedding. Both of us had grown up in fifties and sixties Ireland when liberal notions of young people enjoying their sexuality before marriage were obliterated before they even got to be thoughts, due to the pervasive influence of a Church at the zenith of its power. For sure there were grabbed moments in our young lives when we'd go to the brink but whatever pleasure there was came with a huge dollop of guilt. Now we were a young newly married couple but even within marriage the 'shepherds of the flock' tried to dictate that contraception was only permissible by 'the natural method' of abstention from lovemaking during the fertile phase of the menstrual cycle. Condoms and the use of the pill were considered artificial and as such were forbidden. Occasionally this issue was addressed at Sunday Mass much to our embarrassment and annoyance. We had caught the winds of change blowing through the land and figured out such matters for ourselves.

In the back of my mind was the question of whether or not we would be able to have children at all but this was put on hold because of Bernie's work situation. The custom and practice of the time was for female civil servants to work on for a time after marriage, then to resign and start a family. To encourage this, the marriage gratuity or lump sum became unavailable after two years. This was tax free, worth a year's salary and was an inherent part of our financial plan, but there were two years during which she was 'allowed' to work.

Bernie's job was in Dublin and even though she secured a lift there and back it was seven thirty or so in the evening before she was home, while I was free during term from four o'clock onwards. With time on my hands, I found myself against all expectations taking responsibility for shopping for groceries and preparing meals. We'd been given *Mrs Beeton's Cookery in Colour* as a wedding present and it became my bible as I took to adventurous cooking. The trick, I found, was to study the instructions carefully and to rewrite them in my own words. My favourite was lamb curry, for which I had to ensure we always had the ingredients, including a spoon of plum jam. I can still see the smile on Bernie's famished face when she caught the smell of the curry as she walked in the door.

It was most unusual at the time for a man to be seen shopping with his wife in a supermarket but this didn't bother me one little bit. Over time I became the shopper in the house and because of this I began to notice how my eyes were attracted to certain items on the supermarket shelves and just as interestingly how they were not attracted to others. I didn't realise it at the time but my doing this simple chore was to bestow a significant business advantage to me later in life. We found ways to subsume our individualities into our new situation without too much pain but it wasn't always easy particularly for Bernie who had to make her home in a new place. Also, she had dropped her own surname to take on the Heavey surname. This was and remains the custom, but it must be heart wrenching, especially when one loves their family as much as Bernie loved hers.

That first winter our house was new, raw and very much incomplete. Bare concrete floors with the odd mat here and there were our lot but we were both so happy to be in our own home. However, there was much to be to be done with any spare moment that presented itself. Bernie had lately

Black Taaffe, founding
spirit behind Clongorey
Football Club
1977 - 1987

discovered magnolia coloured emulsion and we purchased
something like ten large cans of the stuff. Most painting jobs I
detested but covering bare walls of our empty rooms with the
newly introduced squeegee roller was easy. Every so often,
Bernadette would come in to check that the emulsion was
applied evenly and that there were no drips. It was this job
I was diligently doing in our soon-to-be-finished sitting room
when I heard someone outside shouting: 'Wellup?, Wellup?'
at the top of his voice. 'Who in the name of God is that?' asked
Bernadette from the kitchen, where she was ironing clothes.

The paths had just been installed but the yard was still rough
and I was afraid whoever it was out there would fall as it was a
dark, dirty night. I went to the door to find Black (Donald) Taffe
standing there in front of me. Black had been centre back on
the Clongorey team that had won the junior B Championship
in1958 and had only recently returned after being in England
for years.

'Black? Come in, come in.' I said.

'No I'm doing the rounds, look we're going to start her up
agin. You're to come to a meeting In Bertie Watchorn's yard
this Sunday morning at twelve o'clock.'

'Start up what again? Can't you come in?'

'No, I've men to see. We're starting up the Clongorey team
agin. Be there on Sunday morning, young Havey.' He turned
on his heel and was gone.

CLONGOREY

I was seven years old when Clongorey beat Kildoon in the 1958 Junior B Championship. Black Taffe was a colossus on that team, as was my father, even though he was at the very end of his football career. Sappy, as my father was called throughout the length and breadth of Kildare, was well known for his feisty performances in the Forties for Raheens and for the County team but the only memory I have of him playing football is his bursting forth from a melee in the blue, black and white hoops of Clongorey and clearing the ball up the field. There were no more than fifty households altogether in the townlands of Clongorey, Blacktrench, Lattensbog and Barrettstown, yet it was one of the best supported teams in the county but when it came to older players retiring there just wasn't the youth to replace them and so it slipped out of existence.

That was then, this was now. I'd played for the county minors and once or twice had been on the panel of a great UCD team but there was little regard for my football prowess in Raheens, where I'd been told I was lucky to be picked for the junior team. I was now twenty five years old and there were several other Clongorey men of my vintage playing for Raheens including PJ Earley, his brother Ken, Jim and Laurence Scott Donoghoe, Black's youngest brother Marty Taffe and the legendary Chicky Mills who had boxed for Ireland. Other Clongorey men played for Sarsfields in Newbridge and there were others who didn't bother playing for anyone at all. Maybe Black was on to something.

Seven or eight of us looked at each other that Sunday morning in Bertie Watchorn's yard. It was a miserable day as cold December rain teemed down on top of us. We moved into an empty shed where we shivered as we stood around. Without preamble, Bertie looked over at me.

'Well Noel you'd better start us off.' He said, I looked back at him. My mind was a complete blank but at the same time I felt excited at the possibility that we might be able to re form Clongorey and play for our own little place.

'So how many footballers do we think we can get?' I asked as I looked around. We started to name the players in the townlands of Clongorey, Blacktrench and Barrettstown. We were going through them house by house until someone asked:

'Why don't we just organise a practice match and see what happens?'

'Exactly,' said Black

The following Sunday over twenty men togged out and played the practice match in Pat Heavey's field behind Lynham's house. It was the first time that 'togged off' footballers had played football in Clongorey for nearly twenty years. We knocked lumps off each other that morning but when it was over we were exhilarated with the turnout and the attitude of everyone there. The news of what we were up to swept through the countryside like a fire on top of the bog. Many thought and said we were stupid to think we could sustain a club but the more this was thought and said the more determined were the few of us who now believed, really believed, that Clongorey could rise up again. Jim Scott Donohoe, who'd won a senior championship medal with Raheens the previous season was now on board and his energy and commitment made a huge difference. Along with PJ and myself he assumed responsibility for giving life to our dream. My father knew someone on the Curragh who procured for us a new set of blue, black and white hooped jerseys, as worn by the men of fifty eight.

There weren't too many used to meetings which in the

beginning were chaotic but before long we had formed a committee. I was asked to be chairman. I was also asked to coach the team on which I fancied myself as a midfielder. PJ, Jim and his brother Laurence also played vital roles on our committee as well as on the field of play. We were busy men as we plotted and planned, discussed and argued among ourselves but all the time we moved inexorably towards getting ourselves accepted as a new club by the county board. We recruited and begged footballers to join us until we were satisfied that we had all the positions covered. Then we raised whatever money we needed with a door to door collection. I had been part of a setup in UCD that trained under Eugene McGee. His were the ways I now adopted. My team mates responded well and after we played a challenge match against Allenwood, we knew we'd be able to hold our own.

When the day came for us to play our first official game fifteen previously disillusioned young men were now a determined ambitious team. I was bursting with excitement and pride as we ran onto a pitch on the edge of the Curragh to take on Athgarvan that first Sunday in March 1977. It was division three of the junior league but to us and our supporters it was the most important match ever played. We won it by six points and that night we gathered up in Mulrennans Bar, just down from the Hill Of Allen to replay every kick and belt given and taken on that day of days.

The next game was against Rathcoffey, after which I had to be brought to the casualty ward in Naas hospital to have my top lip stitched up after it came into violent contact with the elbow of a Rathcoffey man. Our nineteen year old corner back, John Taffe ran fifty yards to drop my assailant like the proverbial 'sack of spuds' with a single punch. Thus was our 'We're not to be messed with' ethos born. That night we again gathered in Mulrennan's bar to savour our second win in two games. Everyone had opinions on the performances of the day and weren't slow about expressing them. I remember spilling Guinness on my good shirt after I had to I had to readjust things to drink through the corner of my mouth in order to avoid the stitches.

We were now being referred to as 'The Cinderella team.' I'm not sure that any of us understood what this was supposed to mean but I started to use it anyway to drive us on more and more as we trained in the field rented from my uncle Martin(Gunner). The week before we played our first home game we readied our pitch to host the first official game in Clongorey for nineteen years. The rushes in the middle of the field were given short shrift with a couple of cuttings with a tractor mower. The big job was to erect the goal posts for which Black had secured the trunks of four pine trees from the Hill of Allen. Everyone lent a hand as we converted the rushy field into a football pitch.

Both teams togged out in cars under the hawthorn hedge. Eadestown were a dour lot. At the end of a really hard fought game, played in a downpour, we had scored three points to their single goal – a draw. The honeymoon was over but we were still unbeaten. After the game some of them asked where they 'could have a wash?' I brought them down to the mearn stream at the far side of the pitch where the cold black water flowed directly from the bog. There the players from both teams washed off the debris of battle as best we could before getting into our cars to drive home.

The following Tuesday night after we'd trained in the field, Larry Kelly of the '58 team approached a few of us with a black sack in his hand. 'I wasn't sure that things would work out but you're to have these. They'll come in handy.' He said as he handed over the sack. The distinctive aroma of mothballs assailed our nostrils as we opened the sack to reveal a set of old blue, black and white hooped jerseys. A couple of them were torn and there were old brown blood stains as well but the spirit of fifty eight was now out of the bag.

My mother who came to all our games that first year used to recite an old rhyme to eulogize the word 'if' and it comes to mind anytime I recall the final minute of our first championship match.

If all the world were apple pie?
If all the seas were ink?
If all the trees were bread and cheese,
Then what would people drink?

Kill, who had burst our bubble in the league after the draw with Eadstown, were out and out favourites to win the Junior B championship. They were our opponents that afternoon in Prosperous. They had scored a couple of goals early on and were coasting to victory albeit by a mere three points when I experienced the most powerful surge of power and focus in all my twenty years of playing championship football. It was in the very last minute of the game during which I'd only been middling but at the very death, a serene feeling of calmness descended on me. This came of knowing exactly what I was about to do and the sure-fire knowledge that nobody in the world was going to stop me. When the ball came towards me, I propelled myself way above the other three midfielders to make an almighty fetch. Landing on the run I soloed a few steps before unleashing a shot from fully forty yards out that was in the Kill net before anyone could react in any way.

Had the consequent kick out come to within twenty yards of me, I'm absolutely certain I'd have it caught and sent over the bar but the referee blew for the draw and Kill went on to win the replay. Many great football moments would come my way in the eight years of championship football still left in me but never again would I experience anything like the majesty of those fleeting seconds. That spring of step and power of limb would never come my way again, but I feel very privileged and thankful to have experienced that single minute of true greatness. If I had it in me to reproduce this in moments of need, I'd have been one the greats of Kildare football. My mother's eulogy to one of the smallest words in the lexicon seemed so apt.

STRAWBERRIES AND BERLIN

Our new house stands on two acres. The strawberries are planted to the right (with polythene cloches). Behind the house is an acre of potatoes that have not yet emerged

S trawberries are a tricky crop to grow and sell. I had made a fair fist of the celery, but the market for this had disappeared. Now I had an acre of strawberries in the ground and I was told I could expect to make over a thousand pounds per annum but the reality was a long way from this. They were easy enough to grow but getting them to market and being paid the price I needed was the tricky bit.

It seemed the easiest thing in the world to show the kids who clamoured for a job that summer how to pick by the stem just behind the calyx but the pay was by the punnet, and their perception was that it was faster to pick the fruit itself. For this reason, it was a constant battle for me to produce berries without bruising. Ned Cross from Pluckerstown also grew them and had done so for years before I 'chanced my arm'. He was a good natured man and his encouragement and advice was very helpful.

Ned introduced me to a man on one of the *produce banks* in the Smithfield market behind the Four Courts in Dublin who undertook to sell strawberries on my behalf. As I walked around the market stands I could see at first hand that other people's produce was more uniform and firmer than mine which consequently sold for a lesser price. The bidding was fast and furious for Ned's produce but when it came to mine, it slowed and the price fell accordingly. It was a difficult but exciting time in my life with big money tied up in a crop I didn't feel all that confident about.

That first morning I drove up to Smithfield I was there before five o'clock. Ned had warned me to be there early to secure a place in the queue as the 'early berries get the best money.' My father had insisted on accompanying me. He was proud and a little excited,but after a half hour waiting in the stationary queue outside the market which wasn't due to open for another two hours, he grew restless and headed off for a ramble, as he called it. There were a few pubs around Smithfield that had licences to open early. He sauntered into one of these and didn't come back until just before seven, by which time he was reeking from the smell of drink. He kept shaking his head in the car muttering:

'Don't fuckin' go into any of them places. The people in there are up to no good.'

He never did disclose exactly what had made such a strong impression on him. I went in a few times after that but all I ever saw were boring old farts. He came up with me most mornings for the first week or so but after that, the novelty wore off. He wasn't with me on a morning I stopped in Inchicore to make a phone call on the way home. The first two phone boxes had their receivers ripped out, but the third seemed OK. I dialled my number without paying attention, but I remember experiencing a squishy cold feeling on the tip of my chin. When I looked down, I could hardly believe my eyes as the mouthpiece was filled to the brim with greenish stodgy material with prominent pieces of undigested carrot in there as well. I recognised the smell of vomit and very nearly got sick myself. Instead I threw the receiver from me and walked quickly to the car at the same time trying to scrape the affected flesh from my chin. Some of it was now on my hand and in my anguish I wiped it on the leg of my trousers. Whether the smell was coming from my imagination, chin or trousers I have no idea but it grew my agitation and I was in a state by the time I reached Newlands Cross. Here, I copped two hitch hikers. Without thinking, I pulled in as was my custom back then, having spent years wagging my thumb there many thousands of times trying to make eye contact with any driver who'd give me a lift down the road.

'Killarney?' he asked as I leaned over to roll down the window.

'Will Clongorey do?'

'Where is Clongorey?' He asked this in a foreign accent.

'It's on the way. Get in quick if you want a lift, I'm in bad form and I'm in a hurry.'

He surveyed me with quizzical blue eyes before looking at his tiny girlfriend who was staring at me. I then noticed that the seats in the back were still down in my Avenger Estate and I had to get out of the car to pull them upright. I was beginning to regret having pulled in, but within seconds the small lady and the huge rucksacks were sitting in the back seat. The blond man with long straggly hair overlapping a similar type of beard, in such a way that they were indistinguishable, sat in the passenger seat beside me.

He spoke slowly and deliberately in his strange accent as we sped down *the dual carriageway*. By the time we reached Naas I had established they were from West Berlin and that this was their first foray away from home. The trauma from my recent experience had by now dissipated, even if the hint of a residual odour remained. I realised I'd warmed to this strange couple and without thinking things through I asked him in earnest if they'd like to come to my home. He turned around and spoke a few words to his lady who shrugged and uttered 'Ja'. He told me his name was Hans and then he formally introduced me to Lotte, who gave me a huge big smile. We turned right without stopping at *The Bundle of Sticks*. They were minutes away from being the first Berliners ever to breathe air in Clongorey.

When I pulled into the yard, he informed me they needed to sleep. Bernadette was at work and warm feeling or not, I daren't let total strangers into our home without me being there. I couldn't stay with them as I had to face into a mountain of work that day. He read my eyes and insisted that he would pitch their tent in the adjoining field. I brought them down to a quiet spot behind the hedge in Stanley's field and bade them adieu, as I went on about the business of harvesting strawberries for the following morning's market.

I actually forgot about them until I drove in the gate that evening, having collected Bernie from her lift. As we got out of the car I heard shouts in the adjoining field and when we looked out, there was the frightened looking Lotte holding her broken spectacles with nothing on her except a skimpy white knickers and a pink bra. All her man had on was a funny looking underpants.

'Wild animals try to kill us,' he roared as he gesticulated his long white arms in the air.

'Jesus Christ,' I said to myself.

Bernadette said nothing, she just stood there gazing in wonder. I went into action mode straightaway and ran to our wardrobe to find them some clothes. He was incandescent with rage as he struggled in vain to find English words to express his anger at what had happened. After a while we went down to the tent to investigate. Ten or so bullocks were grazing in the field close to the tent. He pointed and started rattling on again about 'wild animals'. I whooshed them away. They resumed grazing within a few yards. He was amazed and a little embarrassed. My two guests had been awoken from a deep sleep to find large bullocks with lowered heads snorting and dribbling as they smelt the tent with the two stretched out sleeping bodies inside. The Berliners panicked, never before having seen cattle. When I discovered this I tried to make light of the situation by telling him silly jokes but I think 'they went over his head.' The cattle were used to people and I got him to scratch their haunches to take his mind off their embarrassment.

Lotte demurred from this but they were able to laugh about it as we walked up the field with the rucksacks. It had been a long day and we all ravished the rashers, sausages, eggs and beans put before us by my patient wife. I then brought them up to the spare room to offer them the new bed which we'd purchased the previous week. He said he'd come to the market with me the following morning.

Over the next few days Hans became my shadow. He was about the same age as me and wasn't slow about helping out with whatever I was doing which was mostly trying to get strawberries ready for the following morning's market. He had eyes like a hawk and if he saw fruit being picked incorrectly he'd let a roar out of him which had the desired effect, as the pickers were somewhat afraid of him. The quality and price for my fruit improved from the day he stepped into the strawberry field which was just behind our house. Bernie was now on holidays and she and Lotte became good friends as well. They sewed, baked and gardened in the poly tunnel beside the beech hedge. Lotte was quiet natured but as the time slipped by she came out of herself. Even if she was small in comparison with her man I could see from the start that she was the boss.

Clongorey football team trained on Tuesday and Thursday evenings, Hans came up to the football field with me and after the first evening, he insisted on playing in goals where he took no prisoners. We had been beaten by Kill in the championship, but there were still league matches to be played and the selectors were more than interested in our six foot plus goalkeeper who was told that his name was now Harry Murphy and that he was to be our goalkeeper against Straffan who we were to play that Sunday.

The strawberries season was coming to a close but there was one last big pick on the Friday. That evening after the pick, I brought him down for a swim in the Liffey at Victoria Bridge, where he swam like a giant fish. We dried off and went on down to Coffeys in Caragh to have a pint or two, as we both reckoned it was the least we deserved after the hard week that was now nearly over. Hans took to the Guinness like a duck to water and the one or two, became five or six or maybe more. The ladies were asleep by the time we arrived home. I set the alarm for five o'clock, went to bed and slept like a log. The only problem was I hadn't turned on the alarm and it was half past seven by the time I awoke. I knew that in all probability the fruit auctions would be over by the time we'd travel up to Smithfield.

I woke Hans and we drove off without breakfast and without too much conversation. My worst fears were realised. The auctions were over by the time we arrived in Smithfield. Now I had fifty trays of the nicest strawberries you ever saw sitting in the back of the Avenger Estate, with twelve pounds of fruit in each tray. I drove into town and pulled up on the corner of Stephen's Green, at the top of Grafton Street, where we unloaded half the trays to set up our stall. I started to call out:

'Fresh ripe fruit for sale!'

Hans went about imitating me but after a while it became obvious that this wasn't working. In truth, we weren't of the best appearance or in the best of form for attracting custom. At around ten o'clock or so I reloaded up the Avenger and headed for the red bricked semi detached houses at the back of Rathmines.

'When you ring the bell, step back from the door, when someone answers look down at the fruit and ask. "Would you like to buy some fresh fruit please?" Okay Hans?'

'How much we sell for?' he asked

'Fifty pence per punnet but try to get them to take three for a pound.'

Without further ado, Hans grabbed a tray, went to the nearest door and rang the bell. We worked the two sides of the street. Most of the people were old dears and bought our fruit in most of the houses where the bell was answered. Han's English had come on well in the ten days since his arrival and I had to tell him not to get involved in long conversations as time now was of the essence. Over the course of the morning, I noticed he had to go back to the Avenger more often than me to replenish stock. By the time lunch hour arrived we had sold over thirty boxes but had now started to run out of houses. Bernie's sister Mary lived out in Churchtown and it was to there we now drove. First we stopped in the County Club, where our wedding reception had been, less than a year before. We felt good in ourselves as we tucked into the most deserved and appreciated toasted sandwiches eaten in Dublin that day.

My good spirits had returned. These may have been responsible for the dodgy inspiration that now flashed into my head when we were in the toilet. I didn't need to use the cubicle, he did. I went back out as he waited for a cubicle to become available. After a couple of minutes I returned and pretended to be an impatient Dubliner in urgent need of a cubicle and very much 'under the weather.' I started banging at the door of his cubicle and in a fair imitation of a drunken Dublin accent started to roar in a loud voice:

'Hurry up for fuck's sake, are you going to be in there all day?'

This had the effect of eliciting a string of loud Germanic curses much to the bemusement of regulars who came into the toilet after me. Each time I banged on the door, the Germanic curses became louder. I bolted after I heard the flush and was sitting calm and cool eating my sandwich when he came back in to the bar. Metaphorical steam was coming out of my friend's ears. When he excitedly started to tell me what had happened in the toilet I started to shake with laughter. He looked at me long and hard and I quickly realised I was very close to getting a 'skelp.' I apologised as best I could. He was pissed off with me but this didn't stop him from selling more than me as the afternoon wore on into the evening. By the time we finished, all that was left were four punnets of very tired strawberries and I had over two hundred pounds in my pocket which was more than 'a good whack' of my total profit for the entire three week season.

The following day we travelled to Straffan for the league match. They had a big hardy full forward who stuck his elbow into Hans, now masquerading as Harry Murphy. This immediately elicited the loud string of Germanic curses that I'd heard the day before. I could see them looking at him now with a curious eye. I also knew that if the big full forward went in again he was going to get more than a string of Germanic curses and

Hans would have to give his name when being sent off. We would be brought before the county board and then there would be hell to pay. As well as being chairman, coach and player I was also the County Board delegate and I didn't need this hassle one little bit. I made a sign to the selectors on the sideline and they substituted him.

'Harry' wasn't one bit pleased to be taken off. To compound matters we lost the game and there was a loquacious inquiry held up in Mulrennans Bar that night. We drank more than was good for us and sang songs to beat the band. Hans wasn't as good a singer as Harry was a goalkeeper, but there was no stopping him when he got going.

I left Hans and Lotte to the train station the following afternoon. We have never been in contact since. I often wonder what became of them. We shared the best part of two extraordinary weeks together when two young couples 'with neither chick nor child' and from completely different backgrounds came to appreciate our different ways and cultures. It was a time never to be forgotten.

1978
1. LIFE

For the first year or so of our marriage we took precautions to avoid Bernadette becoming pregnant. It was 'the done thing' at the time for female civil servants to work on for two years after their wedding, then retire with a lump sum free of tax to start a family. During this time we were hypersensitive to snide inquiries from 'smart arse' friends and acquaintances as to whether there was anything stirring?' Quite a few of these found their way into my metaphorical little black book reserved especially for 'the thickest of the thick.'

That was for the first year and a half, now the preoccupation changed to full steam ahead on the baby-making front and while this new scenario had obvious positives there now emerged the doubt that had lurked in the back of my mind. What if we couldn't? I experienced considerable angst as well as exhilaration as we nightly went about our business. Even though I taught biology, I still felt I had to read the relevant chapter of the Well Woman book a few times to fully comprehend the implications of a sexually active woman being 'late, which Bernadette was a few months after our change of tack. Just to be sure she made an appointment to see her doctor, whose surgery was near her workplace in Dublin.

There was only one telephone for the whole school in the Principal's office next door to my Science Room where I taught. I heard it ringing just before lunch but Ray had it answered before I got there.

'It's Bernadette' he said as he handed me the receiver.

I'm not sure whether I hollered or chortled when she confirmed that I was going to be a daddy. Suddenly the world was a different place as I tried in vain not to walk on air. I was now more than half way through my second year of a job that I'd come to love. Ray O'Malley, the principal of the Vocational school in Prosperous had introduced Agricultural Science for the Leaving Certificate. I was the teacher and had taken to this development like a duck to water. Also my father had asked me to take over the responsibility of farming our small holding. I had organised Pat Kane, an elderly farmer and a genial character from Mylerstown, to plough, till and sow our twenty acre field in Barrettstown. This he had done by Saint Patrick's Day. He agreed to my request to come into the school and prepare a half acre seed bed to allow me demonstrate the practical side of what I was teaching and at a cost of little more than the price of the diesel. It was a busy time on his farm and there was no sign of Pat. I fretted that it might be getting too late 'to sow spuds' and said this to him when I called in one evening after school.

'Not at all young Havey, you're time enough as long as you can see a blackbird in an ash tree.' I looked in puzzlement at the big ash he was looking at and we both grinned when I realised, whilst looking at the still intact black buds, that the growing season was still early enough. He completed the job soon after this and I promptly sent his invoice into the County Office for payment. The only outcome of this was a visit from the CEO who berated me for 'not adhering to accepted procedures.' Seemingly I was obliged to procure three tenders before awarding the contract. Six weeks passed and there was still no sign of the money Pat was owed for doing this awkward little job for next to nothing. My solution was to send Pat himself to the County Offices, in his working clothes, immediately after milking to: 'Demand what was owed for the bit of ploughing.' This he did and he was promptly paid there-and-then without further ado.

We had told my own mother and father that we were expecting a baby to be born in November and now Bernadette was most anxious to make the trip to Mayo to tell her own parents, Bessie and Charlie. We arrived down on Friday night and there was great rejoicing at our news. The only trouble was that I had to be back in Nurney by two o'clock on the Sunday because I knew them to be a tough team and it would be wholly inappropriate for me to miss this severe test of our prowess. Bernadette wasn't pleased that we had to leave so early, and I could see why. Life wasn't always easy.

We headed off in darkness before six in the morning and drove into the rising sun. Bessie and Charlie were up to see us off. I'm sure they thought their daughter's husband was quite mad. About half way between Ballina and Foxford, two hares ran straight across the road in front of me. I felt a thud. I pulled in and leapt out to inspect the damage to my newly purchased Kadett. Bernie, who had been snoozing beside me, woke to a litany of loud profanities. The grill was shattered, the bumper bent with water and steam gushing forth from a burst radiator at an alarming rate. There wasn't a sign of either hare.

I drove to a garage which I knew to be but a mile up the road on the outskirts of the Foxford. It was just after half seven and there wasn't a stir but I knocked hard on the window of the attached house. A man with bloodshot eyes eventually came to the window but he just shook his head and told me to go away. There was an old five gallon drum discarded nearby which I filled it with water to replenish the leaking radiator every two or three miles. We drove through Foxford as early mass goers contemplated the steaming crashed Kadett. I pulled in at the next garage on the Dublin side of the town.

Knock, Knock.

Another pair of bleary eyes eventually came to the window and gazed apprehensively into mine.

'I'm in trouble. I have to be in Kildare by one o'clock to play a football match but two mad hares ran into my car and destroyed my radiator.'

The man looked out at the car.

'I can't help you but there's a man out the road who might. His house is three miles out the road, opposite a lake, with a turquoise Kadett in the corner of the garden.'

I could hardly believe my ears.

A few minutes later, I knocked on my third window that Sunday morning and repeated my tale of woe. He changed into his work clothes and without bit nor bite he started to work straightaway even as it lashed rain. While he was at it he swapped bumpers saying he'd straighten out mine when he had more time, all for twenty pounds. That man was the nearest thing to an angel I'd encountered up to that point in my life. Bernadette was bemused by the whole series of events , but she held her peace and was glad when our little car was on the road to Kildare.

I drove hard for the rest of the journey and pulled into Nurney, just as the others were making their way to the dressing room. I had left Bernadette home before the match, as she had decided that the tension and abuse meted out from the sidelines was more than she could bear.

We won but only just. As always against Nurney, it was a tough hard battle. I'd like to say that I was the difference between the two teams that afternoon. The truth was put to me fair and square that night up in Mulrennan's Bar by one of our supporters.

'You hardly got a kick of the ball today, by right you should have been taken off.'

She was dead right.

1978
2. FOOTBALL

Clongorey had recruited well over the winter. John Loney, while still only a student in Newbridge College, was a very good goalkeeper, our most critical position in our founding year. Ken Early had been an integral part of the Raheens set up that had won the previous year's Senior Championship. He could play anywhere and brought with him an extra dimension of steel and cunning. As well as these two, there were Ken's younger twin brothers Colin and Trevor, along with Kevin Scott Donohoe, Sean Kelly and my cousin Martin, who was a UCD student. All these were classy enough young footballers pushing hard for places on the team. Although unbeaten in the League, the Junior B Championship was our main focus. Our first Championship game resulted in a facile win over Sallins second team.

One night shortly after this I answered a call from my mother who beseeched me to 'come down quick.' I left down the phone and was there within seconds. My father's face was grey as he sat in the armchair, exhausted and deeply concerned about pains in his chest. I asked for his keys and as calmly as I could, I ushered him into the passenger seat of his Austin Cambridge. We headed for Naas hospital. He became emotional as we drove along and told me for the first time that I could remember how he was proud of and loved me and to 'look after your mammy if anything happens.' This type of talk frightened me and I didn't want to hear any of it. I was mightily relieved when I drove in through the gates of the hospital, where he was taken from the car in a wheelchair and seen to right away. After a brief examination he was moved to the Cardiac unit upstairs in the old wing.

Over the next few days he was thoroughly checked out and diagnosed with Angina. He was given medication and strongly advised to avoid stressful situations. Within a fortnight he had recovered and was back to his old ways as if nothing had happened. The following Sunday we had to play Sarsfields in the quarter final of the Championship. At our team meeting on the Thursday night, my main concern was that no player should remonstrate with the referee from Straffan, under any circumstances. He had officiated over us during a league game and we had found him highly eccentric and a law onto himself. Other than this, we weren't too concerned about Sarsfield's second string team.

The match was in Allenwood and Sarsfields put it up to us from the throw-in. There was a fair sized crowd and I remember a lot of noise coming from both sets of supporters outside the mesh wire fence surrounding the pitch. I wasn't playing particularly well at the centre of the field and things were not going our way, when I began to hear very loud remonstrations plainly being directed at me. I recognised my father's voice and looked over in his direction. Instantly I became concerned when I saw that his face had become flushed. I trotted over to him on the sideline.

'Are you going to stop this shouting?'

'What the fuck are you talking about?

'You're going to have a heart attack, if you don't stop?'

'Play the fuckin game like I'm tellin you... stay between the fifties and stop running all over the place like a headless chicken.' The colour of his face was a really deep red and I became extremely concerned.

I pulled off my jersey and went to hand it to him. By this stage the game had come to a halt and everyone in the ground was focusing on the drama unfolding on the sideline. We were both close to tears. He stood back from the fence and looked at me without speaking for what seemed a long time..

'Alright Noel, maybe you're right, I'll stop,' was all he said. I put back on the jersey and resumed my position. We were a point or two behind, with Sarsfields mounting another attack just outside our twenty one yard line, when the referee blew for a free out to us.'For Fucks sake, ref!' wailed one of the Sarsfields players. The referee moved the ball twenty or so yards back up the field. A malicious thought formed in my befuddled brain. Before I could stop myself I had roared out:

'You fuckin bollix ref.'

Thinking it was coming from our opposition, he moved it up another twenty yards in our favour. The Sarsfields players were looking around and roaring at each other to shut up. I let out another admonishment and to their consternation the referee moved the ball again. At this stage, I could hear a singular voice above the roars coming from the Sarsfields supporters behind the wire fence.

'It's Heavey ref, it's fuckin Heavey.'

I glanced over to the source of the voice. Rubber Keogh, a Sarsfield legend and staunch supporter was desperately trying to get over the fence, being prevented from doing so only by the stout hearted restraint of several Allenwood officials. Before I could stop myself another surreptitious howl at the referee escaped me. The Sarsfields players were by now ballistic, but mystified as to which of them was the culprit, as the ball was placed on their twenty one yard line for Laurence Scott-Donohoe to kick the free over the bar to level the game. We went on to win by four points. I sought out my father whose colour was nearly back to normal after the game. We put our arms around each other's shoulders and walked towards the dressing rooms.

Next up was Nurney in the semi-final. Our training and

mental preparation now took on an intensity none of us had experienced before. On the Thursday before the game we gathered for our team meeting. We were all there except for the man whose experience and strength held our backline together – Chicky Mills our corner back.

'Chicky's going to go on the beer, someone has to stop him,' said John Taffe, our other corner back.

'I'll take care of it myself,' I said and we continued on with the meeting held to thresh out our plan.

That Saturday morning I drove into Newbridge around eleven o'clock as I wanted to intercept Chicky on the street before he made it into one of the bars. We spotted each other more or less at the same time between The Curragh Inn and Neesons on the Main Street.

'Well Chicky? How'll we go tomorrow? You weren't training Thursday night.' I said.

'No, I couldn't make it. We'll destroy them,' he looked me straight in the eye.'Listen I'm a ball of nerves, come in here with me 'til we have just the one to calm me down.'

'Chicky. It's the semi-final for fuck's sake, come on home with me.' He put his arm around me and his eyes beseeched.

'Just the one sailor, come on in with me for just the one. Then we'll go home.' Against my better judgement, I accompanied him into Neeson's and to my undying shame remained drinking with him for the whole day. We sang songs all the way home that night.

The following afternoon we beat Nurney by a point in Prosperous in as tough a game as I've ever had to play. I could never fully understand how or why but the simple truth was that the two main men for Clongorey that day were myself and Chicky.

We were now in the County Final, against Cappagh, from up around the Meath border. The talk of our place was about

Clongorey 3-8, Cappagh 2-10, 4.45pm, Sunday September 10th, 1978.
We have just been presented with the cup. Players, subs, mentors, and a few true blue supporters
stand and kneel to record our great achievement.
Back, l-r: Trevor Earley, PJ O'Grady, Chicky Mills, Declan Doyle, Larry O'Rourke, John Taaffe, Laddie Earley,
Laurence Scott Donohoe, Tommy Heavey, Ger O'Connor, John Loney, Kevin Scott Donohoe Junior,
Kevin Scott Donohoe Senior, Tom Maguire, Dan Byrne, Seamus Moore, John Currins,
Noel Heavey, Paddy Heavey, a young Sean Kiernan.
Front, l-r: Gaa Kelly, David Kelly, Peter Donnelly, Ned Ivers, Martin Heavey, Sean Kelly,
Dan Earley, Marty Taaffe, Jim Scott Donohoe, John Heavey, PJ Earley Captain, Colin Earley, Pat Duffy

little else, but we remained calm as we prepared for battle. Our plan was simple enough. Get the ball into our full forward line as quickly as possible and attack their possession all over the field with as much intensity as we could muster. Also I knew their centre back, Mick Convey, would come soloing through the centre at every opportunity but we had a fairly basic plan to stop him. Three minutes into the game he strode past me like I wasn't there. But Jim met him fair and square and 'dropped him like a sack of spuds.' To Convey's eternal credit he got up and, moving to centre field, he proceeded to run at me for the duration of the game and more often than not it was left to someone else to stop him.

Mulligan, their full forward came out around the forty yard

line, from where he kicked points to beat the band. Elsewhere we seemed to be in command. We led up until the final few minutes when a mistake let them in for a goal. Immediately after this they took the lead for the first time. The final minutes were a blur before Declan Doyle kicked a wonderful point from well over fifty yards. The teams were now level again and every player on the field would have settled for that. In injury time, we mounted one last desperate attack. I forget who it was that was fouled but from forty yards out Laurence Scott-Donohoe struck the ball directly over the black spot on the crossbar. We had the lead again. A Cappagh player caught the ball from the kick-out but the referee now raised his arms and gave a beautiful long blow on his whistle.

Our supporters now swarmed onto the pitch in a state of delirium. Every player on the field was utterly exhausted. A fabulous warm feeling of absolute joy now welled up inside me, in total contrast to the utter desolation which I read on the faces of each of the Cappagh players who came to shake my hand. I felt for them but the rising euphoria inside me made me laugh and howl and I hugged everyone that came near me. Neutrals who saw the game said it was the best Junior Final in years. We celebrated long and hard, even as we knew there now was the opportunity to contest the Jack Higgins Cup

This is a cup awarded each year to commemorate Jack Higgins, the legendary footballer from Naas. It is played for between the champions of the different grades of junior football in Kildare. This winning of this cup now became our objective.

We were expected to beat Junior C champions Caragh, which we did without too much bother. Junior A champions St Laurence's were seen as 'the strongest junior team to emerge in decades.' One of their team worked alongside several of our supporters and players in the Roadstone Quarry on the Hill of Allen. He had collected a large sum of money and left it as a wager in Mulrennan's Bar. When I heard of this I asked that 'not one penny of this be covered.' There wasn't.

By this stage it was late September and it wasn't practical for us to train in our own field because of the fading light. I brought our team up to the Curragh where we trained harder than we ever trained before using the headlights of our cars as well as the lights from the main road. We were very much the underdogs in most people's opinion but in our own heads we were absolutely certain that we would prevail. One of our moves involved me kicking the ball low into PJ Early on the edge of the square for him to flick into the path of the inrushing Seamus Moore. Once he received the ball at speed, a goal usually was the outcome.

In the dressing room we calmly went through what was expected of each man, as we had done the previous Thursday. There was no shouting or roaring, everyone was calm and focused. It was time to go. As we filed out, the door of the St Laurence's dressing room swung open. Inside they were smiling and joking among themselves; this caused a very strange feeling to come over me. For the first and only time in my life I felt sorry for what was about to befall our opponents. We ran onto the field as the rain drizzled down to be welcomed by roars from our supporters and the smell of the freshly cut grass.

1978: 3. THE JACK HIGGINS

Clongorey 4-4
St. Laurences 3-3

CLONGOREY won the Jack Higgins Cup at Naas on Sunday when they shocked St. Laurences who were the Junior 'A' champions and hot favourites to win this one.

The Clongorey side were in no way overawed by their opponents reputation and within fifteen minutes they had torn the Laurences defence to shreds and put a ten point gap between the sides.

They were yards faster to the ball in all areas and they had the losers defence in the jitters every time they mounted an attack. The Saints got back into the game in the sixteenth minute when the referee awarded them a penalty for some very obscure reason and J. J. Wall belted it to the net. An exchange of points still left seven points between the sides as the 30 minutes ticked over but then Dame Luck again smiled on "The Saints" when B. McLoughlin seemed to have lost control of the ball in front of the goal but drew on the loose ball and found the net with it.

So the interval arrived with but four points between the sides 3-3 to 2-2 and the Saints back in the game with a big chance. The opening five minutes of the 2nd half gave some indication of what was to come when the losers had four wides in the opening five minutes and had to wait until the 10th minute to register their first score of the half a point by B. Higgins.

Within three minutes Clongorey gave them the answer when S. Moore cut through for a brilliant goal, his third of the game, and the cup was as good as on its way to the southern end of Caragh parish. However the drama was not finished yet for in the 20th minute the losers were awarded another penalty. If we thought the one in the first half was "soft" the second one was farcical in the extreme, with the end product of it even more farcical. The kick was again entrusted to J. J. Wall who thumped it off the underside of the crossbar. When he gathered the rebound he looked certain

the rebound he looked certain to score but the goalkeeper brilliantly parried his shot, only to see substitute P. Doyle rush in to hit it to the net.

There was consternation on the losers faces when the referee disallowed the score because the forward was in the small square. The losers never threatened any real danger afterwards and it was Clongorey who almost goaled with only five minutes remaining. A goal for the losers in the final minute was only of academic interest.

So Clongorey who were really the surprise team of the season capped their good work with their best display of all. It was a real team effort allied to a high degree of fitness and stamina and of course having the man of the match in S. Moore whose three goals were brilliantly taken. Others to shine were M. Taaffe, J. Scott, D. Byrne, K. Early, P. Duffy, N. Heavey, D. Doyle and C. Early.

The losers never lived up to their high reputation and too many of their stars failed to shine. The long lay off since the final of the Junior 'A' championship may have taken some of the polish out of their play. No blame however could be attached to J. Ging, T. Gorman, E. O'Brien, M. Kirwan, J. Foley, J. J. Wall or P. Archbold, all of whom tried so hard for the hour.

Another discordant note about the game was the fact that each side had to supply a linesman each and quite a few of their decisions did not meet with general approval. Surely it must be possible to provide neutral linesmen for a tie of this importance.

Scorers: Clongorey — S. Moore 3-0, K. Scott 0-1, L. Scott 0-1, P. J. Early 1-0, C. Early 0-1, P. Duffy 0-1. St. Laurences: J. J. Wall 1-1, B. Higgins 1-1, B. McLoughlin 1-0, P. Archbold 0-1.

Clongorey: J. Lowry, J. Taaffe, J. Mills, M. Taaffe, D. Byrne, J. Scott, K. Early, P. Duffy, N. Heavey, L. Scott, D. Doyle, K. Scott, S. Moore, P. J. Early (capt.), C. Early.

St. Laurences: J. O'Brien, J. Ging, T. Gorman, J. Corcoran, E. O'Brien, M. Kirwan, J. Deacy, J. Foley, B. Higgins, M. Walshe, M. Gorman, P. Keogh, B. McLoughlin, J. J. Walsh, P. Archbold.

The Jack Higgins Cup was presented to the winning captain P. J. Early by Mrs. Higgins after the game.

1978

4. ANOTHER LIFE

I knew that becoming a father was a big deal but a lot of the implications of this went over my head as quite a lot of other things were happening all around me at this time. Both Bernadette and I agreed that we didn't want to know whether it was a boy or a girl until our baby was born. So, we had declined to have our neighbour Mrs Curley swing her pendulum over the emerging bump. Then one August morning after breakfast, as the sun shone through the kitchen window Bernadette with a smile on her face, took my hand and placed it on her belly. I'd heard about 'feeling life' but the little kick I felt registered with me as a mild electric shock. I sat down then and let the full implications of what I'd just felt wash through me. Bernadette said something but all I remember is the way she smiled.

I was a Biology teacher and knew all about gestation or so I thought. I had recently taken to dipping into Bernadette's book called *Everywoman* to try to fully understand what was happening inside her body as that movement inside my wife's belly that morning had thrilled me to the core. I was excited enough to help choose maternity dresses and facilitated her going to breathing classes in between frenetic preparations for championship matches, looking after crops in the ground and the day to day teaching in Prosperous. I became used to the idea of being an expectant father but still received quite a jolt when I saw Bernadette pack a pair of little white babygros into the burgundy weekend case which up to this I'd associated with trips to Mayo.

The Jack Higgins had been won and the due date came and

went but there was still no stir from Bernadette or the baby. After we visited her gynaecologist in Hospital Six, the rather strange sounding moniker for the small maternity unit on the vast campus that is St James Hospital, Bernadette came out to tell me that she was being kept in and that she was going to be induced, whatever that meant. For now I was told it meant I had to bring the burgundy case into the ante-natal ward. Bernadette was one of six expectant mothers and I was very surprised to discover that she was the only married lady in the ward. For the hour or so I sat there, I was struck with how natural and at ease with themselves the other ladies were. I drove home that night, fully realising that I was about to enter a world I knew nothing about, and hadn't really considered up to this.

I was allowed into the labour ward the following day, but it was made clear to me by the nurses that I wouldn't be allowed into the delivery ward, when the time came because of the policy of the hospital. I had absolutely no problem with this. Slowly but surely I adopted to the rhythm of the workings of the labour ward or rather a room in a busy maternity unit. I was allowed hold Bernadette's hand and rub her back when spasms of pain would propel her to take short shallow breaths. Nurses and doctors were coming and going, always checking the foetal heartbeat with a simple little bugle-like apparatus made of grey plastic. There were two changes of shift from the time I had come in but I didn't become at all concerned until I saw the look of surprise on the faces of the nurses who recognised me from being there the previous morning.

Once or twice, when the paediatrician had come in I was expected to step out. This didn't bother me at all except for the shouts and sounds I'd heard coming from the delivery ward, just down the corridor. Eventually things started to happen quite fast and I was told that Bernadette was being taken to the delivery ward. A student nurse brought me down to what she referred to as 'The Blue Room.' At this stage I was in a mild state of delirium, I'm not sure but the student nurse had to lead me down by the hand. There were two other gentlemen in this room. There was no conversation whatsoever between us. Loud sounds, which I knew weren't Bernadette's, were coming from the delivery ward and this made the atmosphere even more surreal. I was close to tears and complete meltdown.

Twice nurses came into the room but in both instances it was to the others. In both instances they left, without so much as a look at me. I was alone when a smiling nurse came right up to me.

'Congratulations, you are the father of a beautiful healthy baby boy. Mother and baby are absolutely fine but your wife is very, very tired.' I remember standing there and looking at that smiling collected lady but cannot remember what I said, or indeed I if I spoke at all. I have though, a recollection of crying and shaking uncontrollably as I silently thanked God from the bottom of my heart.

Bernadette was staring intently at the little bundle in a soft white blanket, beside her in the bed. I went straight to them. When she turned to face me, her eyes were soft with tears in them but her smile was the most radiant I'd ever seen. The nurse took up the bundle and thrust him into my arms. I swayed as tears flowed freely and the warmest feeling I'd ever felt surged through me.

'Can we call him Nollaig?' She asked in a soft whisper. I'd thought of another name, but I now merely nodded.

'KEEP HER GOING SONNY'

My brother Tommy was in the car with me that morning and was trying to engage me in casual conversation, never an easy task when I was reading a newspaper. I particularly loved reading the Sunday newspapers in the car, a habit I'd inherited from my father and had perfected the art of not hearing questions directed at me as I read the sports pages.

We were waiting for the others to turn up for an Old Kilcullen rugby game in Rosetown. I'd given up playing rugby years before but an ex-classmate, Peter Flanagan, was the Captain of the Seconds team and had asked me to play that afternoon. I had trained in the mud on the Friday night and was looking forward to the game which I knew would harden me up for the Gaelic season about to kick in.

My routine for perusing the Sports pages of Sunday newspapers had developed over many years. The first thing I always checked was to see how Manchester United had fared the day before. I'd been to only a couple of soccer games in my life but this didn't stop me from following the fortunes of United ever since the days George Best, and Denis Law.

Because I'd been a serious runner back in my schooldays, I also always checked out the athletic reports written by Tom O'Riordan, who had once written a couple of lines in *The Independent* about how I'd shown great heart to finish second in the Leinster school's cross country championship. His preview in the *Sunday Independent* that morning was about The Quinlan Cup, under a photograph of Frank Cahill, Ireland's oldest athlete. He was in his eighties and had never missed a running of this famous race.

'There's no one coming here today.'

The grumpiness in Tommy's voice cut through my perusal of the sports pages and brought me back to reality. I'd been aware that he was becoming uneasy from his shifting around in the passenger seat. I was now confronted by 'full on grumpiness.' I closed up the newspaper, then looked at my watch, it was coming up to kick off time and mine was the only vehicle in the car park.

'They must have called off the game on account of the pitch being frozen.' I replied.

Nobody had bothered to tell us that the match had been cancelled. Typical! I thought to myself; then almost immediately another idea sprouted in my head.

'Tommy, will you come for the spin to Tullamore?'

'What's on there?'

'There's a road race on that I always wanted to run in. This is my chance.'

'Will we be home before dark?' He asked.

'Yes we will.' With that I was out the gate, on the way, and mad for road.

It'd been years since I'd trained specifically for running but I fancied I was fit enough from all the training I'd done the year before when Clongorey had won the Jack Higgins Cup. Over the years, I don't think I was ever the best footballer on any of the teams for which I played but I fancied myself as the fittest on all of them. Gaelic football or rugby, New York, London, Dublin or in Kildare, someone would always challenge and it was a matter of considerable pride to me that never once had I ever been beaten in the sprint to the finish at the end of the warm up laps.

We arrived in the Square in Tullamore, just as athletes had started to gather for the start. Every colour singlet imaginable in as big a gathering of athletes as ever I'd seen. I changed in the car and then ran up and down the road a few times to warm up. I had allowed my membership of Naas Athletic Club to lapse, had no race number but I was determined to run and I didn't want any truck with pernickety officials. So when I saw runners eyeing up the dirty rugby jersey without a race number I put out the false super confident vibes I used to hold in reserve for this type of situation. I started to act as if I owned the whole town of Tullamore. At the same time I refrained from making eye contact or chatting with anyone, just in case. Even so, I revelled in the buzzy banter of the athletes and the pungent smell of wintergreen as we all packed in for the start.

Distance running in my experience was all about getting away at the start, maintaining the same pace as every other runner for ninety nine per cent of the race, then giving it everything over the last three hundred yards. Not exactly rocket science but a strategy that had served me well back in the day when I used to fancy myself as Clongorey's version of Australia's Herb Elliot, the greatest miler of all time. He had been my hero as was his coach Percy Cerutty, whose training methods I adopted via a book I'd taken out in the library. It had been quite some time since running tactics were in the forefront of my brain but they were there now as silence reigned after we'd come under *starter's orders*.

About twenty or so hotshot runners had lined themselves up to form the very first row. I now barged my way up through the ranks to position myself right in their midst and set myself for the start. I felt giddy with excitement as the adrenaline whooshed through my body. The starter fired his gun. I sprinted as hard as I could for the first two or three hundred yards. Just before we turned a corner I looked around and was shocked to realise I was in the first fifteen with five or six hundred athletes strung out behind me even at this early stage.

'Jesus Christ, I said to myself, 'this could be a big one.'

I pumped the arms as I bounded along inspired by the exalted company I was running in and loving every second of spectators and runners alike wondering:

'Who is your man in the rugby jersey?'

My mind drifted back to the day I went out at the start of the All Ireland Schools Senior 5000m Championship nine years before. I had tucked in behind Eddie Leddy and allowed him to pull me away from the rest of the field. Leddy was the main man that nobody was ever going to beat, but a silver medal in the All Ireland 'schools' would do me nicely. I was coming under a little bit of pressure but still about thirty yards ahead of the third placed runner on the penultimate lap. Suddenly I became acutely aware of searing pain in the soles of my feet. I drifted off the pace and was caught by my pursuers on the second bend of the last lap. I was inconsolable after I finished sixth. Terry Ghent, the hammer thrower from Newbridge came over to commiserate but I was inconsolable. I blamed the new pair of spikes that my father had bought me for the cinders track in Santry, but nobody was interested in my excuses, not even myself.

That was then, this was now. Unlikely but glorious thoughts surged through my brain as I took stock at that first corner. I've always lived a fantastic life in my head. My real life for the most part has been brilliant but not near as brilliant as the one inside my brain.

There were times when reality has bitten hard. Within half a mile of that first corner, I realised it was it was about to bite again. Skinny little men began to pass me in droves.

'No worries' I thought to myself, 'I'll just find a rhythm and a suitable pace to get to the last three hundred yards, then I'll strike for home.' I leaned forward, shortened my stride and imagined I increased the tempo as I pumped the arms and willed my legs to keep up to someone.

Unfortunately no one obliged me by slowing down. All my theories on distance running began to unravel with every step I ran. After the first lap, I knew for certain that glory was going to elude me that day. A new objective now rapidly came into focus: Looks of amusement from spectators on the pavement as they contemplated the fourteen stone man in the rugby jersey and the Dunnes Stores running shoes. My sole objective now was to finish.

Time, finishing position, pain endured and smart remarks became irrelevant. I zeroed in on the absolute necessity of finishing the race. As I cogitated, straggling runners went by me, as if I wasn't there. I had become the invisible man. I continued to pump the arms but my legs were barely moving.

In all my years, I had never dropped out of a race or failed to complete anything I'd started. I thought of my father and mother and the hardships through which they'd persevered all through their lives. Again, I pumped the arms and willed the legs. Sad to say all this produced was a wobble. I took refuge in my fantasy world but three and a half miles were still in front of me.

'Keep her going Sonny.' His words came across as a wheeze rather than an exhortation.

The instant they were uttered, I knew who had said them. Frank Cahill pulled alongside me and in slow motion the eighty something year old man shuffled past me and headed up the road. All cogitations evaporated there and then. The sight of this frail old man running away from caused havoc in my brain. I stopped running altogether. I stood for an instant, then abruptly turned around and walked back the way I'd run suspecting as I did so that my walking pace was probably faster than the running pace the old athlete had just emulated.

It wasn't much fun for Tommy in the car on the drive home.

A grunt was all he got for a reply when he inquired if I was alright. In time I recovered my equanimity and went on to have a good life. I've often thought and talked of Frank Cahill over the years and wondered if he ever realised the devastation caused by his words of 'encouragement.' Somehow I'd like to think that he knew precisely the effect they' have.

JAY

He was always there anytime I went to visit my granny. He often referred to her as the Head Lady and that's exactly what she was. He had been their neighbour but then married my grandmother, a few years after my grandfather died, back in the thirties. By all accounts these were very hard times when Clongorey people had only the bog and their small holdings to sustain them. Hard times they may well have been but I never heard my father or any of my uncles or aunts complain.

It was probably tricky enough when he moved into my grandfather's house. My father was nineteen and the fourth of seven. He never said anything of what he thought or felt about his mother marrying Jay and I never asked. They always presented a united front but where Granny was a positive lady full of the joys of life, Jay was forever giving out about something or other. He thrived on tension and when it wasn't present he would try to manifest it by carrying malicious tales from one household to another within the extended family, until he caused a row.

Still and all he was an integral part of our lives and life was never dull when he was around. Bendigo Twist was the only tobacco he ever smoked, in the crooked pipe that always seemed to be in his mouth or hands. It was forever going out and relighting it was a ritual to behold. He'd strike the match with his right hand, often off the arse of his trousers and immediately join it to his left to form a sort of wren's nest. With the flame protected from even the severest tempest, the cupped hands were raised, then opened, from the bottom to light the rubbed down tobacco in the bowl of the pipe. He'd have started to suck air by pursing his lips, like an inverted bellows, until blue smoke with that familiar whiff spewed forth.

Sometime in the mid-fifties they moved to Gingerstown, the far side of Caragh. This holding, at the end of a long narrow road, was courtesy of the Land Commission. The snag was they had to live there in order to retain it. It was away from the home place but family members were expected to visit and they did.

My grandmother died around the time I became engaged to Bernadette. My sister Marie and her husband then lived in the house with Jay for a while. After they moved to their own new home he became very lonely so he'd cycle up to Clongorey to see his people at least once a week, regardless of the weather.

He always stopped off to visit my mother of whom he was genuinely fond. Here he would get a cup of tea and whatever was going before he'd head on up the road. He would make the rounds of the three houses; my mother's, my uncle Jimmy's and Ivy house where my uncle Gunner lived with his family.

He had become a staunch Clongorey supporter and I often heard his deprecations cutting through the fog of sound that players hear coming from the sidelines when they're in the heat of battle. More often than not he was giving out to the referee. Jay hated referees.

Shortly after I purchased a relatively new Opel Kadett I decided to visit him. On the way, I pulled in to avoid an oncoming car. The other driver, a neighbour of Jay's, hadn't seen me and overreacted, swinging her car into mine. There was nobody hurt and little damage done to the other car but my Kadett was more or less a write off. A few days later, her husband informed me that he wasn't admitting to any liability and didn't see that I should be recouped by him in any way. I was livid and felt much wronged. The following Sunday I came home from a football match 'the worse for wear'. I came in the door to find Bernadette in a bit of a state. Our child Nollaig was in her arms.

'Jay was here.'

'Was he?'

'He was very vexed, he said that you were responsible for causing a rift between his best neighbour and himself and that you weren't to go to his funeral.' Bernadette was flushed and quite upset. Our child, having picked up on this was now crying loudly.

'Where is he now?'

'He's gone up to Gunners.'

'I see.' I turned and walked out of the kitchen.

'Where are you going?'

'I'm going up to see Jay.'

And with that I went out and jumped into my father's Austin Cambridge and sped up the road as fast as it would go 'til I came to Gunner's. Jay was sitting in the middle room beside the Rayburn sipping a cup of tea. My aunt Josie sat on the armchair opposite him.

'Excuse me Josie, do you mind if I have a private word with Jay?'

She looked at me directly for a second or two before answering.

'Alright I'll be out here.'

She closed the door behind her as she went into the back kitchen.

I went up close to where Jay was sitting. I looked at him severely then stuck my finger right close to his nose.

'You are one lucky fuckin man that you are as old as you are.'

'Is that so?'

'Yes, it is so! You've done nothing only cause me trouble since I was a child. You've never had a good word to say about me and always your rotten fuckin lies. If you were only forty years younger I'd take you out to the yard and beat the livin' shite out of you.'

He never uttered a word but his eyes held mine the whole time.

'Don't you ever bother me, my wife or child again you fuckin oul bollix.'

Barely had I finished my tirade when I began to feel guilty for what I now realised was an out and out verbal assault on my father's stepfather, a man in his eighties. I saw Josie's concerned demeanour through the glass door as she stood in her kitchen. I went out to her.

'Josie, I'm so sorry this has happened in your home.'

'Ok Noel, I understand.' I turned and was gone.

A few nights later, Bernadette and I were sitting in our living room watching television when we heard a loud knock, knock on the front door. I answered it and immediately became apprehensive to see my uncle Gunner standing on the step.

'There's a man here to see you,' said Gunner. 'Actually he wants to stay with you for a few days.' With that Jay stepped out of the passenger seat. I was taken aback but said:

'Well then, ye had better come in, 'til we see.' Before I had the words out of my mouth Jay strode past me without even looking at me. He had a small suitcase in his hand.

'Well Jay, you're welcome,' said Bernadette.

He sat down and that was that. At first I didn't know what to think or feel about this sudden turn of events. We drank tea and talked away as if nothing had happened the previous Sunday. Eventually I realised I was relieved and pleased but I didn't let on. The events of the previous Sunday were never spoken of again.

A few days turned into a few months. Over these months Jay integrated into our way of going on and regaled us with stories, tales and lies from the days he was a young man. He loved our baby son, Nollaig and was there to see him take his first steps. I was amazed and delighted the way things worked out. Every so often Bernadette would find a fifty pound note left under his saucer which he insisted she keep.

Jay had a bad shake in his hand which made it very difficult for him to shave himself.

Consequently on most evenings before we went to bed he'd beckon me into the bathroom, where he'd sit himself in front of the mirror for me to shave him. During these times he'd say confidential and important things which for the most part shall remain between the two of us. One night he brought up the topic of his dying which wasn't unusual as for years he'd been complaining that when he'd been very ill after the Head Lady died, and ready to move on himself they'd brought him back from the brink:

'So that I'll have to go through the whole feckin' thing again.'

On this particular night he fixed his eye on mine via the mirror as he jutted out his jaw for me to get a good sweep with the razor.

'I want you to be one of the ones to bury me.'

'Do you want me to do it now or wait 'til you're dead?'

'You needn't be so smart. Will you do it?'

I could see he was deadly in earnest.

He went on to tell me precisely where this was to be in Barretttown cemetery. I knew the spot he was talking about and started to say:

'But sure there's someone buried...'

He cut me off before I had time to finish. His eyes glared and he curled his fists up on his knee.

'That's my grave; the man who is in it was put there without my permission. He died a long time ago. There'll only be bits of bones left. When you come on them, dig a hole in the corner, scrape them in with a shovel and cover them up.' I had stopped shaving him and half his face was still lathered as he turned now to face me directly.

'Will you promise me?'

'Jaysus, Jay!'

'Do you promise?' His eyes bored into mine and he tightly squeezed my lower arm.

'Will you promise me?' He repeated, this time in a desperate whisper. I looked at him for a good while before I slowly nodded my head.

'OK, I'll do it.' He shook me by the hand and gave me a half grin as only he could.

'Good man, now finish your job.'

I was befuddled and had an uneasy feeling, but I let it go. I returned to the shaving and we never spoke of our agreement ever again.

Jay spent that Christmas with us and the following spring, as well as a bit of the summer, but shortly after this he moved back up to Gunners. We were genuinely sorry to see him go out the door with his small tattered suitcase. He didn't come to any of our matches that summer. This confirmed to me that his health was deteriorating. He went into the Jockey Hospital before the following Christmas and died in early January.

Gunner came down to our home that evening.

'He told me you were to be in on digging the grave.'

We drove down to the graveyard. Gaa Kelly was already there. We marked out the plot as Jay had dictated. Chicky Mills and Black Taaffe were also part of the detail. We all agreed to convene for twelve o'clock the following day. I arrived down just before twelve with my spade and shovel. The others were there before me. Chicky and Gaa started to dig, while Black and I kept the soil shovelled back. We swapped jobs every twenty minutes or so and it wasn't long before the grave had taken shape. About an hour after we started Gunner came by to check that everything was going according to plan. He left two bottles of whiskey and four small glasses at the graveside. The banter flew back and forth until Gaa came on a seam of loose soil that had a somewhat richer shade of brown.

'Here, put down that ladder, it's time we all took a break,' said Chicky.

When they came up, they followed Black, who had taken the whiskey and glasses over to the riverbank under the trees. By now I had locked on fully to what I had promised and though I dreaded what awaited me, I was determined to see it through without recourse to drink.

'Lads, ye go on, I'll carry on here.' I said and went back down the hole.

I scraped back the earth with the side of the shovel and hit against something. I recognised the remains of the breastplate of a coffin. My heart now started to pound. Ever so carefully I worked the shovel. Within seconds a skull revealed itself in the soft earth. I could scarcely breathe now and was reduced to panting like a dog. I scraped some more with deadly precision and a ribcage began to emerge. The hairs on the back of my head were now standing on edge. It was so hot and so deathly calm. I became drenched in my own sweat as I uncovered what lay before me. Jay's instructions had been explicit: 'There'll only be bits of bones left. When you come on them, dig a hole in the corner, scrape them in with a shovel and cover them up.'

But I was confronted now by a whole skeleton. Nonetheless, I dug a hole in the corner of the deep grave, about a foot deeper and three feet across at an angle with a corner. The only skeletons I'd contemplated before were in a science laboratory, made of plastic and held together by wire. I wasn't in a science laboratory now and what lay before me wasn't made of plastic. I put the shovel under the little foot bones and was mightily relieved when they separated from the leg bone. I carefully and reverently placed them in the bottom of the hole. When I came back for the leg bones, they disintegrated in front of the shovel blade. All the bones behaved thus except for the skull which remained intact.

My actions now were painfully slow and mechanical as I cleared all traces of bone into the hole and scraped enough clay to cover them. My promise had been honoured by the time the others returned. Drunk and all as they were, they told me I'd done a great job. By this stage, I was in a state of near collapse and unable to process small talk of any description. I shouldered my tools and walked out of the graveyard.

Jay had been an old IRA man and the following day his body received a full military funeral. He would have enjoyed the bugler's playing of the last post and the firing of three volleys over his grave. Before the coffin was lowered, I stared down at the covered hole in the corner. I thought of his half grin the night we shook hands in the bathroom. Then the disquieting thought occurred to me that perhaps the aspect of his funeral that would have given him the most satisfaction was the utter turmoil his simple request had caused in the man, who had so harshly admonished him just a little over a year before.

THE MAN WITH
THE HORRIBLE FACE

After our son Nollaig was born, I became conscious that I needed to earn more money. Besides the obvious fact that Bernadette's salary was no longer coming into the house, there was now our beautiful bouncy baby boy to be looked after. Growing cash crops and utilising my horticultural degree was the route I chose to earn extra cash. So, besides cutting turf and saving hay, around this time I girded myself to grow potatoes, carrots, cabbage and latterly strawberries. These enterprises were labour intensive and in order to look after them, I took on students from my school that were willing to work during the long summer holidays.

I was very pleased with the way my life was going. Nollaig was a wonderful little baby who never caused us any bother and I had settled into teaching really well. The school principal was delighted with the science results of my students. More to the point as far as I was concerned, I very much enjoyed teaching and for the most part, my students seemed to enjoy the way I taught. The bonus was the long summer holidays which allowed me ample time to use my degree to grow crops scientifically.

The field on which our house was built was of about two acres. This meant an acre and a half for me to make my fortune through growing crops and selling the produce. In order to get through what needed to be done; I recruited lads that I knew were interested in working on Saturdays and during the holidays. For the big jobs like planting and harvesting, I recruited young lads mostly from Coill Dubh, which is about nine miles from my house They were great workers and while a fortune wasn't made by me or my workers, that little field kept us all very busy for a good few years.

Bernadette's role in this was to feed the crew. She always took great pride in the empty plates around the tables when she'd cook something substantial when the day's work was done A side benefit of all this enterprise was that it allowed me get to know students on a completely different basis than in the class room. Two young lads in particular, Brendan Byrne and Patrick Hannify, became my 'go-to regulars' when anything needed to be done. They cycled each morning from Coill Dubh and over time they more or less became part of the family through farming, painting, gardening or whatever else needed doing.

Around this time I'd come into the possession of a life-like skin tight mask made of rubber, which I kept secret for a very good reason.

I donned it a few times and dressed up in a ragged coat and tracksuit bottoms, then visited some public houses where I was known well, always with the effect of inducing a resentful silence from friends and acquaintances at a loss to deal with the ugliness of the creature who they had never met or seen before. I made it my business to put them through a quota of misery.

After the horrible looking man stormed out mid drink muttering to himself there would be huge talk and hilarity in the bar.

This was all reported to me when I'd nonchalantly drop in; having whipped off the mask and performed a rapid change of clothes.

To this day I don't think my friends and acquaintances have any idea of the whereabouts or identity of this individual.

In late September I harvested an acre of Kerr Pink potatoes in the field behind our house, courtesy of Johnny Carey, who drove his tractor and spinner all the way from Landonstown to do me the huge favour of 'throwing out' the potatoes. In order to keep the field cleared before him, I had taken on a gang of about seven lads all from Coill Dubh, including John Byrne, the first and only student who had the temerity and ability to beat me in the *Fun Runs,* I used to organise on the roads around the school in Prosperous.

We were all in great form after the hard day's work, as we mulled around after our meal. An idea had occurred to me and I organised with Patrick to take the boys outside, just as darkness encroached. The 'man with the horrible face' duly appeared out of the dusk and scared the bit of daylight that was left out of the lads. They ran into the house to get me to deal with him but I was nowhere to be found.

I was outside doubling over with the laughter and about to disrobe and double back into the house to hear all about their scare when all of a sudden the front door was thrown open and out charged John Byrne with his gang whooping and hollering after him. Now it was the turn of the ugly man to run as if for his life. I'm not at all sure what would have happened had not Patrick called them off. Luckily for me, he did. The 'man with the horrible face' retired after this and never ventured forth, ever again.

THE APOGEE

Dreams weren't talked about much in 1979. Certainly I didn't speak much about mine, except that one time in the Clongorey dressing room. We had won all before us in the junior ranks the previous year and now we were to play in the intermediate grade. My dream was to win this championship, then sweep to victory in the Senior Championship the following year and as County champions to have a cut at becoming kingpins of Leinster. First though, there was Rathangan, who had been favourites to win the Intermediate Championship for years.

Father had come up around noon that Sunday, just as I was about to leave the house. He tried to be as diplomatic as he could. He said he was concerned. A friend of his from Rathangan had just rang to say that Chicky Mills had been drinking in Rathangan the previous day and had said to all and sundry that if his opposite number as much as looked like scoring a point, then Chicky had orders to break his legs. I was no longer the coach in question but I knew this was a load of codswallop. Instead of laughing it off however, I responded with a string of expletives leaving him and Bernadette totally bemused as I stormed out, slamming the door behind me, which woke our baby and made him cry.

I calmed down before I reached Newbridge and grinned to myself at the *shenanigans* of Chicky, the master of mental warfare. We went through our game plan in the dressing room, at the end of which I spoke of my dream. Rathangan had a lethal forward known as *The Sheriff*. Dan Byrne had been instructed to keep 'within half an arm of him at all times for every single second of the full sixty minutes.' I had every confidence that Dan would do just that. We scored three goals within the first ten minutes, and were well on the way to a famous win when I heard a shout.

'Dan Byrne has gone off.' I looked around, Dan was nowhere to be seen.

'He's sitting in the Rathangan dug-out,' someone else shouted., I think it was John Taaffe. I looked over, there was Dan sitting in the middle of the green and white hooped Rathangan men. I couldn't believe what I was seeing. I ran over.

'Dan, what are you doing in there?'

'I'm doing my job' said Dan, 'Now you go and do yours.'

I just couldn't understand until I noticed he was beside the player he had been detailed to mark. Seemingly *The Sherrif had* walked off the field complaining that he couldn't play football with the digs he was getting from the fellah who was following him everywhere he went. When his opposite number walked off, Dan suspected some sort of trickery and followed him into the opposition dug-out. Dan slipped back onto the field of play after a few minutes. There was no sign of the Sherriff. Chicky's direct opponent didn't score anything either. We pressed on, and won the game handily enough.

A league game against our neighbours Ballyteague was next up. At the time they were a senior team and quite formidable. Their players to a man had supported us on our glory march the previous season but we were under no illusions as to the severity of the test in front of us as we togged off before the game. As it turned out we beat them fair and square and most importantly we took what punishment they doled out and met their fire with fire of our own.

The only problem was we lost *Colin Earley*, now a key player to injury. He was unavailable for the championship semi-final against Suncroft, the following Sunday. This we lost by a point kicked from a free in the last few seconds of another terrific contest. It was our first defeat in an important game in over two years. I wasn't to know it at the time but this was our apogee, the high point of our existence; I would go on to play for Clongorey for seven more years and have some great moments in good games but we would never again be a team that others feared. It was the nearest we were to come to achieving my dream.

A SATURDAY EVENING
IN AUGUST

There was one particular Saturday evening I well remember when I was thirty. I had gone down to Woodbine House to see my mother around four o'clock in the afternoon after I'd finished up my jobs for the day. Tommy was driving the red Ferguson tractor away from the turf shed. I knew from the gimp of him that he was none too pleased. My father was sitting in the trailer. When he saw me come in the gate, Tommy drove the tractor hard until he jammed on the brakes and pulled up beside me, before I could get into the house. Father was pitched forward in the trailer.

'For fucks sake, will you take it easy?' he roared at Tommy, before he turned to eyeball me.

'The very man. We've only the one jog left up here, will you come with us' he said this in a soft beseeching tone.

'Typical, fucking typical' I thought to myself. I'd just finished after being 'on the go' since eight in the morning. I was looking forward to a cup of tea and a scone with my mother. If I'd dallied with Bernie and little Nollaig up at our own house for even one extra minute, they'd have gone up the road and I'd have had my mother all to myself, along with scones and strawberry jam that she'd made from fruit I brought down to her three weeks before. I loved Mother's jam. Instead, I now jumped up on the trailer.

Tommy turned around. He was now shaking his head with laughter. I'd been caught. He pushed down the throttle and drove the Ferguson as hard as it would go, as we passed Curleys. My father was grinning as well. He knew what was going on in my head. There wasn't much talk as we drove

A happy mother, Bernadette, with Nollaig learning to pose and a pensive father in our newly established garden

One year old Nollaig helps his Dad sow seeds

Father, a rabbit and Nollaig, his first Grandson

Back Row L-R, American visitors Gerry and John Dinan,
my father holding Nollaig, Bernadette and cousin Valerie.
Front Row L-R, Marie with baby Nicola, my Mother and Veronica with baby,
Brian, under the big Beech tree in the garden of Woodbine House

up the road. Someone had given him an Afghan hound that summer. He ran behind the trailer with big loping strides. Every house along the way had at least two dogs. This gauntlet the hound had to run, but he managed.

It was probably the fasted load of turf ever loaded on Clongorey bog. I know it was the second week in August because Tommy said on the bog that he was in a hurry to get home 'to clean up' as a couple of lads were calling and they were going out to celebrate his twentieth birthday, which is on the twelfth. The vexation at being caught to go to the bog had well left me as my father and I climbed on top of the load for Tommy to drive us home. The thing about working on the bog is it is almost a pleasure when there is plenty of help, and it helped also that there was only three quarters of a load left. In fairness to Tommy he took it fairly handy as we drove out the car-way onto *The Bog Road* for a couple of hundred yards before turning left at Kelly's Cross to drive down into Clongorey.

As we arrived home Bernadette waved at us. She was wearing the maternity dress, I liked best, the one with a tapestry of large golden petals on a black background. She was ambling down to Woodbine House, holding our son Nollaig by the hand. She had one month to go.

I'd noticed Andrew's car parked beside the porch as we drove in the gate. He is from Monastrevin and is married to my youngest sister Veronica who now smiled broadly and waved from the sunroom as Tommy drove into the yard. She held her baby, Brian in her arms. Andrew came out to give us a hand and was throwing off turf before Tommy dismounted from the tractor. The trailer was unloaded even faster than it had been loaded.

Mother had the tea on the table by the time we came in, along with two plates of buttered freshly baked scones, dripping with the strawberry jam, she knew I loved. Veronica loved coming home as often as she could and was always very bubbly when she'd come. We all sat around the table and scoffed scones. The two plates were cleared just as our other sister Marie drove into the yard with her daughter Nicola strapped in to the back seat. Nicola was only six weeks younger than Nollaig and was also well able to squawk and toddle around the place. Marie noticed that all the scones were gone and started to give out. Mother had a particular place at the table that was nearest the sink, the range and the press. She reached behind her to the bread bin on the press and produced a quarter of currant cake.

Mother loved her family and loved nothing better than when we were all together. The three toddlers had learned to walk, but were all still in cloth nappies. This made our' family get togethers' into events not for the faint hearted. In the middle of the mayhem, the phone in the hall rang. Father answered it. He was only a minute before he came back in. He was somewhat excited.

'Bertie has a dog running in Shelbourne Park. He wants me to go up with him.'

'Did you not tell him, you can't go?' Pleaded my mother.

'He is going to win.' There's no way I'm not going. He says he'll be here inside twenty minutes.'

'Jesus Christ, I hate them bloody dogs.' Responded my mother.

Tommy had gone up to the bathroom to get ready for his night out, but was now ordered out of it by my father.

'Wait 'til you hear? Said Mother 'Where's my shirt? Where's my socks? Where's my shoes?

Three minutes later, the shout came down the stairs.

'Where's my shirt?'

Mother took a fit of the giggles and couldn't answer.

'Did you not hear me, where is my fuckin shirt, please? The dog has to be kennelled by half past seven, it's not a fuckin laughing matter.'

By this stage Mother was in complete hysterics. Luckily Marie or Veronica went up to him. It was now getting on a bit and the toddlers started to let their presence be felt as the heat of a long day began to take it's toll. Nappies had to be changed, toddlers fed and readied for the night. In the middle of this, Bertie's car pulled up outside.

Beeeeeep Beeeeeep Beeeeep

'Tell him I'll be there in a minute' Father looked at me. I handed him his shoes which I'd just polished and shined. I went out to Bertie who was bristling with impatience.

Another car pulled into what was now a fairly congested yard. I recognised Toddy Conlan and two other friends of Tommy's who had worked with him in Conlan's garage in Rathangan, where he'd served his time as a mechanic.

Beep Beep.

My father and Tommy walked out the door together. Both were dressed for action, far from the bog they'd just left. They hopped into the separate cars. Bertie pulled away first, and was immediately followed by the car with Tommy in it. I walked inside where mother, sitting at her spot at the table, was still laughing.